Black Oot Here

'Black Lives Matter' street art in Glasgow, 2021. Photograph by Najma Abukar

Black Oot Here

Black Lives in Scotland

Francesca Sobande and layla-roxanne hill

BLOOMSBURY ACADEMIC
LONDON • NEW YORK • OXFORD • NEW DELHI • SYDNEY

BLOOMSBURY ACADEMIC
Bloomsbury Publishing Plc
50 Bedford Square, London, WC1B 3DP, UK
1385 Broadway, New York, NY 10018, USA
29 Earlsfort Terrace, Dublin 2, Ireland

BLOOMSBURY, BLOOMSBURY ACADEMIC and the Diana logo are trademarks of
Bloomsbury Publishing Plc

First published in Great Britain 2022

Cover design by Adriana Brioso

A catalogue record for this book is available from the British Library.

A catalog record for this book is available from the Library of Congress.

ISBN: HB: 978-1-9134-4133-3
        PB: 978-1-9134-4134-0
        ePDF: 978-1-9134-4135-7
        eBook: 978-1-9134-4136-4

Series: Blackness in Britain

Typeset by RefineCatch Limited, Bungay, Suffolk

To find out more about our authors and books visit www.bloomsbury.com
and sign up for our newsletters.

Dedicated to those 'oot (t)here'.

Contents

Illustrations

Preface

The process of writing this book together has been punctuated by many moments of both joy and pain in our lives, and those of people close to us. Our collaborative project first emerged long before the COVID-19 (Coronavirus) pandemic and galvanizing global Black Lives Matter (BLM) activism in 2020, of which the effects of both are still ongoing. Our plans to spend a portion of that year together, immersed in archives and conducting interviews face-to-face, were detoured by the realities of multiple crises, how they collided and crept into our every day. In other words, our approach to writing *Black Oot Here: Black Lives in Scotland* was inevitably influenced by what was happening in our own lives and around the world. There are many words that surface when thinking about such times, but two that often spring to mind are chaos and care. Perhaps, *Black Oot Here* reflects aspects of both.

Our book may be best described as at once messy and mindful. From our unyieldingly long 'introduction', to our focus on questions concerning an ethics of care, when writing this work, we weathered the storm of life by embracing (some) disorder and disruption, as well as stillness, support, and the absurd. Essentially, when working on this together, while in the throes of crises, we let go of our potentially perfectionist preconceptions concerning what this book *had* to be. What our book has *become* is shaped by our experiences of turmoil and togetherness during this time.

While it is grounded in survey responses, interviews with people, photography, and analysis of media and archived material, *Black Oot Here* also features our random ruminations that arose in reaction to the temperature of the times, which took us in different directions that we never could have anticipated. Ultimately, what we mean to say is that although our book has some structure or may appear to be linear in nature, it is a collage of considerations and meandering, yet meaningful, musings (often initially communicated via lengthy voice notes and a plethora of emojis).

Our words may mirror the chaotic yet care-full backdrop of our lives. Our words may meet you in ways that (un)settle assumptions or paint a(n) (un)familiar picture of Scotland. Our words may spark more questions than those that they answer. Overall, while our words could never completely encompass the fullness of the lives and history at the core of this work, we hope our book highlights what it *can* mean to be *Black Oot Here*.

Francesca and layla-roxanne

Acknowledgements

We acknowledge and thank the Society of Authors for a grant award in support of us writing this book. For more information about the Society of Authors, please visit: www2.societyofauthors.org

We also acknowledge and thank the School of Journalism, Media and Culture (Cardiff University) for a seedcorn grant in support of our research which informed this book.

Thank you to everyone who spent time completing our survey on Black Lives in Scotland and to everyone who spoke to us about their own experiences and knowledge of Black Scottish history. We really appreciate all that you do and share.

Thank you to Tomasz and Nayiri at Bloomsbury for your support and to Zed Books for believing in the book project.

Thank you to our friends and families who supported us in the writing of this.

Thank you to Najma Abukar, sister and comrade, whose beautiful photographs feature as the 'foreword' and throughout this book.

We acknowledge Black people in, from, and connected to Scotland who are in their teens, 20s, 30s, 40s, 50s, 60s, 70s, 80s, 90s, 100s, and of course, the bairns and weans.

We acknowledge Black people in Scotland who have been (t)here for decades, and those who have been (t)here for seconds, minutes, hours, days, weeks, or months.

We acknowledge Black people in Scotland who do not consider it to be home, as well as those who do but may still navigate an uneasy relationship with the place.

We acknowledge Black people who identify with a sense of Scottish national identity, as well as those who do not.

We acknowledge Black people in Scotland who did not find themselves in Scotland out of choice, as well as Black people in Scotland who made the decision to move (t)here.

We acknowledge Black people in Scotland who chose to leave, as well as Black people in Scotland who were forced to.

We acknowledge Black people who have never been to Scotland but who have ancestral connections to it, including connections that may be marked by pain, violence, and oppression.

We acknowledge Black people in, from, and connected to Scotland, and whose lives are so much more than our words can ever express.

Abbreviations

ACWA	African & Caribbean Women's Association
BAME/BME	Black, Asian, and minority ethnic
BBC	British Broadcasting Corporation
BIPOC	Black, Indigenous, and people of colour
BLM	Black Lives Matter
BWC	Black Workers' Committee
CARF	Campaign Against Racism and Fascism
CCIs	Creative and cultural industries
CND	Campaign for Nuclear Disarmament
COP26	Conference of the Parties 26 (The 26th United Nations climate change conference held in Glasgow, November 2021)
CSR	Corporate social responsibility
EDI	Equality, diversity, and inclusion
EIS	Educational Institute of Scotland
EU	European Union
FOI	Freedom of Information
GWL	Glasgow Women's Library
LBF	Lothian Black Forum
LGBTQIA+	Lesbian, gay, bisexual, transgender, queer, intersex, asexual (and other people who are not heterosexual and/or cisgender)
NASS	National Asylum Support Service

NGO	Non-Governmental organisation(s)
NHS	National Health Service
NRPF	No Recourse to Public Funds
NUJ	National Union of Journalists
POC	Person of colour (or people of colour)
PPE	Personal protective equipment
QTIPOC	Queer, trans, and intersex people of colour
SACC	Scotland Against Criminalising Communities
SNP	Scottish National Party
SPF	Scottish Police Federation
STUC	Scottish Trades Union Congress
UK	United Kingdom
US	United States
WOC	Woman of colour (or women of colour)

Tis 'ere tae: A long and winding introduction

I feel like I'm tolerated but only if I keep quiet and accept my circumstances. I was told by another teacher, whose ethnicity is ambiguous, but I can say is not white, that living in Scotland and being of colour means that I should just expect the fact that I would experience racist behaviours directed at me. I don't want this to be my life and choose not to accept this as the default.

27 October 2020 (26–35 years-old)

Racism in Scotland exists. Specifically, such racism includes the persistence of antiblackness. Contrary to mainstream media, marketing, and tourism messages that mobilize 'post-racial'[1] perspectives, racism is not something that is just visible over there and elsewhere – tis 'ere tae (it's here too), in 'bonnie' Scotland. The opening words of this chapter form a comment which was shared in response to our 2020–2021 survey for Black people on 'Black Lives in Scotland'. As is illustrated throughout our book, such an experience of encountering anti-Black racism, and being expected to 'keep quiet' and 'accept' it, sadly, can be a common occurrence for Black people in Scotland. Hence, presenting Scotland as a supposedly 'post-racial' utopia in comparison to England and other parts of the United Kingdom (UK) is inaccurate and dismisses the reality of racism experienced (t)here.[2]

In the words of Jonathan Wilson, a branding expert, public speaker, and marketing scholar of Caribbean and Scottish descent, who spoke to us about his experience of living in Scotland in the 1990s – 'I love Scotland and I love the dream, the fantasy, the mythology associated with Scotland, but along this awakening, I'm also acutely aware that there's a lot of embarrassing past and history that's been uncovered to me'. We contend that Scotland is shaped by intersecting inequalities and a matrix of oppression related to racism, classism,[3] ableism, sexism, misogyny, xenophobia, homophobia, transphobia, Islamophobia, and many other interlocking forms of systemic harm and violence. Furthermore, extensive work highlights that Scotland *is* still distinctly impacted by disparities and deeply entrenched forms of discrimination (Bassel and Emejulu 2017;

Christoffersen 2020; Davidson, Liinpää, McBride, and Virdee 2018; de Lima 2012; hill and Sobande 2020; Meer, Akhtar, and Davidson 2020).

Simply stating that structural racism in Scotland exists is far from being a radical act. However, efforts to meaningfully record and respond to the realities of racism and racialized[4] people (t)here are often resisted by individuals and institutions that deny Scotland's colonial and racist legacy. In other words, acknowledging the existence of racism in Scotland, without seeking substantive actions to address it, is *not* revolutionary. Nevertheless, naming and examining racism in Scotland can pose a potent threat to the palatable 'post-racial' position that is sometimes strategically projected onto the nation. Still, we recognize and affirm the words of scholar Katherine McKittrick (2021) whose vital book *Dear Science and Other Stories* includes discussion of the unsustainable nature of the 'logic of knowledge-to-prove' (McKittrick 2021: 4).

Oor way: fowk, nae jist percentages

When writing our book, we did not do so to *prove* the existence of anti-Black racism, nor to prove the existence of Black people in Scotland. Instead, we wrote with an acute awareness *and* experience of anti-Black racism and being Black in Scotland. Therefore, perhaps unsurprisingly, we note the redundancy of research and writing that patronisingly ponders whether anti-Black racism and Black people are indeed present in Scotland (*spoiler alert*: *both* are). Throughout history Black people have faced various iterations of a burden of proof which is often buttressed by anti-Black assumptions of the falseness of Black people's claims and knowledge. Although some of what is articulated in our book may be interpreted as forms of 'proof' (e.g. of Black people's perspectives), our work was not written in response to an impulse to prove or persuade. Instead, *Black Oot Here: Black Lives in Scotland* was written from a place of pausing, processing, piecing together, and, also, peering back from Black living archives.

This research and writing project of ours acknowledges the nuanced and expansive nature of many aspects of the lives of Black people in, from, and connected to Scotland. As such, our work is shaped by the poignant words of interdisciplinary scholar and artist Derrais Carter (2018: 40) on 'Black Study', who states that 'Blackness somehow remains both in and out of time, pushing against the attempts to be ordered in the present, revisiting and reimagining the past, and producing future possibilities'. We also draw on Black geographies work, including the revitalising scholarship of Lioba Hirsch and Naya Jones (2021) who co-edited a *Transactions of the Institute of British Geographers* intervention – 'Incontestable: Imagining possibilities through intimate Black Geographies'.

While writing this book we thought about conversations and experiences that are seldom deemed to be forms of knowledge because they do not receive the institutional seal of approval or because they occur in spheres that are not cowed by the territorialism of academia and institutions seeking to be *the* authorities on Black history and Black lives in Scotland. Relatedly, the clarifying collective work of scholars Azeezat Johnson, Remi Joseph-Salisbury, and Beth Kamunge (2018), who co-edited the crucial collection *Fire Now: Anti-Racist Scholarship in Times of Explicit Racial Violence*, is a reminder of the ways in which writing is always much more than just words on a page (Kamunge et al. 2018: 2):

> We write to make sense of this moment as the speed at which these unrelenting, traumatising events are unfolding has been breath-taking, requiring new frameworks that seem constantly behind current events.

When working on our book we remained cognizant of common ways that Black people's experiences of Scotland are merely reduced to conversations concerning race, racism, and trauma, without due attention being paid to different dimensions of what it can mean to be a Black person in, from, and connected to (t)here. While the lives of many Black people in Scotland may be affected by antiblackness and interrelated forms of oppression, this does not exclusively define who such people are and how they experience the world. In writing *Black Oot Here: Black Lives in Scotland* we seek to reckon with the relentlessness of anti-Black racism in Scotland, while also reflecting on many other facets of Black people's lives which are rarely foregrounded in writing and research regarding Scotland, as well as writing and research related to Black lives and history in Britain. For example, we acknowledge some of the different perspectives of Black people in Scotland and push against the essentialist idea that *all* Black people in Scotland share the same political views, activist inclinations, and social values.

As part of such discussion, we consider how the material conditions of Black people in Scotland can drastically vary and are influenced by the nexus of issues concerning race, class, migration, and asylum-seeking, among other matters. In taking this approach, we draw on feminist methodologies that are based on 'the idea that feminist research involves something more than adding women and stirring or simply controlling for gender by means of a single variable. Feminist research requires a shift in how we approach research ...' (Harnois 2013: 5), including in ways that centre analysis of the entanglements of various inequalities and Black women's experiences.

The many topics and issues covered in *Black Oot Here: Black Lives in Scotland* include the following:

- How the histories and lives of Black people in, from, and connected to Scotland are shaped by *both* the specific nature of Scottish socio-political settings and the relationship between Scotland and Britain (including perceptions and experiences of the distinction between Scottishness, Englishness, and Britishness).
- How anti-Black racism, xenophobia, and interconnected oppressions impact Black people in Scotland and solidarity building.
- The currents of contemporary political and public conversations concerning racism, multiculturalism, Scottish Independence, Black people, and the notion of 'New Scots' in Scotland.
- The educational experiences of Black people in Scotland, as both teachers and learners.
- The development of Black activism in Scotland.
- Black people's experiences of, and engagement with, the creative and cultural industries (CCIs) in Scotland.
- The COVID-19 (coronavirus) pandemic experiences of Black people in Scotland.

Writer, storyteller, and researcher Jen Katshunga's (2019) article 'Too Black for Canada, too white for Congo: re-searching in a (dis)placed body' offers a crucial and reflexive discussion of matters regarding Black geographies, knowledge production, and institutional violence. In the words of Katshunga (2019), '[r]e-searching considers and reckons with systemic and structural violence, but it also necessitates that we answer where and how care (in all senses of the word) exists'. Our approach to this book is shaped by the care-full work of Katshunga (2019) which generatively distinguishes between researching and *re-searching*, while being attentive to an ethics of care.

When choosing to include a survey as part of our methodological approach to this research we were mindful of the potential for such a research method to result in work that places a harmful emphasis on quantifying Black people's lives. We wanted to avoid reducing the rich words and perspectives shared by Black people to dehumanizing 'data' points that make the fullness of who they are disappear. Therefore, we created a survey that mainly featured open questions to learn about the lives of Black people who we may not have otherwise had the chance to connect with and hear from, particularly due to the pandemic circumstances that we navigated while doing this work.

We decided that when reflecting on survey responses we would do so in a predominantly qualitative way that involved us carefully considering what people's comments may suggest about the experiences and lives of Black people in, from, and connected to Scotland. Questions that featured in the survey included, but were not limited to, the following:

- Please describe your experience of living in Scotland as a Black person and how Scotland has or has not changed during that time.
- What are your thoughts on the media representation of Black people in Scotland and/or their experiences in the media industry?
- Are you aware of any organizations or groups in Scotland that specifically focus on the lives of Black people there? If so, please provide a brief explanation.
- Are you aware of the movement for Scottish Independence and, if so, what are your thoughts on it?
- How has your life been impacted by the COVID-19 global pandemic?

We received survey responses from people aged 18–77+ years-old. Most responses were from people aged 26–35 years-old (approx. 42% of respondents), which is perhaps partly due to the 'snowball effect' of sharing our survey with people we knew, who then shared it with people they knew, resulting in many respondents who are relatively close to us in age. As the survey was predominantly shared via digital forms of communication and was created during the COVID-19 pandemic, it was not accessible to everyone, and we acknowledge this as being one of the limitations of such an approach. That said, importantly, creating the survey still afforded us the opportunity to learn about different views and experiences regarding being a Black person in, from, or connected to Scotland.

People who responded to our survey described their racial identity and ethnicity in many ways which included the following:

- Black African
- Black British African
- Black Caribbean
- Mixed race – Scottish and Ghanaian
- Black American
- Black and white mixed, Scottish, Nigerian, Irish, Jamaican and Brazilian
- mixed race (zambian-scots)
- Black African/Scottish

- Black mixed POC
- West African
- Mixed race Jamaican Scot
- Black Welsh
- Mixed Black African/White English
- Afrikan of Caribbean descent
- Black

Approximately 90% of people who responded to the survey are currently based in Scotland and the others have previously lived there or have an ancestral connection to it. The many different parts of Scotland that people who responded to the survey currently live in or have previously lived in include the Highlands, Bo'ness, Edinburgh, Falkirk, West Lothian, Glasgow, Renfrewshire, East Dunbartonshire, Hamilton, East Lothian, Peebles, Fife, Aberdeen, Stirling, Inverclyde, Perthshire, Argyll, Motherwell, St Andrews, Lanark, and Helensburgh. Most people who completed the survey have lived in Scotland for over 10 years (approximately 63% of respondents) and everyone who completed the survey had lived in Scotland at some point for at least seven months.

We share this information in the spirit of openness, but in doing so we also seek to state that this is not a book mainly based on statistics, nor do we claim that the responses to our survey represent the views of *all* Black people. Instead, we view the value of the survey responses as being rooted in the vivid and detailed reflections that people shared and which should not be dismissed on the basis that such reflections cannot capture the experiences of all Black people in, from, and connected to Scotland.

We are aware that many statisticians and positivist-inclined researchers may regard the 54 responses to our survey as not constituting so-called 'valuable data', but we reject notions of value that are rooted in research cultures that place more of an emphasis on numbers than the realities of people and ensuring they are not presented as little more than percentages. Also, the limited nature of disaggregated societal data regarding Black people's experiences in Scotland should not be confused for there being an absence of Black experiences that are impacted by both the specifics of race and gender.

Over the years we have witnessed others articulate claims of 'insignificance' when seeking to challenge the value of research and scholarship that foregrounds Black people in Scotland, often based on the assumption that because Black people 'only' constitute just over 1% of Scotland's population (Scotland's Census 2011) their perspectives are irrelevant to efforts to learn about lives (t)here.

Therefore, we aimed to steer clear of predominantly positivist language and logics in our book, and we reject expectations that we wrap our writing in elitist academic rhetoric and abstract theorizing that frames people and their experiences as nothing more than 'data'.

Essentially, we affirm the importance of meaningfully engaging with the words and lives of Black people in Scotland, on their own terms. So, we refuse to reinforce ideas about the perceived value of Black people's perspectives that are based on restrictive (and often harmful) attempts to quantify, count, and measure, and which fail to attend to the descriptive details of Black people's daily lives. As such, we are inspired by the work of scholars including Chisomo Kalinga (2021) whose writing highlights the importance of oral histories. Thus, in addition to drawing on responses to our survey, our book is based on discussions that were part of in-depth, semi-structured, and intergenerational interviews with Black people in, from, and connected to Scotland, including Mary Osei-Oppong, Gary Younge, Charmaine Blaize, Kubara Zamani, Jonathan Wilson, John R, and someone who chose the pseudonym Nikko Dingani. *Black Oot Here: Black Lives in Scotland* is also heavily shaped by our ongoing collaborative approach to combing through a range of archives in Scotland and online, as well as moments when we have reflected on some of our own and shared experiences and ephemera from our decades in Scotland.

This opening chapter contextualizes our book and provides a brief roadmap of significant moments and events in recent history that have impacted the contemporary social and political context of Scotland – a country within the UK with a population of approximately just short of 5.5 million people (National Records of Scotland 2020). Referring to responses to our 2020–2021 survey, as well as interview excerpts, this chapter also introduces key themes and topics that are explored in detail in our book, including some of the concerns and experiences of Black people in Scotland which relate to education, health and wellbeing, history, and work and labour.

Keekin back tae keek forwards: Looking back to look forwards

Very little [that I know about Black history in Scotland], other than general awareness of Scottish contributions to slavery and its in situ New World advancement of same.

2 May 2021 (56–65 years-old)

Africans have been part of Scottish life since the 16 century ... learned this through my personal research.

7 February 2021 (46–55 years-old)

All I was taught in school was that slavery is black history. I'm not well versed in Scottish black history at all.

3 February 2021 (26–35 years-old)

I don't know much [about Black history in Scotland] except that there were rich merchants who profited (many times tangentially) from slavery. I know more about the history of Christian missionaries from here because they had schools in my home country. I think courses that teach about this should be free to Black people here.

25 November 2020 (36–45 years-old)

... to be honest, it's only in the last few years where I learned more about black history in Scotland.

10 November 2020 (26–35 years-old)

Not much [that I know about Black history in Scotland]. I was made aware of Frederick Douglass and realised that half of the streets in Edinburgh/Glasgow were named about slave plantation owners.

27 October 2020 (26–35 years-old)

These comments by people who responded to our survey reflect frustrations regarding the scarce provision of opportunities to learn about Black history in Scotland. Many survey responses emphasized the need for more critical discussions of how Scottish missionary work can be understood as an iteration of paternalism, global power, and harmful colonialism. Such perspectives echo those that have been voiced by literary anthropology, storytelling and health-HIV/AIDS, illness, medicine, women, and sex researcher Chisomo Kalinga (2021) who has done essential work on 'making sense of silenced archives', and has carried out extensive archival research on the writings of the first medical missionaries from the Church of Scotland to settle in the Nyasaland Protectorate (Malawi). In the words of Kalinga (2018):

More Malawian scholars are incorporating indigenous knowledge systems into a praxis of care that reflects the nation's rich cultural history and reverence for the integration of healing and the arts in society with biomedicine. In precolonial times, the 'land of fire' or the Maravi empire as it was known, held the healer in the community with great reverence. Shortly after the arrival of Dr David Livingstone, a Scottish missionary, the colonial engagement in the region was initiated by medical doctors from the Church of Scotland in 1874, who sought to establish the British Protectorate of Nyasaland as a medical missionary colony.

In addition to highlighting issues such as those poignantly outlined by Kalinga (2016, 2018, 2021), various responses to our survey included comments that conveyed an interest in learning more about Black history from the twentieth century onwards, which is the time period most strongly foregrounded in our book:

> I would say I know certain areas in depth rather than a great breadth. I work in museums, and my personal interest is always Black history, so I seek it out. I would love to learn more about 20th century Black history, particularly post-War.
>
> 5 February 2021 (26–35 years-old)

As well as expressing their frustration concerning the lack of Black history taught in Scotland, people who responded to our survey expressed their gratitude for the work and knowledge-sharing of Black-led groups and organizations in Scotland such as Jambo! Radio, Fringe of Colour, Project X, The Edinburgh Caribbean Association, and Yon Afro Collective – of which we were two of several co-founders in 2016, following on from key related events that we were involved in, such as *Black Feminism, Womanism and the Politics of Women of Colour in Europe*[5](University of Edinburgh, 3 September, 2016) led by Akwugo Emejulu, and *Black Women and the Media – National Union of Journalists* which took place a month later (Glasgow, 6 October 2016).

In the years since such events occurred, there have been some shifts in terms of the visibility of Black-led groups and grassroots community-orientated activities in Scotland. Nevertheless, as the words of those who responded to our survey allude to, there is still a long way to go to tackle the scarcity of Black history in Scotland that is taught in formal learning, teaching, and educational environments, as well as a long road ahead to ensure that Black-led grassroots work in Scotland receives sustainable sources of support that do not require Black organizers to be tokenized and compromise their political principles, autonomy, and liberationist goals. Such issues are investigated in detail in Chapter 2 which involves us *(Re)inspecting Scotland's Black History*.

As we discuss in Chapter 4 on *Black Scotland in the Media and Public Life*, the increasing visibility that surrounds the lives of certain Black people and grassroots groups can result in commercial and political organizations opportunistically aligning themselves with them to improve their own corporate social responsibility (CSR) public image (hill and Sobande 2020; Sobande 2020a 2020b;

Sobande 2021a), or undermine the political aims of Black groups who have been identified as presenting a threat to the Scottish socio-political status quo.

A theme woven throughout our book is that visibility and public praise of a select few should *not* be mistaken for structural changes that improve the lives of *all* Black people. For these reasons, as part of the build up to our deeper discussion of matters related to visibility and *Black Scotland in the Media and Public Life*, in Chapter 2 we attempt to untangle elements of the relationship between capitalism and racism. To be precise, we consider how racial capitalism (Gilmore 2020, 2021; Quan 2019; Robinson 1983) which relates to the relationship between racism and the 'organisation of labor under capitalism' (Robinson 1983: 3) is implicated in the different degrees of visibility afforded to Black people in Scotland, and Black people's experiences of work in Scotland.

Indeed, our research involves an attempt 'to understand how the lives and representations of Black people are impacted by the whiteness of ever-present institutional gaze and marketplace structures that seek to simultaneously commodify and obscure Blackness' (hill and Sobande 2020: 1170). But throughout our book we also aim to reflect on Black interiority and intentionality which involves considering how the personal lives, feelings, thoughts, and experiences of Black people in Scotland occur in ways removed from a scrutinizing and structurally white gaze.

Black Oot Here: Black Lives in Scotland is emphatically about the past and present-day experiences of Black people of African descent in, from, and connected to Scotland, including those who are Caribbean and/or Black and 'mixed-race'.[6] Our approach to this work involves being alert to how 'Black mixed-race people are positioned as the palatable version of Blackness' (Lewis 2019a), particularly when they are perceived as embodying a proximity to whiteness. The extensive research, writing, and ongoing work of sociology scholar Chantelle Lewis (2019a, 2019b, 2020) highlights the importance of mixed-race people being 'attentive to intersectional specificities' and 'entangled proximities to whiteness' when reflecting on their/our experiences and lives. Therefore, in Chapter 3 which focuses on *Multiculturalism, 'New Scots', and Black Women's Lives*, as well as other parts of our book, we consider how the lives of *some* Black people in, from, and connected to Scotland, are shaped by the particularities of mixed-race identities which are undeniably part of Black Scottish life and history but should not be mistaken as representing *all* Black experiences.

In *Black Oot Here: Black Lives in Scotland* we use the terms *antiblackness* and *anti-Black racism* when referring to the ways that Black people in Scotland are targeted and oppressed due to reasons related to racism, ethnonationalism, colourism, colonialism, Afrophobia, and xenophobia. It is important to observe that such forms of interlocking oppression are structural in nature and can be inherent to how certain institutions (e.g. education, healthcare, housing, policing) operate, but this does not detract from the fact that individuals *are* still responsible for their own oppressive actions and their maintenance of inequalities in the context of interpersonal relations.

In our book, '[w]hilst we use the terms, "Black women" and "women of colour", the distinct differences that exist between both are recognized. This includes those related to the antiblackness that can be perpetuated by [non-Black] women of colour and which can constrain the scope for interracial solidarity in certain contexts' (hill and Sobande 2018: 113). We affirm important critiques of the term *women of colour* (WOC) which is a term that is sometimes uttered in a manner that denies or distracts from the specifics of Black women's experiences, and erases the powerful activist work that this term is intended to be embedded in. Depending on its use, WOC is a term that can function in ways that are detached from any clear liberationist, coalitional commitment, and can dismiss distinct differences between women from a range of different racial and ethnic backgrounds.[7]

Still, also, given that the term WOC originated from grassroots solidarities in the US forged between Black, Asian, Latinx, and other racialized women, but which also include international solidarities, we use the term when discussing similar activism in the setting of Scotland where the phrase 'women of colour' has even become part of the lexicon of various mainstream media and political spheres (BBC 2021a; Mcilkenny 2021). It would be simplistic to assume that our engagement with the term WOC is indicative of an import of North American concepts. Instead, the discussion of the term WOC in our book is reflective of the fact that the term has now been part of the Scottish terrain for years.

Also, we observe the crucial history of collective organizing across racial differences and rooted in a shared anti-capitalist, anti-racist, anti-sexist, and anti-imperialist political commitment (Emejulu and Bassel 2018). The term, women of colour, has never just been about race, gender, and ethnicity. Instead, it was always also about a coalitional liberationist approach that involves acknowledging differences but working together despite them; such coalitional organizing *does* exist in Scotland but is peripheral to the political centre.

We are intentional in our avoidance of solely using the language of 'race, racism, and anti-racism' in relation to the lives of Black people in Scotland, as the exactitudes of Black people's experiences are rarely sufficiently understood or articulated with the use of such terms, alone. Moreover, as we discuss in the chapters that follow, amid the landscape of conversations concerning race and racism in Scotland, Black people's lives and perspectives are sometimes glaringly marginalized or discussed without due attention being paid to class struggles and interconnected struggles against xenophobia. Contrastingly, at times, it seems as though the *only* topics Black people are encouraged or 'allowed' to discuss in Scottish media and public spaces concern race and racism.

On a related note, in our experience, within academia in Britain, critical scholarship on race and racism in Scotland is often treated as inconsequential in contrast to critical scholarship on race and racism in England. Mentioning this should not be confused with suggesting that critical research on race and racism in *any* part of Britain, or the UK, for that matter, should take precedence over another. Nor do we suggest that there is anywhere in the UK where critical research on race and racism is not marginalized within academia and society more broadly. Rather, we note the relatively peripheral position of scholarship on race and racism in Scotland within British studies of race and racism, in comparison to that which occurs in and/or on England, as this issue reflects how reporting and research on race and racism in the UK appears to be impacted by the socio-political dominance of England in relation to the other constitutive nations (Northern Ireland, Scotland, and Wales), and the subsequent politics of who and what is regarded as representing Britain and Britishness.

Make no mistake about it, in this book we do not imply that hegemonic and imperialist dynamics that exist within the UK between its constitutive nations are similar to the forms of racism, anti-Black violence, and colonialism that the UK (including Scotland!) inflict(ed) on Black people and places outside of it. Instead, we acknowledge how the legacy of such interrelated, yet *different*, issues concerning the British Empire impact the lives of Black people in, from, and connected to Scotland today, as well as how such dynamics affect contemporary discourses on race and racism in the UK.

Additionally, our book grapples with how borders 'are indisputably sites of violence' (Cowan 2021: 1), including by considering the multitude of ways that borders affect Black people in Scotland. As hill (2018) has argued elsewhere:

> Borders are everywhere in our lives: not just at the extremities of superpowers such as the European Union, or those of post-imperial epicentres like Britain, nor in detention centres and immigration raids. They are in schools and universities, hospitals and letting agencies, where successive waves of legislation require workers to check the immigration status of students and renters, to turn away anyone who may not meet the rules, and to force them underground.

Furthermore, when writing about the different lives of Black people in, from, and connected to Scotland, we reflected on the work and words of precarious migrant, researcher, teacher, and mental health advocate Furaha Asani (2020):

> Given the UK's current hostile environment policies, undocumented migrants, asylum seekers, and refugees do not have the right to access healthcare. Currently, there is no firewall between the NHS database and the Home Office. This means migrants without a visa are at risk of not receiving medical treatment, being charged for medical procedures and/or being deported. Recent data has shown that BIPOC are disproportionately affected by Covid-19. It is fair to speculate that the actual numbers could be higher when we consider the fact that many migrants without a visa will not seek medical help out of fear of being detained and/or being deported.

Our discussion of how borders affect Black people in Scotland is also based on an understanding of borders as being 'invisible and tangible, felt and (re)imagined, enforced and challenged, reproduced and recreated, online and offline' (Sobande 2020a: 103), and often constituting 'barriers between one place and another, (de)constructed differences between people and cultures, containers, confinement, separations and edges, to be near or adjacent to, limits placed upon the contents of something, somewhere, or someone' (ibid.).

Mair o' it than afore: Growing work on race, racism, and Scotland

Despite critical research and collective action related to race and racism in Scotland arguably being overlooked and obstructed in academia and public life in Britain, such work has considerably expanded since the 1990s. Texts that examine how racism takes shape in Scotland, who it impacts, and how, include *African/Caribbeans in Scotland: A socio-geographical study* (Evans 1995), *Challenging Racism in The Early Years: The Role of Childcare Services in Scotland and Europe* (HMSO 1994), *The Enlightenment Abolished: Citizens of Britishness* (Palmer 2007), *No Problem Here: Understanding Racism in Scotland* (Davidson et al. 2018), *It Wisnae Us: The Truth about Glasgow and Slavery* (Mullen 2009), and *New Shoots Old Roots: Volume II* (African & Caribbean Women's Association – ACWA 2020).

The growing volume of work on such matters also includes the *Retrospect Journal*'s June 2021 special issue on the theme of 'Race in Retrospective' which in 'collaboration with RACE.ED (a cross-university network concerned with race, racialization, and decolonial studies' (Gemmell 2021: 4), 'charts an unofficial genealogy of race and racialization at the University of Edinburgh' (ibid.). The publication features writing by a range of scholars across various contexts, such as Kalinga's (2021) on 'Making Sense of Silenced Archives: Hume, Scotland, and the "debate" about the humanity of Black People', as well as the essential work of Azeezat Johnson and Katucha Bento (2021) on 'Spoken Gems: When Academia Meets Self-Care – A Conversational Piece'.

Of special note among work over the decades on Black history in Scotland is *African/Caribbeans in Scotland: A socio-geographical study,* a comprehensive research project undertaken and submitted as a PhD thesis by June Evans, a Black Guyanese woman studying at the University of Edinburgh in the 1990s. Evans' research is underpinned by two principle objectives, as stated in the abstract (1995: iv), 'first to make the African/Caribbean presence in Scotland visible and secondly to challenge the prevailing view that racism does not exist in Scotland'. *African/Caribbeans in Scotland: A socio-geographical study* not only achieves these objectives, but also provides an invaluable resource to Black Scottish studies, to which we hope *Black Oot Here: Black Lives in Scotland* will also considerably contribute.

There is much crossover between Evans' (1995) work and ours, demonstrating what has changed and what has not in the decades in-between. Also of note, is the last of the previously mentioned books, *New Shoots Old Roots: Volume II,* which features the work of visual artist Sekai Machache on its cover and puts the focus squarely on the lives of Black African and Caribbean women in Scotland. Volume II, which foregrounds the perspectives of 18 women, builds upon the first iteration of such writing which originally involved interviews with eight women from the African & Caribbean Women's Association about five decades of life in Scotland, resulting in elements of such interviews forming audio/visual work which in 2015 featured as part of Luminate Festival (Scotland's Creative Ageing Festival) and Black History Month (ACWA 2020).

Among the stories and experiences outlined in Volume II are 'issues of racism, discrimination and triumph over adversity. The contributions offer a reflection on how the immigrant story has changed for the better through the years in some respects; while in other areas, many challenges remain the same' (Iredia 2020: 5). Mary Osei-Oppong, who is the current chair of ACWA and author of *For the Love of Teaching: The Anti-Racist Battlefield in Education* (Osei-Oppong 2020), kindly agreed to be interviewed in 2021 as part of our research. Excerpts from Mary's generous interview feature in our book and include insightful comments such as the following that convey the complexities of some of what has, and *has not*, changed for Black people in Scotland over the years:

Now ... I can see a good number of Black people of African heritage in Glasgow and also in Scotland as a whole ... but not a lot ... and everyone's experience will be different. Even for my children ... my three children ... their experiences are different. But for me ... I belong to three groups. So, I'm part of the African & Caribbean Women's Association and just quite recently I have been elected as the Chair. I'm also part of African-Caribbean Elders in Scotland, and as a Ghanaian, I belong to the Ghana Welfare Association, and I was the Secretary for two years for them ... so through this I have listened to a lot of African people and understand their suffering their anxiety ... the trauma they suffer. I would say in terms of maybe employability we have moved on ... you can see one or two ... you can see African faces in some places, but mostly in nursing and maybe in social care, but in education it's lacking ... The only difference is because now we are here in number wise more than the early 80s, so if I have to equate it ... I would not say much has changed [since then] ... for me, anyway, I speak for myself and what I've come across ... racism, micro-aggression (a form of racism) ... in the workplace and in society in general ... we have to work hard ...we have to understand one another. For example, if you have Black employees and you want to improve their health and wellbeing in your organisation and your company, you cannot just go and devise any strategy and think that will work for them. You have to sit with whatever the group is that you're working with ... and talk to them ... ask them what do you need in order to make you comfortable here ... I think that is what is lacking.

The words of Mary Osei-Oppong echo elements of the sentiments of work by the Mwasi Afrofeminist Collectif, a French-based collective fighting for Black liberation, who has written about the need for 'those who fight for us' to ensure that their efforts do not occur 'without us' (Mwasi Collectif 2019). As the excerpt from Mary Osei-Oppong's interview makes clear, there is a need for work intended to support Black people in Scotland to consistently foreground Black people's perspectives and priorities throughout the process.

Over the last decade there has been an expanding number of conferences, events, and symposia that focus on issues regarding race and racism in Scotland, such as 'Racism: From the Labour Movement to the Far-Right' (University of Glasgow, 5–6 September 2014), 'Borders, Racisms and Resistance' (Abertay University, 6 September 2017), 'Women of Colour Researchers: A Mentoring Symposium' (University of Glasgow, 22 September 2017), 'Resisting Whiteness' (Edinburgh, Pleasance Theatre, 22 September 2018 and 28 September 2019), 'Telling our Own Stories: People of Colour in Scotland's Media' (Kinning Park Complex, 27 September 2019), and 'Tackling Scotland's Racism Problem' (University of Glasgow, 10 May 2020).

March 2021 saw the creation of the new role of Lecturer in Black British History at the University of Edinburgh which, the job advert suggests, may involve the appointed person expressing 'a willingness to develop a Scottish dimension of Black British histories to research, teaching and knowledge exchange' (University of Edinburgh 2021). Such a job advert, which refers to 'a Scottish dimension of Black British histories' (University of Edinburgh 2021), is one that neither of us have come across before in Scotland, 'where the nation's racist and colonial legacy is scarcely institutionally acknowledged' (Sobande and Wells 2021: 11). Perhaps, the job advert reflects the gradual increasing recognition of the specifics of Black Scottish history across institutions including universities, as well as the emergent and expanding scholarly area of Black Scottish studies which may include forthcoming work by US-based scholar Jeanette Davidson, who was born in Scotland, and the Black male studies work of Tommy J. Curry, who moved from the US to the University of Edinburgh in 2019. That said, although scholarship on race, racism and Black history in Scotland is simultaneously somewhat established and burgeoning, seldom are the lives of Black people of African descent the central or sole focus of such work. Further still, scarcely is such scholarship led by or embedded in the work of Black people of African descent in and/or from Scotland.

As sociologists Leah Bassel and Akwugo Emejulu (2017) highlight in their landmark book, *Minority Women and Austerity: Survival and Resistance in France and Britain*, 'we are witnessing important divergences between England and Scotland in relation to multicultural citizenship' (Bassel and Emejulu 2017: 3). As such crucial work suggests, to treat the Scottish context as the same as an English one would be a misguided approach to research regarding Black people's lives. Black people's experiences in Scotland are far too frequently subsumed under broader discussions of race and racism in Britain which fail to acknowledge and wrestle with the geo-cultural and socio-political traits that are particular to Scotland. Returning to the illuminating words of Bassel and Emejulu (2017: 3–4):

> [l]ike England, it [Scotland] shares the principle of liberal pluralism and actively promotes an idea of Scottish multicultural citizenship. Like the rest of Europe, Scotland is also experiencing an upturn in nationalist sentiment. In stark contrast to other European countries, however, Scotland combines its nationalism with multiculturalism to advance a civic multicultural nationalism and national identity.

Bolstered by such analysis, we penned our book with an understanding of how the experiences of Black people in Scotland are affected by internal regional and national political dynamics, as well as those that take shape within Britain and link to its fractious relationship with Europe – namely, the European Union (EU). In taking such an approach we affirm that '[p]art of the difficulty with the dominant cultural formation of Britain is the inability or reluctance of its institutions to accept that European racism was and is a constitutive feature of British nationalism' (Hesse 2000a: 18).

Influenced by aspects of the Black studies work of Cedric J. Robinson (1983) on *Black Marxism: The Making of the Black Radical Tradition*, in the chapters of this book we also ponder the relationship between nationalism and racial capitalism, while thinking about how this may be made manifest in Scotland. We reflect on Robinson's (1983: 3) view that '[n]ationalism, as a mix of racial sensibility and the economic interests of the national bourgeoisie' was a powerful 'ideological impulse' (ibid.) enmeshed with the development of capitalist structures. Inspired by many aspects of the Black radical tradition, our book draws on the work of Black African diasporic people in various places, as even 'place-based liberationist struggles' (Gilmore 2020) which attend to the needs of individuals in a particular part of the world require 'an approach to solving problems, that no matter how particular and local they are, involve an international dimension because it [racial capitalism] is an international problem' (ibid.).

As is asserted by critical race, gender, and leadership studies scholar Philomena Essed (2009: xii), when reflecting on *Black Europe and the African Diaspora*, '[i]t is important to understand the significance of women's groups in European antiracism and ethnic emancipation movements. Many of the women's groups consisted of feminists who had been part of the larger, white-dominated women's movement. From questioning the "we" of the "we women's movement" emerged antiracist organizations among women'. Relatedly, the 1989 paper, 'Black Woman, White Scotland' written by multicultural and anti-racist education scholar Rowena Arshad and Mukami McCrum who has worked for the Scottish Government as policy manager in Gender and LGBT Equality and Violence Against Women, and was the chief executive of Central Scotland Racial Equality Council, stated, 'Scottish thinking has in general shifted from a stance of total complacency about racism to one that accepts, be that grudgingly or willingly, that racism is not a problem confined to areas of high black populations e.g.: Birmingham, London'.

Arshad and McCrum (1989) were critical of the equal opportunities policies, racism awareness/multi-cultural/anti-racist training programmes and commissioned studies implemented by local authorities and the voluntary sector to address this. Such strategies, they persuasively argued, had yet to occur across the board, nor had such strategies radically affected existing policies, 'it is immaterial if there was none, one or one hundred blacks [sic] per square mile, as the issue of equality within policies and general combatting of racism still exists' (Arshad and McCrum 1989: 207).

Decades later, in 2018, authors and scholars Neil Davidson, Minna Liinpää, Maureen McBride, and Satnam Virdee (2018: 9) asserted that '[i]n contrast to England, there has been relatively little public discussion about the historical or contemporaneous structuring power of racism in Scotland'. This statement, alongside Arshad and McCrum's (1989) remains relatively applicable to public discourse in Scotland in 2021 (and, now, in 2022), but there is also a need to recognize some significant shifts that have occurred in recent years, including due to the increased momentum and visibility of anti-racist and Black Lives Matter (BLM) social justice movement organizing in Scotland since 2020.

In Britain '[a] conjunctural moment can be identified at the very end of the 20th century where the concept of institutional racism suddenly arrived into the political arena in an unprecedented way' (Nwonka 2020: 7). Additionally, in the years since Davidson et al. (2018: 9) reflected on how 'this narrative of an absent racism in Scottish history has become even more entrenched in the course of recent developments . . ', public discussion about racism in Scotland has moved on in some (un)surprising ways which we consider in our book.

Although *Black Oot Here: Black Lives in Scotland* is based on interviews with other Black people, a survey that we conducted (2020–2021), photography, and analysis of archived material, it is also the outcome of decades of our own experiences and those of family members and friends. In writing this book, we reflect on aspects of our individual and shared encounters when discussing issues such as Black and anti-racist organizing, as well as the media representation and workplace experiences of Black people in Scotland.

Our book is undoubtedly influenced by our own lives, including the many years that each of us has spent in parts of Scotland such as Glasgow, Edinburgh, Hamilton, Dundee, and Dunoon. Since meeting in Glasgow in 2016, after being introduced to each other by Akwugo Emejulu, 'we have continued to collaboratively reflect on and research issues related to race in Britain, particularly in Scotland where we have both spent most of our lives, in addition to Wales which is which is where one of us [Francesca] now calls "home"' (hill and Sobande 2020: 1169). Still, *Black Oot Here: Black Lives in Scotland* is not a collaborative autobiographical account of living in Scotland for several decades – where one of us migrated from Nigeria in the 1980s and is still based, and where the other was born in the early 1990s and lived until 2017.

The history and many different experiences of Black people in Scotland cannot be understood and supported by referring and deferring to a handful of individuals and archived sources. Hence, while we do not shy away from the fact that our book is impacted by who we are and how we have experienced life in Scotland as Black (and 'mixed-race') women of Nigerian descent, we attempt to avoid centring ourselves in the chapters of our book. After all, many of our own experiences drastically differ to those of Black people in Scotland who are the most structurally stigmatized and oppressed.

Black people in Scotland – and anywhere, for that matter – are far from being one homogenous demographic. The details of their/our lives cannot be comprehended by simply being grouped under the umbrella label of *Black, Asian, and minority ethnic* (BAME) or *people of colour* (POC). Because of this, instead of exclusively focusing on terms including *BAME* which often serve 'as a rhetorical device used by politicians, policymakers, and media professionals' (hill and Sobande 2019: 110), we aim to more precisely articulate Black people's experiences by tarrying with the meaning and use of words and identity descriptors such as *Black in Scotland, Black Scots, Afro Scots,* and *Black Scottishness.*

When referring to these terms we do so with an understanding that they do not resonate with all Black people in, from, and connected to Scotland, including for reasons related to different experiences of/(in)access to nationality, the nation, the state, and citizenship. As writer, photographer, and broadcast journalist Johny Pitts (2019: 1) explains in the book *Afropean: Notes from Black Europe,* '[l]abels are invariably problematic, often provocative, but at their best they can sing something into visibility'. Likewise, as historian Olivette Otele (2020: 8) explains when outlining key terms that feature in the book *African Europeans: An Untold History,* many words 'have been significant in particular places and at specific times in history'. In Chapter 3, we take the time to consider how labels and language function in Scotland in ways that impact Black people and the (in)visibility that surrounds such lives. When accounting for these matters, we attempt to untangle how such (in)visibility connects to different material conditions that Black people in Scotland deal with.

We refuse to fall into the neoliberal and tokenistic trap of being marketed as representing and speaking on behalf of *all* Black people in Scotland. Instead, we acknowledge that our book offers *one* account of Black life in Scotland. Nevertheless, it is still a multivocal and intergenerational account that draws on the perspectives, experiences, and knowledge of many people. For all that is included on these pages is much more that is not, which is why we hope that when reading *Black Oot Here: Black Lives in Scotland* you treat it as part of the ongoing narrative(s) of Black people (t)here, including those who came before us and those who are yet to be born.

What are the contemporary experiences of Black people in Scotland? In what ways are these impacted by how notions of nationhood, home, and belonging have been shaken up by the past Scottish Independence referendum in 2014 and Britain's European Union Exit (Brexit) which officially commenced in 2020? How have the lives of Black people in Scotland been affected by longstanding structural inequalities that were exacerbated by the COVID-19 (coronavirus) global pandemic which 'exposed an uneven economy that has undervalued the work of ordinary people and punished the poorest for far too long' (Sangha and hill 2020: 21)? To what extent is antiblackness in Scotland recognized and addressed amid mainstream media, politics, and public discourse, and has this been shaped by the increased visibility of Black social justice movement organizing in recent years? In *Black Oot Here: Black Lives in Scotland* we pose and consider these questions, and more.

Nae jist aboot race: Race, gender, sexuality, and class

One of many aspects of racism that is necessary to understand is that racism intersects with other forms of oppression (Bilge 2013; Collins and Bilge 2016; Collins 2000; Crenshaw 1989, 1991; de Lima 2012; Johnson 2020). We are no doubt stating the obvious, to some. However, unfortunately this point requires reiterating due to the prevalence of racism, sexism, classism, and xenophobia being framed as completely unrelated issues in Scotland. From the start, our book emphasizes that racism and how it impacts different people's lives, is interconnected with sexism, classism, misogyny, ableism, homophobia, xenophobia, Islamophobia, colourism, transphobia, and other interrelated types of structural oppression. It is important to acknowledge that the pervasiveness of antiblackness *and* transphobia results in vitriolic forms of abuse and violence that are directed at Black trans and non-binary people who may even encounter such oppression within Black-led spaces.

We affirm the view that '[t]he construct of gender binary is, and has always been, precarious. Aggressively contingent, it is an immaterial invention that in its toxic virality has infected our social and cultural narratives. To exist within a binary system one must assume that our selves are unchangeable, that how we are read in the world must be chosen for us, rather than for us to define – and choose – for ourselves' (Russell 2020: 6–7). Rampant transphobia in Scotland continues to be inadequately addressed by many Scottish politicians and public sector organizations that claim to be advocates of social justice. Furthermore, although there appears to have been an increase in public discourse concerning intersectionality in Scotland over the last few years, typically it seems to be the perspectives of cisgender women that are foregrounded, rarely the perspectives of people who are Black. Thus, many of Scotland's claims of progressiveness and commitment to equity and social justice are yet to be substantiated in ways that move beyond centring the opinions, experiences, and work of a select few whose lives rarely resemble those of the most oppressed.

Here, key work that has guided ours, again includes the detailed research of Emejulu and Bassel (2015: 86) which explores 'how well third sector organisations, policy-makers and social movements have responded to minority women's perspectives and needs arising from austerity and racism'. We are also informed by the inimitable research and writing of social geographer Azeezat Johnson (2020: 801) whose work foregrounds the lives of Black people, particularly Black Muslim women, and whose journal article 'Refuting "How the other half lives": I am a woman's rights', offers an incisive analysis of how normative notions of womanhood are irrefutably tethered to whiteness:

> The popularity of phrases like 'women and PoC (People of Colour)' or 'women and BAME (Black Asian Minority Ethnic)' are illustrations of this problem: the category of 'woman' becomes implicitly attached to white women while non-white women are subsumed within a racialised homogenous Other ...

Additionally, we take stock of some of the perspectives shared in the book *Grit and Diamonds: Women in Scotland Making History: 1980–1990* (Henderson and Mackay 1990). Written texts, images, and ephemera that are accessible at Glasgow Women's Library (GWL) also played an invaluable role in our research – particularly press clippings that provided a glimpse of some of the ways that issues related to race, gender, sexuality, class, and Black people were discussed and dismissed in Scottish media and public life in the twentieth century.

One of many revealing findings from the GWL archive which reflects how antiblackness and misogyny has influenced education in Scotland for decades was a 27 July (1989) clipping from *The Glasgow Herald* (simplified to *The Herald* since 1992). It featured the title 'Colour Coding' and words from a letter that a reader sent on 21 July 1989, expressing their concern that two Scottish colleges where electrical engineering was taught were apparently using the following words when teaching students how to remember coding resisters, 'Black Bastards rape our young girls but virgins go without. Bad Boys rape our young girls but Violet goes willingly'. In addition to, arguably, being evidence of misogyny and rape culture, such words reflect the gendered and violently anti-Black stereotypes that surround certain ideas about Black men in Scotland, who are oppressively framed as hypersexualized, predatory and aggressors.

Other clippings accessed at GWL include those that are part of a Scottish Women's Aid Collection Box that highlight work that occurred in the 1980s as part of an effort to tackle racism in Scotland. A piece by Sarah Nelson for *The Scotsman* on 5 May 1986 acknowledges the work of The Educational Institute of Scotland (EIS), referred to as having 'committed itself at the weekend to far-reaching policies aimed at fighting racism in education. Fundamentally, it accepted that racism is a serious issue in Scotland as a whole, and within the education system in particular'. Another part of Nelson's piece in *The Scotsman* in 1986 is illustrative of how the experiences of Black people in Scotland have often been treated as a separate issue to the experiences of women – as though Black women in Scotland do not exist: '[t] hese ideas are less familiar in Scotland … Black activists faced questions acutely familiar to women's campaigners, despite the different situations'.

In *Black Oot Here: Black Lives in Scotland* we seek to emphasize the intersecting nature of oppression and discuss some of the particularities of the experiences of Black women in Scotland, including Black women campaigners such as Mary Osei-Oppong and Charmaine Blaize. We also focus on some of the anti-Black and gendered stereotypes and forms of oppression that impact the lives of Black men and can contribute to their experience of the Scottish criminal justice system, as well as forms of police brutality.

As the COVID-19 pandemic emerged at a significant point in our archival research timeline we mainly turned to personal and digital resources to learn more about the history of Black people in Scotland. A key online archive that we accessed was that of *The List* – 'a digital guide to arts and entertainment in the United Kingdom'. Searching this archive with the use of keywords such as 'Black African' (which returned 20,776 results in April 2020) and 'Black Women' (which returned 25,513 results in April 2020) enabled us to trace aspects of Black people's involvement in and contribution to the creative and cultural industries (CCIs) in Scotland.

In recent years, while *The List* publication was under the editorship of Arusa Qureshi (2018–2020) who is a writer, editor, 'general music person', and author of *Flip the Script: How Women Came to Rule Hip Hop* (Qureshi 2021a), there was notable coverage of the creative work of Black women that is typically omitted in mainstream media in Scotland. In Chapter 4, we connect to the writing of Qureshi (2021b) who ran a six-month project on the experiences of people of colour in the CCIs in Scotland, which involved a series of interviews with individuals from different arts genres who were asked: '*What can be done to get more creatives of colour involved in the arts in Scotland in a way that is genuine and not tokenistic, with attention also given to sustained support?*'.

When doing research via *The List* archive, we encountered articles about the exhibitions of Black women artists and creatives in the late twentieth century and early twenty-first century (France 1992; Patrick 1990). As part of this project we also read writing regarding Black art and creativity in Scotland over the last decade (Folorunso 2020a), and contributed to, and, experienced, some of this creative work ourselves (hill and Sobande 2018; hill and Sobande 2020a). Overall, this resulted in us gaining a greater understanding of challenges that Black artists and creative practitioners have faced (t)here for a long time.

Our prior work has considered 'issues regarding the encounters of Black women and women of colour in relation to arts and cultural spaces in Scotland' (hill and Sobande 2019: 107), including 'to emphasise the need for their narratives to be archived, creatively expressed, and publicly acknowledged' (ibid.). Further still, since first meeting in 2016 we have been glad to witness and be involved in the growing work of Black people in Scottish media and CCIs contexts. However, we are still hyperaware of how such work is frequently pigeonholed, underfunded, trivialized, short-term, and seldom involves Black working-class people being substantially and sustainably supported. After all, the time it takes to even complete a grant application is sometimes time that the most marginalized in society do not have the luxury of spending on anything other than different survival strategies and work (both paid and unpaid, including care work). Also, we have noted how the term 'Black Scottish' is sometimes used by CCI organizations in ways that are disconnected from the lives of local (particularly, working-class) Black people, and involve predominantly platforming the work of middle to upper-class Black diasporic people who are based elsewhere and are deemed to be part of a 'global Afropolitan' creative world.

As film studies scholar Clive Nwonka (2020: 1) notes, '[d]espite the continued presence of racism, black British identities have found the UK's creative industries particularly opportune as a site of cultural representation, which at varying moments have performed as both the vanguard of post-multicultural racial inclusion, and an enabler of the circulation of hegemonic narratives of blackness, often under the equally contested logic of cultural diversity as a policy rationale'. Nwonka (2020: 1) advances that the term 'black neoliberal aesthetic' is one that 'points to a visual mode in which popular, mediated constructions of blackness are narrativized and presented as positive black representation' (Nwonka 2020: 4). A more detailed explanation offered by Nwonka (2020: 8) includes the following:

> *The black neoliberal aesthetic* operates as the nomenclature defining such a phenomenon when, both in the public sphere of narrating blackness and the

voluntary participation of blackness in its production of images, moments and vernaculars of black social and cultural interest, a dynamic is achieved where the proactive response by the screen industries to black moral panics, requires the involvement and uptake of blackness itself in its narrating. When conceived under the rubric of diversity, black cultural value and social analysis, the dynamic can be legitimised and telegraphed as a collaborative *black self dramatisation*. My use of contradictions refers to the aesthetics' ability to sustain the values of liberalism, diversity and racial progress, while being equally committed to neoliberalism by serving a broader audience's desire for the hegemonic version of the black 'social condition'.

We recognize the salience of *some* Black British identities (e.g. some associated with life in major cities in England, and, even, at times, Scotland) amid elements of the creative and cultural industries in Britain. However, we also observe the distinct dearth of other Black people in and/or from Britain in the creative and cultural industries (e.g. the scarcity of sustainable industry support that is accessible to Black working-class, disabled, and LGBTQIA+ people, including Black people in rural parts of Scotland).

We do not dispute Nwonka's (2020: 1) acknowledgement of 'a hybridising of neoliberalism and themes of black consciousness in the UK screen industries'. However, we emphasize the significant differences that can exist between the screen and creative/cultural industries in the UK's constitutive nations (England, Northern Ireland, Scotland, and Wales), which can be impacted by 'the influence of variations regarding regionality and rurality' (Sobande 2020a: 29) – including a lack of understanding and recognition of Black Scottish film (which is distinct from Black film that is simply shown in Scotland) and creative practice across the UK.

Accordingly, when examining matters to do with Black lives in Scotland and the CCIs in more detail in Chapter 4, while drawing on the work of scholars such as Hesse (2000a, 2000b), and Brown (2009), we pay attention to some of the differences between notions of Black Britishness and being Black in and/or from Scotland. In turn, we reflect on 'the role of regionality in experiences of Black life in Britain, especially in parts where distinctly few Black people live' (Sobande 2020a: 34). Consequently, we call for more specificity in naming whose/what experiences are typically foregrounded in and by contemporary discourse on Black Britishness, and whose/what experiences such a term often does not encompass.

We do not contest the existence or meaningful use of the terms *Black British* and *Black Britishness*. Instead, we aim to contribute to expanding discussions about the differences between the lives and identities of Black people across various nations and regions within Britain, especially as such differences are, at times, obfuscated by the ways that the term 'Black British' is used and functions.

Black fowk maitter: Black lives matter in Scotland

… Scotland needs to come to terms with racism in it's society, both historic and contemporary, perhaps even more so than in England, where it's so obvious, and as a result have done more to counteract this. For example, Black-focussed cultural, health and political resources across the country. This is obviously also a result of having more Black communities.

5 February 2021 (26–35 years-old)

Since we started to write *Black Oot Here: Black Lives in Scotland* years ago, a lot has changed, and a lot has not. Among the many changes that took place was the COVID-19 global pandemic which resulted in government-enforced 'lockdown' measures in Scotland and many parts of the world in 2020 and 2021. During that time, we also watched as Black Lives Matter (BLM) and the Black social justice movement galvanized in the US, and globally (Taylor 2021), in response to fatal violence and police brutality inflicted upon Black people such as George Floyd, Tony McDade, Breonna Taylor, and Ahmaud Arbery.

As outlined by writer, historian, scholar, and activist, Barbara Ransby (2018: 1), 'Black Lives Matter began as a social media hashtag in 2013 in response to state and vigilante violence against Black people, sparked by the vigilante murder of Trayvon Martin in Sanford, Florida, 2012, and the police murder of Michael Brown in Ferguson, Missouri, 2014. The slogan has evolved into the battle cry of this generation of Black youth activists … The breadth and impact of Black Lives Matter the term has been extraordinary. It has penetrated our consciousness and our lexicon, from professional sports to prime time television, to corporate boardrooms, and to all sectors of the art world'. The sentiments of Black Lives Matter have been felt and upheld by some in Scotland for years, including in the form of protests following the death of Sheku Bayoh, a Black man who died following police contact in the Scottish town of Kirkcaldy in 2015.

Even though BLM sentiments and expressions of solidarity have been present in Scotland for years, we began working on our book at a time when neither of us could have imagined the size of BLM social justice movement gatherings that occurred in Glasgow, Edinburgh, Dundee, and other parts of Scotland in June 2020. Ahead of a BLM event in Edinburgh at Holyrood Park on 7 June 2020, more than 9,000 people on Facebook had indicated their interest in attending it. This was certainly the first time in both of our lives that we had seen the coordination of multiple events on this scale, ostensibly related to tackling antiblackness in Scotland and globally. As scholar and activist Adam Elliot-Cooper (2021: 172) writes in the book *Black Resistance to British Policing*, 'these would become the largest anti-racist protests in British history, with hundreds of thousands of people taking to streets in cities, towns and villages across the country . . . their sheer scale made them impossible to ignore'.

During that first fortnight of June 2020, we found ourselves frequently messaging each other about how Black activism and anti-racist action appeared to be gaining momentum where we lived at the time – Glasgow in Scotland and Cardiff in Wales (hill and Sobande 2020). Social media served as a way for each of us to attempt to connect with what was happening on the ground where the other was based.

1 'Black Lives Matter' signage in Glasgow, June 2020. Photograph by layla-roxanne hill

2 Glasgow, Scotland – 23 June: Black Lives Matter graffiti is seen in Glasgow, Scotland. Photograph by Jeff J Mitchell/Getty Images

3 Edinburgh, United Kingdom – 7 June: Black Lives Matter protest in Holyrood Park. Photograph by Jeff J Mitchell/Getty Images

4 'BLM' sprayed in black on street box in Edinburgh, August 2020. Photograph by Francesca Sobande

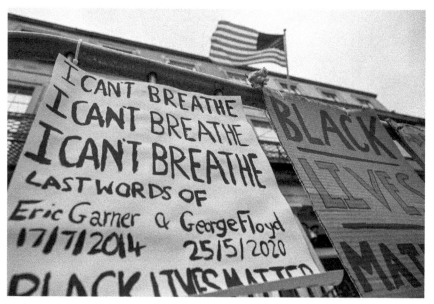

5 Edinburgh – 4 June: Members of the public view messages remembering George Floyd. Photograph by Jeff J Mitchell/Getty Images

As current chair of ACWA and author of *For the Love of Teaching: The Anti-Racist Battlefield in Education*, Mary Osei-Oppong, said when asked about her thoughts on the rising discussions about BLM and Black activist organizing in Scotland:

> I think Black Lives Matter made an impact because I don't think that we have ever seen anything like that in Scotland. To see young people ... Black, white, whatever ... came together to fight for a cause. I've never seen anything like it, apart from maybe say the Union ... EIS (Educational Institute of Scotland), their pay fight for teachers, but to see young people coming together with such force ... is something that ... it will be with me forever and ever. I think for me it signifies a cultural shift ... that people are tired ... we have to listen to the young ones, and I think that we have not seen the end of it, and, maybe, I believe, that has changed the conversation ... and now every organisation wants to be part of it, which to me is a good thing but it should not be just for a 'smokescreen'. It should be something ... that they take it seriously and believe in it and work towards that to improve everybody's wellbeing ... because the disparities in society are just too much.

Like Mary, we were heartened by such BLM events and activity in Scotland. While we are hopeful, we also remain sceptical of the extent to which substantial change in Scotland regarding addressing antiblackness and white supremacy will be supported in a sustained way at a structural level. As freelance writer and creative Tomiwa Folorunso (2020b) rightly points out, '[p]olice brutality against black people isn't shocking or surprising' to those who have long been aware of the prevalence of antiblackness and white supremacy, globally. Therefore, a relatively recent focus on it in aspects of Scottish media should not be mistaken for suggesting the newness of such issues.

During early June in 2020 we observed how organizations, institutions, and individuals in Scotland who have previously participated in forms of antiblackness rushed to issue public statements that implied they were invested in tackling racism and inequalities. Often, such statements seemed to amount to little more than unsubstantiated messages propped up by sufficiently ambiguous rhetoric and nebulous representations that evade articulating an intention to address antiblackness and white supremacy, locally and globally. Put differently, some of the actions of organizations may be interpreted as examples of cosplaying as community (hill 2021), or evidence of how 'ideas regarding "intersectional" approaches to feminism and Black activism are drawn on in marketing content related to the concept of being "woke" (invested in addressing social injustices)' (Sobande 2020b: 2723).

Many comments on the impact of BLM were made by people who responded to our survey. These included words such as the following in response to the question 'Has your experience as a Black person in Scotland changed since the recent Black Lives Matter organizing there? Please explain':

> It has made me more aware of the different advocacy groups in Scotland. Also, my current professional role is a direct result of the Black Lives Matter reigniting in 2020.
>
> 4 May 2021 (36–45 years-old)

> Not sure because of lockdown but there seems to be a readiness to listen, look back and reflect.
>
> 19 March 2021 (56–65 years-old)

> Yes and no. I realised how my neighbours think of me. they believe that racism does not exist in Scotland.
>
> 17 February 2021 (56–65 years-old)

> Somewhat people tend to be a bit more sympathetic for want of a word. Still looking to Black people to come up with solutions and educate white people which has its pros and cons. Knowledge is there for everyone . . . its not hidden.
>
> 10 February 2021 (46–65 years-old)

> Yes. More awareness on racism among the Scottish population. But still lots of work to be done.
>
> 7 February 2021 (46–55 years-old)

> Has changed in the way where I have less friends as I was sick of people's indifference to what we face on a global scale. I've become more unapologetic. I have even less patience for white nonsense. I've engaged and connected with more black creatives in Scotland, which I really appreciated as up until a couple of years ago I felt very isolated in the industry.
>
> 3 February 2021 (26–35 years-old)

> Not really, but I have noticed my children's lives change. They are more involved in wanting to make change and call out racism so much more.
>
> 29 January 2021 (36–45 years-old)

> While most people support BLM, most don't want to deal with difficult topics. In fact there seems to be resistance to look at these issues.
>
> 13 January 2021 (46–55 years-old)

Such perspectives make clear that racism, and, more specifically, antiblackness, is not something that can be addressed with a 'tick box' corporate Equality,

Diversity, and Inclusion (EDI) approach which is typically little more than an exercise in maintaining the public image of organizations and managing reputational risk rather than tackling structural oppression. Time and time again, shallow attempts to address racism, or at least, appear to care about addressing it, are operationalized as a way for organizations to market themselves rather than challenge white supremacy, which would likely require the upending of at least some of such organizations.

When we were scanning institutions' stock 'BLM' statements that were issued on social media in Spring/Summer 2020, and, in some cases, may have been meticulously crafted in an attempt to distract from track records of antiblackness, the signature line of cynical and comedic Scottish TV character Olive Actory (played by Karen Dunbar) in *Chewin' The Fat* (1999–2002) continually came to mind – 'I can definitely smell shite . . .'.

When messaging each other back and forth in June 2020 and attempting to make sense of how issues related to racism and antiblackness in Scotland were being framed in the press, we discussed being thankful for the writing, analysis, and grassroots work of Black people in Scotland that made its way to us online and through different channels at the time. Yet, we also reflected on our frustration at revisionist Scottish media and political narratives that despite acknowledging anti-Black violence in the US, conveniently stop short of fully interrogating antiblackness (t)here in Scotland.

There are still individuals and institutions who peddle 'the myth that Scotland does not have a serious racism problem' (Davidson and Virdee 2018: 9), or who engage in conversations concerning race, gender, and intersectionality, but without daring to name antiblackness and white supremacy. However, since the Spring and Summer 2020 wave of BLM protests in Scotland, to some degree, and in certain contexts, a newfound stigma and sense of cynicism surrounds flimsy claims of Scotland's lack of racism. As one person put it:

> While the Black Lives Matter movement has been very visible in my area (loads and loads of window posters) I have not seen much change on the ground. The discussion over the Dundas monument in Edinburgh has been influenced by it but overall I don't see it as a particularly high priority issue in Scotland. . . .
> 12 March 2021 (aged 36–46 years-old)

Expanding on the considerations addressed in *No Problem Here: Understanding Racism in Scotland* (Davidson et al. 2018), we argue that on the rare occasions that issues to do with race and racism *are* central to public and political discussions in Scotland, such discourse often predominantly or exclusively

6 'Blacks out' carved into children's climbing frame in a Scottish playpark, June 2021. Photograph by layla-roxanne hill

focuses on Scotland's past involvement in slavery, without also paying due attention to connected contemporary experiences of antiblackness and interrelated oppressions. If public discourse on race and racism in Scotland is only preoccupied with its past there is a risk that such discussion stymies work to address present-day oppression and is weaponized to enable individuals and institutions to absolve themselves of their part played in antiblackness *right now*.

Put briefly, we call for public, political, and policy conversations and strategies concerning race and racism in Scotland to avoid restrictively focusing on the past, at the explicit exclusion of addressing how racism, including, anti-Black violence, manifests in the present. Indeed, Scotland's colonial legacy and connection to the enslavement of Black people *must* be acknowledged and addressed in meaningful and honest ways that disrupt attempts to deny such history. Yet so too should current experiences of antiblackness in Scotland. We are aware of how elements of the lives of Black people in the twenty-first century including the oppression that is inflicted on them, are, at times, cloaked and concealed by the amorphous language of 'colonial legacy' and an analytical lens that does not make links between Scottish history and the here and now. So, throughout *Black Oot Here: Black Lives in Scotland*, we seek to centre both the past and present experiences of Black people, and to write about Scotland's history in a way that clearly connects it to today and the living people and archives that are part of it.

Tak the high 'n' low roads: Book roadmap

Chapter 2 continues our considerations concerning the lives of Black people in Scotland by focusing on Scotland's Black history. This next chapter includes discussion of Scotland's connections to the transatlantic slave trade, in addition to addressing the distinct scarcity of opportunities for people to learn about Black history in Scotland in formal educational contexts – ranging from primary school to university settings. Chapter 2 establishes our understanding of racial capitalism and some of our key arguments regarding how racial capitalism is evident in Scotland and in ways that inherently oppress Black people. Chapter 2, as with the other chapters of our book, features a range of photographs including some of our own, and work by Somali-born, Glasgow-based photographer Najma Abukar, whose photography features at the start of our book and whose photographic work documents cultural and gender identities, the African diaspora and immigrant experiences within the Scottish landscape.

In Chapter 2 there is discussion of how '"Black" as a political signifier has at times been used to identify those who experience structural and institutional discrimination because of their skin colour; namely peoples of African, African-Caribbean and South Asian origin' (Maylor 2009: 360). We consider how this notion of political blackness, even when operationalized in a well-meaning way, can obfuscate forms of anti-Black oppression faced by Black people of African descent. However, we do not avoid recognizing the anti-capitalist, anti-imperialist, and anti-racist roots of politically Black positions which have played a central role in elements of union organizing in Scotland and elsewhere in Britain.

Chapter 2 also focuses on some of the educational experiences of Black people in Scotland, as both educators and learners, as well as how the COVID-19 pandemic has impacted Black people in Scotland. Following on from the penultimate part of chapter 2 which attends to elements of Black activism and collective organizing in Scotland, as well as ideas about Scottish Independence, the chapter closes with reflections on the relationship between notions of Britishness and Scottishness.

Chapter 3 examines the landscape of language related to race in Scotland, and what lessons can be learnt from the (in)effective use of certain terms (e.g. POC, BAME, WOC) as part of efforts to address racism and intersecting inequalities in this setting. This part of the book involves an in-depth discussion of the rise of 'broadly sympathetic statements made by elite politicians in Scotland about migration and the "New Scots"' (Davidson and Virdee 2018: 10).

Encouraged by the words of Davidson and Virdee (2018) who remind us that '[i]t is crucial to remain alive to the disjuncture between elite discourse on migration and the lived reality of racialised minorities in Scotland' (ibid.), Chapter 3 scrutinizes the ways that the notion of 'New Scots' does (and does not) further anti-racist efforts and attempts to challenge intersecting oppressions such as xenophobia, antiblackness, Islamophobia, and classism. We ponder over the question of who are 'Old Scots' in relation to those who are positioned as 'New', and what might such distinctions reveal about perceptions of Scotland, identity, belonging, and permanence? Our analysis of such issues is sculpted by an understanding of 'the politics of race as nation' (Hesse 2000a: 6) and involves a review of recent strategy content that has surrounded the discourse on 'New Scots' in Scotland.

Chapter 3 also includes writing on Scottish Independence and some of the various perspectives of Black people on this topic. In addition to this, the chapter features a section based on our experiences of archiving elements of Black life and history in Scotland, such as the importance of intergenerational oral histories. Such discussion foregrounds an in-depth interview with Nubiart Diary editor, presenter/producer/scriptwriter and activist Kubara Zamani.

Chapter 4 focuses on Black people's experiences and representation in the media and public life in Scotland. Such discussion deals with changes to Scottish media and politics over the last couple of decades, including the number of Black people and non-Black people of colour pursuing public political positions, and how political parties have (and have not) attempted to 'diversify' and/or make a commitment to address racism.

Chapter 4 features writing about Black women's lives, as well as the role of digital culture and technology in some of the media experiences of Black people in Scotland, who may feel connected to a wider and global Black diaspora. As well as focusing on it in chapter 4, aligned with how Black feminism has shaped our approach to this work, in other parts of *Black Oot Here: Black Lives in Scotland* we also consider the specifics of the experiences of Black women. Finally, Chapter 5 brings together the various themes, questions, and considerations that are articulated throughout our book, and which may impact the future of life in Scotland for Black people, including the wee yins (younger generations), aulder wans (older ones), and everyone in between.

Scottish exceptionalism, naw: (Re)inspecting Scotland's Black history

The only black history I know about in Scotland has been from personal study. We didn't learn anything in school. I have learned about Glasgow and Scotland's ties to slavery, I was interested to know about Scottish ties to Caribbean plantations and what role they played there. I don't know much about black history in Scotland in more recent years. I have come to understand that this is also not taught in the curriculum up here. I think our education needs to be entirely rethought.

12 December 2020 (36–45 years-old)

Before embarking on writing *Black Oot Here: Black Lives in Scotland*, we thought through and with the words of many Black people who spoke of the glaring absence and inadequacy of Black Scottish history taught at schools, colleges, and universities. We also considered how Black people's images, ideas, experiences, testimonials, and thoughts have appeared on the pages of books in ways that can reduce such individuals to tired tropes, (mis)representations, and (re) traumatizing commentaries that obscure the multitudes of Black people's lives.

As such, we critique prior writing such as the work of Hargreaves (1994: 129) on 'African Students in Britain: The Case of Aberdeen University', which features the dubious claim that 'any embarrassment' experienced by such students in Aberdeen in the late nineteenth century was 'likely' to have been 'caused by uninformed benevolence rather than racial malice' (ibid.). Hargreaves (1994: 134) then goes on to state, without using the word *racism*, '[a]lthough inevitably there were some cases of racial conflict or misunderstanding, memory suggests that most Africans found their studies in Aberdeen a positive experience'. We view accounts such as that chapter by Hargreaves as being part of the post-racial myth of exceptionalism that has been projected onto Scotland in ways that unabashedly overlook anti-Black racism and Scotland's colonial legacy.

Other accounts that seem to suggest that Scotland is a tolerant place that is free from racism, include the framing of parts of the book *As Good as Any Man: Scotland's Black Tommy*. Such work focuses on the life of soldier Arthur Roberts who during the first quarter of the twentieth century served in the King's Own Scottish Borderers and was then transferred to Royal Scots Fusiliers (Miller et al. 2014). The book includes jarring 'gotcha!' style statements such as the following in the introduction, '[t]hose who seek evidence of racism and discrimination will be disappointed' (Miller et al 2014: 14). Also, Chapter 1 of that book refers to the Race Riots of 1919 in Glasgow as being '[f]uelled by economic desperation and community distrust' (Miller et al. 2014: 15), with no explicit mention of racism in relation to those events.

We recognize that Black people's experiences of oppression and life in general in Scotland can distinctly differ. However, when encountering writing which in various ways implies that racism was *not* a distinct issue that Black people in Scotland faced in previous decades, we parse such work with scepticism, scrutiny, and sighs. This is particularly true, when detailed accounts by Belizean forestry workers, brought to our attention by June Evans' (1995) PhD thesis, *African/ Caribbeans in Scotland: A socio-geographical study*, offer an alternative view of living and working in Scotland as Black people during roughly the same time period. As Belizean forest worker Amos Ford (1985: ii), himself writes:

> It is this one-sided recording of history which this book has set out to correct the picture from the foresters point of view before the general public. Throughout, the black foresters, unlike the forestry contingents from Australia, Canada, Newfoundland and others were made to appear most unsavoury and worthless to say the least. For the writer, who was an active participant of the British Honduran Forestry Unit (B.H.F.U.) the official records made disturbing reading.

Documentation such as *Telling the Truth: British Honduran Forestry Unit in Scotland, 1941–44* make clear the unfounded nature of claims of Scottish exceptionalism that suggest racism is not part of the nation's history.

Relatedly, the reflections of individuals we interviewed, such as Jonathan Wilson who is a branding expert, public speaker, and marketing scholar, starkly contrast with post-racial perspectives. Such interviews offer unique insights concerning Black history in Scotland, including by documenting what life was like as a Black man of Caribbean and Scottish heritage studying in Dundee in the 1990s:

> So, Scotland was good to me, in that I think I became quite conscious of my Black identity, being one of the only . . . there were very few Black kids in Dundee;

you could count them on one hand. I ended up getting spotted at a gig and doing the voices and writing some rap songs for the Grand Theft Auto videogames, so it worked out in my favour, being the only Black rapper in Dundee, that they then thought, 'cool, we need him to be in our Grand Theft Auto videogame . . .'. University was a complete awakening because I had this romantic view of Scotland and being Scottish and having a kilt. I remember the first time I wore a kilt in Scotland at a university ball, and most people were basically, 'why are you wearing one? Like, what gives you the right to wear one, you're *not* Scottish?'. And that is on appearance. And not to mention the other things, of people trying to stick their hands up the kilt to find out 'how Black you are . . .' – and I think you know what I mean – that I actually fell out of love for a period of time with being Scottish. I remember giving my kilt away to my little brother and not really feeling Scottish in the way that I used to. I was feeling more affinity with East Coast hip-hop and that got me through that period.

The closing words of Jonathan allude to a Black diasporic experience. This means that for some Black people in, and, from Scotland, clear connections are made between their own lives and cultures, and those of Black people in other parts of the world, including as expressed in resonant 'East Coast hip-hop'. Other remarks of Jonathan's also emphasize that Black diasporic experiences in Scotland can be distinctly different to those in England and elsewhere:

I think Scotland seemed like it was in a time warp. Coming from Manchester and what we had, with our football and our music and everything I knew, whether that's the Caribbean baker where I could get a patty and a chat and they had the newspaper from my mum's island and stuff, there was none of that in Scotland. Scotland seemed dead like that . . . What I saw then was that being in Scotland and being into hip-hop, no-one could say, you can't be into hip-hop in the same way as they could say, you can't be into wearing kilts, or you can't be into rock music because I *was* hip-hop. And then along the way, that consciousness of Malcolm X, and all of those other things that rappers were talking about explicitly, just opened my mind. I remember when I was up in Dundee, there was one member of the Black Panther Party that came to give a talk at Dundee and I think only ten people turned up . . . I think hip-hop gave me a window to another place and that became, I guess, my dream/fantasy world. Scotland was no longer that place because I knew Scotland explicitly now. I'd travelled the length and breadth and, Stornoway to Inverness to Aberdeen. I'd seen all of these places and I'd see people look at me and follow me, so it didn't have any allure to me anymore. It gave me legitimacy to feel proud that if someone said, are you Scottish? 'Yes, I am. I've lived here'. I'd got all those things, but I kind of felt I had done Scotland, and this hip-hop thing was really fascinating to me.

Following on from the remarks of Johnathan Wilson, the comments of someone else who we interviewed, named John R, also point to the realities of racism in Scotland and the need to challenge claims that it is not an issue (t)here. In the words of John R, who migrated to Scotland from the US and has a background in law:

> There is racism in Scotland. You can find racism in the very expression of the idea that racism doesn't exist. You may like to think of yourself as not racist but when you deny the fact of racial differences, you're denying the history of what that means. The reality is that the Americas and North America, and the United States in particular, has always had to deal with the original sin. The reality is that race exists here [in Scotland], not as toxic as elsewhere, but that doesn't diminish its potency, and it certainly doesn't diminish the imperative to root it out and address it in whatever way we can. With respect to the media, that's obviously one way to start.

Focusing on this point regarding the relationship between race, racism, and the media in Scotland, our book considers how the Scottish media landscape has changed in ways connected to Black people's lives and their involvement in the industry. Before moving towards such discussion, we now take the opportunity to provide insight into how and why media (to be specific, photography) is incorporated into our book.

Th' power o' photies: 'Picturing' Black lives in Scotland

When writing *Black Oot Here: Black Lives in Scotland* we re-read the words of humanities, modern culture, and media scholar Tina M. Campt (2017: 7) on *Listening to Images*:

> Listening to Images explores the lower frequencies of transfiguration enacted at the level of the quotidian, in the everyday traffic of black folks with objects that are both mundane and special: photographs.

We knew from the start that we wanted to include photographs in this book but during our conversations about Black lives in Scotland, archiving, and visual culture, we consistently considered the capacity for certain images to feed into the Othering spectacularization of Black people, and potentially result in them facing harm. Of course, Black lives are embodied, and in some circumstances involve navigating such embodiment 'within the context of whiteness' (Yancy 2008: xv), but the encounters of Black people are not solely seen, understood, and experienced through a physical body or representations of it. Furthermore, in the poignant words of writer and curator Legacy Russell (2020: 8): 'We use "body" to give material form to an idea that has no form, an assemblage that is abstract. The concept of a body houses within it social, political, and cultural discourses, which change based on where the body is stated and how it is read.'

We exercised caution when choosing to include visuals in our book and we opted to mainly feature images of places and seemingly mundane, yet meaningful, inanimate objects and spaces, as opposed to many images of Black people.

Our approach to including images in our book was influenced by our understanding of 'the racial dynamics of visuality and photography' (Sobande et al. 2020: 166) and how '[p]hotography and related archival collections have historically been enlisted in political projects of social disciplining and hierarchy maintenance' (ibid.). Furthermore:

> As a writer, whose work is mainly published in Scotland, I [layla-roxanne] am often conflicted with how much of my own experiences of race and racism I should include in my writing. Photography and visual, creative practices provide a different way for me to reflect on and represent such issues. When taking photographs with 35 mm cameras or on my phone, I feel more able to express understandings of identities, social constructs and racism, particularly within Scotland. Though I am conscious digital images stored on a cloud and photographs taken on film become accessible to others, elsewhere, when used as

7 The front of an African shop on King Street in Glasgow. Photograph by Najma Abukar

part of my practice and incorporated with text, the images become able to confront racism, Western power structures and shared practices of liberation'.

hill and Sobande 2020: 1169

Although we do not make use of many images of Black people in our book, we still recognize the importance of such images, including when recalling the words of artist, feminist, and the co-founder of the Glasgow Women's Library, Adele Patrick (1990: 67), who for *The List* wrote the following about an exhibition of Glasgow-born Maud Sulter's creative work and a group show of Black artists from the US and UK in 1990:

> Nine black women encircle the walls of the Streetlevel Gallery. Each figure is participating in the symbolic imaging of her life history, making a statement about her own creativity and power through portrait ... Disparate voices form a chorus from the black women's diaspora ... The portraits do not encourage us to consume complacently the representations of black women; they succeed simply within the terms of their own self-imagery. Each look is a confrontation with the unequivocal evidence of photography's white, patriarchal history. Photography is after all Fine Art, it too has sought to colonise and misrepresent the body and mind of women, and in particular the black woman.

Our decision to mainly make use of images that do not depict people in this book was also guided by us noting how, following the BLM protests in Scotland in June 2020, Black people were, to some extent, notably hyper-visible (t)here, resulting in images of Black people sometimes being (re)framed and (mis)used by media and organizations in ways that promoted narratives potentially intended to neutralize critique of antiblackness in Scotland. Additionally, when deciding on which visuals would feature in *Black Oot Here: Black Lives in Scotland*, we turned to the insightful work of Zuleka Randell Woods and Anthony Kwame Harrison (2021: 28):

> ... learning more about the person behind the lens and getting some sense of who they recognize (and don't recognize) as a worthy subject of the photographic gaze enhances our understanding of the relationship between visuality and race. Obviously, race is largely recognized through the visual field. But understanding the terms of this recognition – what is seen and how it is interpreted – tells us a good deal about the differing meanings we attach to race.

At times, the images included in our book specifically relate to the following:

> ... the power of photography to illuminate issues regarding the relationship between race, antiblackness, intersecting oppressions, activism, marketing,

media, and the aesthetics of public spaces ... questions concerning who and what is (un)seen and (re)presented in images of marketplace and public space contexts. Utilising critical reflexivity, we observe and (re)view the myriad ways that the practice of photography – the framing of the lens as well as the (re)production and distribution of photos – captures, capitulates, and counters hegemonic understandings of (y)ourselves and other Black and racialised people in spaces of 'consumption',

hill and Sobande 2020: 1169

We continue our book by considering how Black history in Scotland has (and has not) been made visible in media, education, public, and political contexts. Beyond mere questions of visibility, and by going into more detail, we think about how Black history in Scotland has (and has not) been experienced by Black people (t)here.

Slaverie ''n' 'aw that stuff' in the past: Slavery and Scotland's history

In October 2020, BBC Scotland released a documentary about 'Scotland, Slavery and Statues' which is described as 'following the four-year debate over how Henry Dundas should be remembered on the inscription of the Melville Monument in Edinburgh' (BBC 2020a). The documentary featured eminent life sciences scholar and current Chancellor of Heriot-Watt University, Geoffrey Palmer, who was born in Jamaica, moved to Britain as part of the Windrush generation, and became Scotland's first Black professor in 1989. In 'Scotland, Slavery and Statues', Palmer carefully examines aspects of Scotland's relationship to the 'transatlantic slave trade'. The documentary focuses on how the statue in Edinburgh which depicts Dundas (who Dundas Street in Tkaronto / Toronto, Kanata / Canada, is named after) evades acknowledgement of how he disrupted efforts to abolish the transatlantic slave trade by arguing for its 'gradual' rather than immediate abolishment in 1792.[1]

Abolition of the slave trade in the British Empire eventually happened in 1807 but the ongoing impact of Britain's involvement in the enslavement of Black people did not end there. Also, as Otele (2020: 2) reminds readers in *African Europeans: An Untold History*, 'The black figures who are remembered are only part of the broader story of a fight against exploitation. The connections between these various stories have been forgotten because physical subjugation was accompanied not only by a rewriting of the oppressor's history but also by a shaping of the story of the oppressed.'

'Scotland, Slavery and Statues' is one of a small, yet expanding number of mainstream media documentaries that explicitly deal with how Scotland is implicated in the history of slavery. Other examples of such media include the BBC's two-part documentary 'Slavery: Scotland's Hidden Shame', which features film, television, and stage director David Hayman travelling to three continents as part of an exploration of how Scotland was involved in the transatlantic slave trade (BBC 2019c, 2019d), during which Hayman stakes the claim that '... now is the time to acknowledge our past and begin to rewrite our historical narrative'.

The first of these documentary examples ('Scotland, Slavery and Statues') opens with footage of BLM protests in Britain in 2020, hinting at how current efforts to tackle antiblackness in Scotland connect to the nation's legacy of being embroiled in the history of the enslavement of Black people. Shortly after such footage, First Minister of Scotland Nicola Sturgeon (Scottish National Party – SNP) features saying, 'I do think we should have a long hard look, and perhaps not that long a look, but a hard look at this as a country ... and the question I would start with is why do we want to continue to have statues and celebrations and street names of people who profited in and traded in abject human misery? This is a big debate and long overdue debate'.

The words of the First Minister of Scotland (Nicola Sturgeon) when speaking about 'statues and celebrations and street names of people who profited in and traded in abject human misery' signal that issues regarding antiblackness and slavery are increasingly being acknowledged by the Scottish government (2020a) and amid party politics. Indeed, in *Protecting Scotland, Renewing Scotland: The*

8 Dundas Street signage in Tkaronto (also known as Toronto), Kanata (also known as Canada). Photographs by John Foley

9 A statue of Arthur Wellesley (1st Duke of Wellington) with a traffic cone on its head and located in the front of the Gallery of Modern Art in Glasgow which has strong ties to the transatlantic slave trade. Photograph by Najma Abukar.

10 Statues in Scotland draw scrutiny for links to slave trade. Photograph by Jeff J Mitchell/Getty Images.

11 Inside National Museum of Scotland, Edinburgh. Photograph by Najma Abukar.

Government's Programme for Scotland 2020–2021, a commitment has been made to, 'sponsor an independent expert group to recommend how Scotland's existing and future museum collections can better recognise and represent a more accurate portrayal of Scotland's colonial and slavery history'. Additionally, several of Scotland's political parties referred to supporting the teaching of Scotland's legacies of empire and colonialism in their manifestos for the Scottish Parliament 2021 elections.

The relatively recent nature of some public institutions acknowledging Scotland's involvement in the enslavement of Black people is evident when reflecting on a statement on the National Library of Scotland's website, '[t]he role played by Scots in the slave trade and in its abolition has only recently been recognised. We hold both printed and manuscript resources recording Scotland's links with slavery'. In addition, the words of the Coalition for Racial Equality and Rights (CRER), Cllr. Graham Campbell, and Hoskins Architects & Stuco Design (2020a) which feature on a Black History Month Scotland 2020 website highlight that Scotland's involvement in slavery is evident throughout the country, '[i]n every city there are many hidden stories. Our buildings, statues and the names we give to places often contain links & clues to past events and forgotten people. From the 17th century, Scotland was significantly involved in the transatlantic slave trade'.

During that time, 'England, and then Britain, colonized parts of Ireland, North America, the Caribbean, Africa and Asia, strategically positioning itself at the centre of a plethora of economic and political networks' (Virdee 2014: 1). Discussion, debate, and research on Scotland's role in the building of the British Empire and the transatlantic slave trade is (re)surfacing, however, little has been said about the nation's participation in settler colonial systems. Unlike other forms of colonialism, settler colonialism continues as an ongoing and unfolding event/structure which 'replaces' Indigenous populations and develops its own distinct identity and sovereignty. Scotland and its people were – and still are – active agents of settler colonialism in countries such as Aotearoa (also known as New Zealand) and Kanata (also known as Canada).

From Perth, Cessnock, Ben Lomond and Stirling in Australia, to the Irvine and Lochaber located in Canada – made famous in *The Proclaimers* song *Letter from America* – these few examples of place names show that the Scottish Lion was indeed rampant. Though *Letter from America* references the Highland Clearances and draws parallels to the de-industrialization of the West of Scotland in the 1970s and 1980s – which often forced emigration of Scots to so-called 'New Worlds' – it is important to note that not all Scottish emigration took place as a result of forceful displacement.

Many of those who left Scotland, were 'skilled'[2] workers who were able to access financial assistance and recognized the 'New World' as a place which rewarded their whiteness. As Black feminist and scholar, Hazel Carby (2019: 193) notes, 'In 1905, under the direction of Frank Oliver, Minister of the Interior and Superintendent-General of Indian Affairs, Canadian immigration policy became more racially and culturally restrictive, favouring "Anglo-Saxon" immigrants who were deemed "most able to assimilate". Over 100 years later, the 2016 Canadian census shows those of Scottish ethnic origin totalled approximately 11% of the Canadian population. Some of these 11% will be

12 A line drawing of steps in the snow and stick people moving up and falling down the steps, drawn on the ground by someone in Edinburgh, 2013. Photograph by Francesca Sobande.

descendants of those who first travelled to the 'New World' and many will be the result of recent emigration.

Carby (2019: 193) asks of those who left in 1905, 'How many realized that their whiteness opened up opportunities they thought their poverty had foreclosed? How many came to believe that they were, justifiably, rulers of the earth even if they didn't have enough to eat?'. Though the conditions leading to Scottish (e) migration may have changed since then, settler colonialism remains an ongoing process of erasure and obfuscation, heavily reliant on the trading of whiteness – or closeness to it – for access to an international, multi-cultural 'New World'.

'While Britain's role in the transatlantic slave trade is increasingly the subject of scrutiny, Scotland's inclusion in, and collusion with, this, has received comparatively less attention. Yet, this is gradually changing, as is suggested by the University of Glasgow publishing a report on the institution's historical links with slavery' (Sobande, forthcoming). Furthermore, the University of Glasgow's Runaway Slaves project – 'a searchable database of well over eight hundred newspaper advertisements placed by masters and owners [sic] seeking the capture and return of enslaved and bound people who had escaped' – shows enslaved Black people (re)located across Scotland, confirming the involvement of Scots in the enslavement of Black African people. Though many of these Scots were located in Glasgow and Edinburgh, the database highlights areas such as the port town of Greenock and smaller places like Almrycross (near Arbroath) and Inverary in Argyll and Bute as places where enslaved Black people had been (re)located and had run away from. The Runaway Slaves project has also produced a graphic novel, *Freedom Bound*, which follows the interconnected stories of three enslaved people living in Scotland in the 1700s.

Though this work is necessary, it is essential to note that June Evans, a Black person from Guyana who lived and studied in Edinburgh in the 1990s, undertook similar research which was published in the 1995 PhD thesis, *African/Caribbeans in Scotland: A socio-geographical study*. Evans' pioneering study provides an account of African/Caribbean people living in Scotland and acknowledges their long-standing presence for at least four centuries. Evans (1995: 24), 'scanned every newspaper issue from the 18th century that could be obtained' and court records, to produce a chapter in the thesis which 'provides original evidence of African slaves in Scotland during the period of slavery in the 18th century and discusses their resistance to slavery, their sale and their baptism and some aspects of their social and demographic characteristics' (Evans 1995: 18).

That chapter in Evans' (1995) thesis also includes an account of the historical African/Caribbean presence beginning with their presence at the Scottish royal court of James IV and later as servants of the Scottish aristocracy. Newspapers during this time, Evans (1995: 24) argues, 'were on the side of slaveowners [sic] and planters and served the interest of the merchants and slave owning classes, not the enslaved', and were utilized to share information between enslavers with an understanding that newspapers would rarely be read by enslaved Black people. However, as demonstrated by Evans' and the Runaway Slaves project, depending on the publication, newspaper resources can be subverted to firmly place the history of Black people in Scotland, 'today, their testimony is on the side of the African slave/servant for they now tell the world of the historical African presence in Scotland' (Evans 1995: 24).

Despite Evans' (1995) ground-breaking research providing an unmistakably essential foregrounding to the Runaway Slaves project, such work does not appear to be referenced. Evans' (1995: iv) research was undertaken to document and challenge the ongoing and intentional invisibility of Black people in Scotland, 'whose contemporary as well as historical presence frequently remains unacknowledged and ignored', yet it seems that such vital work is due much more acknowledgment within Scotland than is currently evident.

Other examples of concerted efforts to reckon with Scotland's connections to the enslavement of Black people include the creation of 'Ghost', a 'new immersive app exploring slavery and empire in Glasgow's Merchant City' (National Theatre of Scotland 2021) which has been described in the following way:

> A young man in 18th Century Glasgow, leads us on an atmospheric journey of over 500 years of resistance through the streets of the Merchant City down to the River Clyde. Audiences are invited to download a bespoke app, to plug in their headphones, and immerse themselves in this poetic storytelling experience, exploring the myth of Scotland's collective amnesia of slavery and racialised wealth, of empire and identity ... A lament to lives lost and an impassioned call to action in the present day.

Scotland's legacy is inextricably linked to the so-called Enlightenment period in the eighteenth– early nineteenth century which is typically societally framed as being a turning point in terms of significant intellectual, philosophical, and scientific innovations and developments. However, as hill (2019) has discussed when writing for the Scottish online publication *Bella Caledonia*, such a point in time is also one marred by violent and colonial endeavours:

> The roots of the ideology of civilisation that informed Victorian colonial policy and practice lie in Edinburgh. In eighteenth-century Scotland a theory of historical development was elaborated by a number of thinkers and writers, most notably Adam Smith, David Hume, Adam Ferguson and John Millar. Scotland had joined with the Act of Union in 1707 and the civil strife centred on conflict over religion in the previous century would have been difficult to forget. The establishment of the Kingdom of Great Britain, would have represented an opportunity to construct an identity of civilisation and project an illusion of political stability, particularly with the ever-increasing threat of the Jacobites. The construction of an identity of civilisation crucially necessitated the construction of savagery and the savage 'Other'. New societies across the world, encountered by Victorians were to be found right across the savagery and civilization spectrum, affirming the notion of those most advanced in civilisation had a moral responsibility to civilise savage nations which displayed progressive tendencies. The view of savagery and civilisation was a clever theoretical construct and its many empirical failings were ignored or overlooked, not due to an inconvenience to British colonisers to recognise pre-existing societal structures but owing to the binary of civilisation and savagery being able to define who colonisers were – as a civilised peoples.

As twentieth century contemporary English literature scholar Joseph H. Jackson (2020: 2) states: 'Scottish physicians, scholars, philosophers and writers produced many of the key racializing texts of the British Empire.' Furthermore, 'Edinburgh was once the pre-eminent intellectual environment for the eighteenth- and nineteenth-century invention of race' (Jackson 2020: 7). Scotland's history of racism and its connection to the transatlantic slave trade is undeniable. However, this is rarely recognized within formal education contexts where the history of Britain and, more precisely, Scotland, is frequently taught without naming and critically examining the nation's links to slavery and violent forms of anti-Black oppression.

In the words of researcher and writer Churnjeet Mahn (2019: 119) who has written about 'Black Scottish Writing and the Fiction of Diversity', 'the displacement of politicised histories of racism to the broader British context, coupled with Scotland's own framing of colonial and colonised history, has de-emphasised race as a significant marker of difference in Scottish literary criticism, while Scottish writing by ethnic minorities has produced a more ambivalent relationship to race and nationalism. This contradiction reflects some of the ideological tensions around teaching race in Scotland'.

Moreover, when attempts *are* made to acknowledge Scotland's racist and colonial history, even in the form of small gestures – such as name changes to streets and buildings, a practice which has occurred with regularity throughout the years (including the renaming of St George's Place to Nelson Mandela Place in 1986) but has arguably drawn less attention than protests in the form of marches –there is often a backlash. This is evident considering the uproar that surrounded the 2020 University of Edinburgh announcement that a university building, David Hume Tower, where one of us once attended university classes, would instead be known as 40 George Square in acknowledgement of the racist words and work of philosopher, historian, and economist Hume in the eighteenth century.

As Kalinga (2021: 9) puts it:

> The decision to rename the building, and hold a review on the way forward prompted much commentary – a great deal of which encouraged a reckoning with what David Hume means to the University, its staff, and students. These ideas include the full extent of Hume's views on humanity, to establish whether he maintained any possible links (ideological or participatory) to the slave trade, and the role of Scotland in the African slave trade.

The university's decision regarding the building was announced as part of a statement on the work being done by its equality and diversity committee and race equality and anti-racist sub-committee (BBC 2020b). Unfortunately, it does not take long to find many disparaging responses to the announcement online, including half-baked articles published by mainstream media organizations that fed into frenzied backlash against the perspectives of people of colour, which is indicative of the far-from-'post-racial'-status of the nation.

13 40 George Square. Photograph by Francesca Sobande.

Returning to related reflections on Black history in Scotland, and the dearth of formal teaching on it, we now turn to the comments of several people who responded to our 2020–2021 Black Lives in Scotland survey. These words were shared in response to the question, 'What do you know about Black history in Scotland and how did you learn about it?':

> I know quite a bit about the sugar trade and emigrants from here to the Caribbean. I am personally interested in history and architecture. I have visited many stately homes and I regularly read about the history of any areas that I visit

or watch tv programmes. It's not specifically to do with being black, I am just genuinely interested in how villages, towns and industries have come about.

5 April 2021 (56–65 years-old)

More than I did as a child, but still less than I would like. I know about Glasgow's connection with the transatlantic slave trade, that thousands of enslaved Black people were docked at Port Glasgow (just fifteen minutes up the road), that Merchant city was built with the wealth generated by slave labour. On the plus side, I know that Maud Sulter (Glaswegian and Ghanaian) was the first Black woman to have a showing at the Tate. That our Poet Makar, Jackie Kay, has blazed a trail in more ways than one.

13 January 2021 (26–35 years-old)

I know that the African & Caribbean slave trade had a big impact in the development of Scotland and Glasgow in particular. Many slave merchants and plantations owners were from Glasgow and their names are celebrated in street names through the city. I read books about the history of the Black British community, and the British colonial deeds . . . also have had conversations with local black Scottish about it.

10 December 2020 (26–35 years-old)

I do not know much about black history in Scotland. I have not had the opportunity to hear about how other Black people's experiences of living in Scotland have impacted on their lives. I have not really been aware of any literature that deals with Black people's history in Scotland.

6 December 2020 (46–55 years-old)

Self taught. My mother made a huge effort to research Scotland's history when we first moved here. I have carried that on. Some of the information is not easily accessible but it's there. So many Black pioneers across Scotland. Interesting notes for some that were well known and revered in their communities.

11 October 2020 (26–35 years-old)

I know only that Scotland enslaved Black people, especially in the Caribbean. My father is from the West Indies and we are descendants of enslaved Africans. He even has Scottish DNA, (he tested his DNA recently), which is a testament to the proximity of Scots to our enslaved ancestors.

10 October 2020 (46–55 years-old)

I don't know much. But started exploring it more as I was curious about general Black British histories. I remember reading about Black merchants coming to Glasgow. So I wish there was more available information on this, and that it would become a much more significant part of public education.

9 October 2020 (26–35 years-old)

While the perspectives of those who responded to our survey vary, among the key themes that emerged from their words were the following: (1) critique of the scarce nature of Black history education provision in Scotland; (2) frustration concerning the focus of Black history in Scotland often mainly, if not only, being on large cities such as Glasgow and Edinburgh; and (3) the central role of personal, familial, and intergenerational oral histories in the documenting and unfunded archiving of Black history in Scotland. In other words, although the responses to our survey and interview questions highlight a range of views and experiences of being Black in Scotland, repeated points made emphasize that despite the clear existence of Black history in Scotland it is, arguably, yet to be meaningfully acknowledged, engaged with, or taught in many spheres of Scottish public life. So, throughout *Black Oot Here: Black Lives in Scotland*, we seek to contribute to the care-full and ongoing archiving of Black history and contemporary experiences, which is work that far too often is assumed to be reserved to those with so-called 'personal detachment' from these matters.

As part of our project, we have taken stock of both the very visible and far from public ways that Black people and racial justice activists have sought to push back against racism and the illusion of Scottish exceptionalism. Hence, we note that:

> '[i]n June 2020, against the backdrop of the COVID-19 crisis, the Merchant City has become a site for reconcilement and transformation. Activists in solidarity with Black Lives Matter organizing and the Movement for Black Lives, and as an acknowledgement of Glasgow's – and Scotland's – often underplayed role in the British Empire, have taken to the streets of the Merchant City, symbolically placing the names of Black campaigners and those who have died in police custody, below existing street names'.
>
> hill and Sobande 2020: 1173

As Otele (2020: 3) puts it, '[t]he notion of exceptionalism is an interesting tool with which to understand history. It is used in history writing to shed light on histories that intersect with class, gender, religion, race and so on. A pitfall of the term is its suggestion that one story, circumstance or character is better than another'. Additionally, '[e]xceptionalism can lead to a thorough analysis of the tensions between what has been forgotten and lurks on the outskirts of the discourse (those forgotten or untold histories), and how history is presented and transmitted for various social, cultural and, of course, political reasons' (Otele 2020: 5).

Many myths of Scottish exceptionalism involve the promotion of the false idea that, unlike in other parts of the world, such as England, Scotland is not

14 A sign renaming Cochrane Street as Sheku Bayoh Street. Photograph by Andy Buchanan/AFP via Getty Images

15 Glasgow, Scotland – 9 June: Anti-racism campaigners have renamed streets in Glasgow city centre that have links to the slave trade. following the worldwide Black Lives Matter protests on 9 June 2020 in Glasgow, Scotland. Photograph by Jeff J Mitchell/Getty Images.

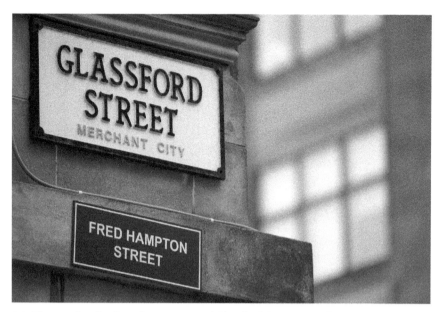

16 Glasgow, Scotland – 9 June: A view of Glassford Street, one of Glasgow streets linked to slave owners in the city. Glasgow and its historic ties with the transatlantic slave trade and slavery have come under recent scrutiny following the worldwide Black Lives Matter protests. Photograph by Jeff J Mitchell/Getty Images.

17 Glasgow, Scotland – 9 June: A plaque near The Tobacco Merchant's House in the Merchant City on 9 June 2020. Photograph by Jeff J Mitchell/Getty Images.

somewhere where racism remains. 'In the renaming of streets, Harriet Tubman, Rosa Parks, George Floyd – though since removed – and Sheku Bayoh are made visible, sitting alongside tobacco merchants and enslavers' (hill and Sobande 2020: 1173). As we have previously argued:

> '[t]he inclusion of Sheku Bayoh is significant, reflecting an understanding of antiblackness and arguably, contesting notions of Scottish exceptionalism. Sheku Bayoh was a Black man who died in police custody in 2015, after being arrested in the Scottish town of Kirkcaldy, and his death remains the subject of an ongoing public inquiry . . . The renaming of Merchant City street names demonstrates an understanding of the link between capitalism and racism, perhaps even antiblackness. Statues and street names remain visible and can be changed'.
>
> ibid.

More recent strategies to organize and protest outside of traditional spaces such as public squares, also connects capitalism and racism. Some activists recognize the ability to disrupt the making of profit as more powerful than targeting sites of institutional power as Elliot-Cooper, (2021: 169) argues, '. . . privately owned spaces are often more familiar to young people than the government buildings traditionally targeted within earlier campaigns against police racism'. Furthermore, 'in a society where public spaces are being decimated, and shopping and transport have become central to public life, shutting them down is likely to attract far more public and media attention than other forms of protest . . . Traditional demonstrations, typically outside public institutions often barely receive a mention, but novel political actions that differ from the usual A-to-B march catch the eye of the press' (Elliot-Cooper 2021: 169).

However, 'public spaces and marketplace contexts continue to be sites of struggle, including due to how the grassroots work of individuals calling for and contributing to structural change concerning antiblackness is reframed and subsumed by commercial organizations that perform a false proximity to particular demographics and social movements' (hill and Sobande 2020: 1176). In the words of one person who completed our survey and reflected on the impact of BLM events in Scotland in 2020:

> The black community has no political influence in Scotland so nothing in that spectrum has perceivably changed, on a social level a new generation became aware that racism exists and affects real people, and it's part of their community. Many claim to support the BLM movement either for clout or true compassion, but I have not seen this reflected in actions other than demonstrations.
>
> 10 December 2020 (26–35 years-old)

As another person who responded to the survey put it: 'Black people face discrimination in housing, education, health, employment and the justice system. Robust policies to address these will be a step in the right direction.' Such a perspective parallels that of race, ethnicity, and health scholar Gwenetta Curry, whose work emphasizes the fact that '[c]urrent structures throughout the UK have relegated ethnic minorities to the more deprived area and created challenges for them to have equal access to quality health care and education. According to the Office of National Statistics, Black African (20%) and Arab (17%) groups had the lowest rate of home-ownership compared to white British (63%) populations'.

In the words of someone else who responded to the survey question 'If you have experienced racism in Scotland, please describe the impact of this on your life':

> It has definitely caused a lot of mental scarring and only in the past year have I realised that racial PTSD exists. As racism is rampant in Scotland, I find myself cutting out people in my life who refuse to be antiracist. At times, I would try to tone down my blackness at job interviews, or made myself smaller for the comfort of white people. Due to the racism at a young age, I deliberately moved to a more diverse area to raise my family and actively look for diverse baby and toddler groups for my children's benefit, in a bid to prevent my girls going through what I did. As I was a shy kid (the othering was a big part of that), I'm instilling confidence in my babies from a young age.
>
> 3 February 2021 (26–35 years-old)

Such discrimination has not emerged out of nowhere. Instead, sadly, it is steeped in the history of Scotland, particularly the parts of it that many Scottish institutions are reluctant to acknowledge. As one person wrote when reflecting on the impact of racism on their life in Scotland: 'Isolating. hurtful. demeaning. reminiscent of my apartheid/colonial experience.' Further still, as someone else put it:

> I learnt about Scotland's race issues and involvement in the Transatlantic Slave Trade only through my own research, and because of the social media outpouring to the murder of George Floyd. For the most part, Scotland has tried to minimise and downplay its very part in the racism we see in history and today.
>
> 17 March 2021 (26–35 years-old)

Arguably, there is a paucity of academic institutional support regarding scholarship by and about Black people in, from, and connected to, Scotland. However, the relatively scarce nature of such scholarship should not be mistaken for an absence of this sort of work occurring, commonly in unfunded ways and outside the context of formal educational settings.

Learning, politics – 'that's no fur me', 'n' makin: Education, politics, and the arts

In the Series Editors' Preface to Jackson's (2020) book on *Writing Black Scotland: Race, Nation, and the Devolution of Black Britain*, the editors write:

> It is more urgent than ever to understand how the historical and contemporary construction of Scottish identities intersects with questions of race, gender and class: yet Scottish cultural studies are dispersed across conflicting traditions of ethnographic, sociological, historical and aesthetic enquiry.

On a related note, as Arshad and McCrum (1989: 223) state in 'Black Women, White Scotland':

> [m]ost research carried out on black women has been done south of the border and mainly from a white perspective, be that male or female, middle or working-class. This has allowed an assumption that black women's experiences are uniform and coupled with the popoular [sic] view that Scotland has 'good race relations because there is no racism here' has meant that not only is the position of black Scottish women been ignored, but it is also worse. It also raises the question as to why the majority of research has been carried out by white academics.

Such questions raised remain relevant today, particularly as we are witnessing a range of Scottish institutions, including universities, express more interest in this topic than before, but seldom in ways that involve connecting to or foregrounding the experiences of local Black people, as knowledge producers in their own right.

While the series editors who wrote the preface for Jackson's (2020) *Writing Black Scotland: Race, Nation, and the Devolution of Black Britain* assert that 'Scotland's past and present continue to demand critical analysis, the detachment of the scholar combined with the commitment of the activist', we call for more embracement of Black Scottish scholarship that does not claim or feign any detachment and which is emphatically rooted in a clear sense of connection and commitment to the matters researched and archived. The notion of the 'detachment of the scholar' is not a neutral one, and, unfortunately, can be operationalized in ways intended to obstruct Black Scottish scholarship, particularly that which is undertaken by Black Scottish people, for whom detachment from this history may never be possible nor preferable.

Roles such as that recently advertised (in March 2021) Lecturer in Black British History position, which may involve the appointed person demonstrating 'a willingness to develop a Scottish dimension of Black British histories to research, teaching and knowledge exchange' (University of Edinburgh 2021), may signal that more Scottish educational institutions are invested in, or, at least, interested in, doing more work to acknowledge and teach Black Scottish History. However, institutions will need to approach such efforts in a long-term and sustainable way which will involve ensuring that more than one person is expected to do the work of developing and teaching courses that relate to Black Scottish History. These institutions must also ensure that such appointments cover the full range of lecturer levels (e.g. Lecturer, Senior Lecturer, Reader, Professor) to avoid treating Black Scottish history as a footnote in British history and to avoid foreclosing opportunities for career progression for educators who work in these areas. We are glad to see early signs of some institutional work to address this, and we hope that such work far surpasses the first quarter of the twenty-first century.

Although Black history in Scotland is very rarely explored and taught in detail in many educational environments (t)here, the efforts of several groups and grassroots initiatives within educational settings have challenged the intentional erasure of such history. For example, in 2019, Edinburgh Black Studies presented a short course that consisted of four seminars on Black Studies and the Africana radical tradition. Also, since 2016 Project Myopia (founded by Rianna Walcott and Toby Sharpe) has done crucial ongoing work across Britain to revolutionize pedagogical practices and, since 2018, the work of individuals involved in the collaborative student-led archival project at University of Edinburgh (UncoverED) has yielded insightful information related to the stories of Black alumni.

Other examples of such generative work include that of the Anti-Racist Educator, a collective of students, teachers, parents, academics, and activists working towards building an education system that is free of racial injustice, as well as the Glasgow School of Art People of Colour Collective which lists, 'collective learning in order to expand our knowledge beyond the white, cis-het, Eurocentric male syllabus' and 'centering the voices of black people, whilst actively combatting the continued exclusion of black folx from the arts' amongst its aims. In addition to this, established as a partnership between the Glasgow School of Art, GSA's Students' Association (GSASA) and GSA Exhibitions, the Race, Rights and Sovereignty programme has been developed 'to create opportunities, and forums, to engage with and unpack ideas and issues related to race, rights & sovereignty; particularly in the contexts of creative practice'. Also, two 'Resisting Whiteness' events in Edinburgh (22 September 2018 and 28 September 2019), organized by a collective of QTIPOC activists with the common goal of discussing and facilitating anti-racist action, highlighted and covered many issues regarding racism in Scotland, including in relation to education.

We are conscious that many well-known, but not all, initiatives to address racism in Scotland have been formed from – and remain rooted in – academic or educational institutions, which can sometimes fail to connect to grassroots groups and initiatives which exist outside of these spheres, or indeed, replicate systems of extraction and oppression when they do. The issues raised by those located in academic and educational environments can often appear to be part of a Black collective struggle; however, some of these issues – and solutions – may only benefit a minority, and not the *many* Black people who have been struggling against oppression for decades and in intergenerational ways. As scholar Steven Osuna (2017: 21–22) puts it:

> Schools, colleges, and universities reproduce the social relations of oppression and exploitation. Interventions from radical scholarship that identify the root causes and structural conditions of exploitation and oppression and that prioritize the interests of aggrieved communities are vital, and will occur only if scholars and intellectuals are in conversation with these communities. This is easier said than done, however. Professionalization in academic institutions distances many scholars and intellectuals from people and communities in radical social movements who are struggling against oppression. Instead of engaging and building with social movements that are seeking solutions and strategies to combat the ravages of racial capitalism, scholars and intellectuals remain entangled in bourgeois academia.

Despite the scarcity of funding that is often made available to them, there are countless individuals and groups who educate and share knowledge, such as Chief Gift Kofi Amu-Logotse at the African Arts Centre in Glasgow and the work of the African Women Group Scotland in Aberdeen, who receive little recognition of their efforts in providing Black history education. Black educators within educational and academic institutions undertaking Black history education, should build and contribute to the rich Black Scottish canon already being created by people engaged in such work. However, given Osuna's concerns, the transience of some students and of those employed within educational and academic institutions, as well as the temporary nature of funding for such initiatives, these efforts should be focused not only on combatting the ravages of racial capitalism but ensuring the non-erasure of such knowledge and work, by offering an additional avenue for archiving and documenting.

The Museums Galleries Scotland (MGS) 2020 appointment of Sheila Asante as Project Manager for Empire, Slavery & Scotland's Museums: Addressing Our Colonial Legacy, and Glasgow Life's 2020 appointment of Miles Greenwood as Curator (Legacies of Slavery & Empire) signals some changes in terms of Scottish institutional efforts 'to continue to tell the story of the impact the transatlantic trade in enslaved Africans and the British Empire has had on Glasgow' (Glasgow Life 2020). As asserted by Glasgow Life (2020), a charity that delivers cultural, sporting and learning activities on behalf of Glasgow City Council:

> The legacy of the extraordinary wealth that Glasgow accumulated on the back of enslaved labour is woven into the city's physical environment and material culture. In the 19th century, Glasgow's connection to slavery was obscured. As a consequence there are few objects that directly relate to slavery in the city's museums. Greenwood's remit as Curator (Legacies of Slavery & Empire) will include developing a programme of community engagement and collaborative research to reshape understandings of the connections between the slave trade and colonialism, and their contemporary legacies. Across Glasgow Museums, Greenwood will, with colleagues, curate new displays to clearly demonstrate the impact slavery and empire had on all aspects of the city. Working with local communities and existing specialist curators he will shape a public programme of talks, tours, handling sessions and other activities that reflects the legacies of slavery, empire, race and globalisation.

As we have outlined, one of many key themes that emerged from our 2020–2021 survey on Black Lives in Scotland was the strong desire among Black people for Black history in Scotland to be properly taught and recognized in formal education contexts, as well as various other institutional settings which involve the recording of Scottish history. In addition to wanting there to be more robust efforts to ensure that Scotland's connections to the transatlantic slave trade are acknowledged as part of educational curricula, many who responded to our survey expressed a desire for Black history in Scotland to be taught in a way that involves discussion of many different aspects of Black people's lives. As six people put it:

> Education reform. Include global history, literature, politics and culture in an equal way, that decentres Scotland and the Western world. (Although I don't think we should rely on the powers that be to implement this).
>
> 5 February, 2021 (26–35 years-old)

> I believe a lack of education around the lives and knowledges of Black and other people of colour leads to a lack of intersectional policy. So I think, while this

wouldn't address the issues *today* the education curriculum needs reforming and addressing and there should be a mandatory Black British and BAME history taught.

17 January 2021 (26–35 years-old)

It [policy change] should start with something that tackles education, and this is for Britain in general, they have to teach history properly in schools, acknowledge their past and be openly ashamed and not celebrate it. Aggravate penalties for the crime of racism such as imprisonment time.

10 December 2020 (26–35 years-old)

[I want to see] [c]hange of the school curriculum- I think education is part of how we get lasting change moving forward. Better education of our collective history will be helpful for members of the diaspora in knowing who we are, the richness of our pasts and things we have achieved. We are under appreciated on a large scale in many ways. For non-black people educating themselves is necessary for them to lean into anti-racism and understanding their privilege, and how they benefit from a racist society . . . I feel that people up here believe it is more tolerant and fall into the trap of saying 'it's different up here' where really Scottish exceptionalism provides an excuse for people not to actually look at their racism and how colonialism etc still effects our lived existence today.

12 December 2020 (26–35 years-old)

Mandatory education of Scotland's role in Slavery and colonialism. Mandatory education of Black Scottish pioneers, peoples across the world etc. Mandatory education regarding the push and pull factors of migration. This should occur from primary school to high school. Not as an optional subject but mandatory. Scotland lives in denial. Since Black history in context of the enslavement of Black people is only ever taught Scotland's educational system avoids addressing the true history of it's people and impact on the world. As a result bias is prevalent and truths are never addressed or highlighted from an early age. This allows ignorance and action in context of white supremacy to sit comfortably in Scotland's society where ignorance is bliss and denial is acceptable.

11 October 2020 (26–35 years-old)

Teach Black history in schools, and not just slavery and colonialism.

9 October 2020 (26–35years-old)

Though addressing Scotland's role in the building of the British Empire is becoming increasingly prominent within Scottish consciousness and, indeed, jobs are being created to raise awareness of that perspective of Black history, we should consider who has a stake in promoting this narrative and the way in which its framing sometimes turns the focus away from more contemporary histories and experiences of Black people in Scotland. This is of particular importance when much of the contemporary lives of Black people in Scotland is made visible only through their experiences of racism. Furthermore, Black history in Scotland should not only look beyond solely focusing on slavery and colonial legacies; these histories must also go beyond city peripheries and to different places where Black people have lived and have contributed to the geographies of the area. As Evans (1995: 3) states,

> During the Second World War American soldiers, black and white, became a part of Scottish social life. Thus, the black presence was no longer confined to the port areas of British cities, as American soldiers were based in towns and villages. In the 1980's several African-Americans were still based at RAF Edzell so there is a small concentration of African-Americans from Edzell to Dundee. Dunoon, another American base, which once had several African-American residents has now been closed but left Afro-Scottish descendants such as the jazz singer, Suzanne Bonnar.

Located in Dunoon, where some of these descendants remain and where one of us spent a significant part of their childhood, is a painted rock known as the 'Jim Crow' rock. For decades, the rock has had a black grinning face with bright red lips and the words 'Jim Crow' painted onto it. When the rock attracts attention, such as when Neville Lawrence, the father of teenager Stephen Lawrence who was murdered by racists, expressed his disappointment upon seeing the rock when visiting Dunoon (Learmonth 2017), attempts are made to paint over it, though these are short-lived, with 'Jim Crow' quickly reappearing.

More recently, following the BLM protests in 2020, the rock was painted over again, with BLM replacing the racist imagery and commitments were made by the local council and MSP to change the rock permanently. Amongst the arguments in favour of maintaining the 'Jim Crow' rock is that it allegedly relates to a Jim Crow who owned a builder's yard in the area and has nothing to do with either the anti-Black racist depictions of African-Americans in minstrel routines or the Jim Crow laws which enforced segregation in the United States. However, given the location of the rock and its close proximity to the port town of Greenock, where enslaved people were located, and the placement of the United States Navy base at the nearby Holy Loch from 1961 (whilst segregation laws were still in place in the US) to 1992, which had African-Americans amongst the personnel, it is unlikely the rock was painted in such a way to commemorate either the mysterious builder's yard or the James Crow who died whilst swimming in the area (Dundee Courier 1875).

Not far from the 'Jim Crow' rock, and from the West of Scotland Convalescent Seaside Home where James Crow was staying at the time of his death, is Hunter's Quay Holiday Village and Hafton Castle. James Hunter, who built and owned Hafton Castle, is listed as an awardee of the Slave Compensation Act 1837 in the University of London College's Legacies of British Slavery database. Hunter's association with Trinidad 1754 (Palmira Estate), which held 54 enslaved people, 'earned' him a share of £2858 13s 7d, equating to approximately £328,231.66 in today's money. Furthermore, the creation of the West of Scotland Convalescent Seaside Home was developed with the support of both James White of Overtoun and Sir Peter Coats (Hillhouse 1909). White's chemical manufacturing business, J & J White Chemicals located in Rutherglen, exposed its workforce and the surrounding areas to a contaminated and potentially lethal atmosphere (Walker 2005) and Coats' firm, J&P Coats, based in Paisley was once the leading maker of cotton thread in the world.

In recent years, the town of Paisley has seen events such as Africa: Paisley 2021 (Paisley, Paisley Town Hall, 21 July 2018) and Taste of Africa (Paisley, Paisley Town Hall, 21 November 2010), designed and organized to celebrate African cultural heritage and 'give the people of Paisley a flavour of African culture, food and fashion' (Rennie 2010). There has also been the establishment of various African-led groups such as, the Association of African Communities in Renfrewshire and Pachedu, both of which aim to improve community integration, promote African and minority ethnic cultural identity, and build capacity within those communities.

Focusing on related questions concerning the experiences of Black people in different regional and rural parts of Scotland, we now turn to Nikko Dingani's reflections on Black history outside of cities in Scotland:

> I like it sometimes when I travel in the Highlands, you read something in the stone about Scots and it's so exciting. And you think, where's mine? Of course, this is Scotland and I'm not saying we should see all the Black people's history in the Highlands. I'm just saying it's nice when you read something, history about Scots. I'm interested to learn Scotland's history as equally as the Black history.

Places like the Highlands and East Linton, where Belizean forestry workers were sent to work as part of the World War II effort, as referred to in Evans' (1995) research, or Dunoon, located outside large cities and towns, already struggle to find a place in mainstream discourse. This also means Black histories in Scotland are kept hidden, allowing the notion of Black people being located only in urban areas, and for anti-blackness to persist, on shores and in hills, the exact places

18 'BLM' painted over the 'Jim Crow' rock in Dunoon 2020. Photograph by layla-roxanne hill

19 Hilly Scottish area in the distance, surrounded by a blue cloudy sky and tall strands of grass in the foreground. Photograph by Francesca Sobande.

20 Shadows and sunlight on a field in Fife. Photograph by Francesca Sobande.

where Black people are not expected to be. As Black feminist theorist, urban ethnographer, and political storyteller Zenzele Isoke (2013: 95) states: 'the politics of homemaking is a politics of *not* forgetting, of *not* looking away, and, most importantly, creating *new* spaces to affirm black life, black struggle, and black survival.'

In her interview for this book, Charmaine Blaize, mother, Ifa/Orisa spiritualist, human rights and social justice activist, IT Health Management professional and co-founder of Women of Colour Scotland, compared her daughter's learning of Black history in Scotland, to her own in Trinidad:

> When you are born in a former English colony – I was born in the 60s, so that's post-independence, that's all we knew. Post-independence, in the 70s, you had Black Power revolution, that's what we grew up in. Kwame Ture, you know – Stokely Carmichael, our first prime minister – Eric Williams – he wrote, *From Slavery to Capitalism*, and the likes of Walter Rodney – these are all Caribbean intellectuals who influenced some of our thinking. But, here, after a whole pandemic, a whole period of George Floyd, my daughter goes back to school and there is nothing about activism or human rights. There is nothing. Nothing. They

are doing World War II. They are studying world wars. I said have they taught you anything about the Civil Rights Movement, anything about Martin Luther King even? No, she said 'no'. And that's our young people. We have to start with them. They are our future policy makers. It has to start with the young people. We have to find ways to create spaces where our young people – especially in Scotland – can realise that there is more to life than just being white Scottish.

Another person who responded to the survey wrote: 'I think the racist experience, particularly of pupils is because of ignorance which, I think, can be redressed by teaching appropriate history which makes them understand the world today – especially colonial history and the British Empire'. While we remain wary of claims that racism is merely the result of ignorance, we do support calls for effective and sustained education in Scotland which explicitly and critically acknowledges colonial history, the British Empire, and structural racism.

Perhaps in the future the Scottish government will push for changes beyond those stated in the Scottish National Party (SNP) Manifesto 2021 to 'fund an online programme on Scotland and the UK's colonial history throughout the world that can be delivered to schools, and we will encourage Local Authorities to adopt the programme in all schools'. Such future changes may involve adopting something similar to what was recently announced (March 2021) in Wales, where all pupils are to be taught about racism and the lives of BAME people in school (Clements and Flint 2021; Huskisson 2020). These planned changes in Wales were announced following the creation of a petition to 'Make it compulsory for Black and POC UK histories to be taught in the Welsh education curriculum' which was signed by 34,736 people and was debated in The Senedd in November 2020 (Senedd Cymru Welsh Parliament 2020). There is a long road ahead before it will be possible to determine to what extent, if at all, such changes contribute to effective efforts to tackle racism. However, for the time being, many rightly remain hopeful about the potential impact of these anticipated school curriculum shifts.

The work of Black women such as teacher, author, and human rights campaigner Mary Osei-Oppong has played a central role in changes regarding discussions about and approaches to education in Scotland. Osei-Oppong's (2020: 5–6) book *For the Love of Teaching: The Anti-Racist Battlefield in Education* features insights including the following:

> *For The Love of Teaching: The Anti-Racist Battlefield in Education*, does not set out or dress itself up to be an account of every teacher's experience, nor the complete story of the Scottish Education System. The content comes from my experiences and observations during my time of service as a secondary school

teacher. Throughout my career, I sought to help close the gap in the disparity that exists in Education. I have done so by encouraging multiculturalism in my classroom and through campaigning for diversity in the teaching profession. It has never been acceptable for people to say they are not racist and have black friends, when their actions cause racial harm. I urge all of us regardless of race, gender, religious affiliation, sexual orientation or socio-economic class, to work together towards equal opportunity for all in society.

When reading the words of Osei-Oppong (2020) we thought about different perspectives and experiences of multiculturalism in Scotland, which led to us considering how Scottish politics connects to contemporary conversations concerning race, inequality, the legacy of slavery and empire, and the lives of Black people.

In 2018, Davidson and Virdee put forward the perspective that the Scottish National Party (SNP) are particularly at the helm of a 're-imagining of Scotland as different (and arguably more progressive) than England' (9) which 'has been crafted in such a way that the historical role which Scotland played in Atlantic slavery and colonial conquest has been consigned to what George Orwell referred to in *Nineteen-Eighty Four* as the "memory hole", thereby giving the impression that it never happened' (ibid.). Echoing some of the sentiments of Davidson and Virdee (2018), we recognize that Scotland's political spheres are enmeshed with narratives related to race and racism, but rather than attributing post-racial narratives of 'progress' or myths of racial inclusivity to a particular political party, we understand such discourse as being co-constructed by a variety of institutions and market actors in Scotland – including, but not limited to – those involved in Scotland's tourism strategy, creative and cultural industries, higher education marketing, and work to secure the nation's positive image on a global and digitally mediated stage. As argued by scholar David Millar (2010: 106) in *Who Rules Scotland? Neoliberalism, The Scottish Ruling Class and its Intellectuals*, 'Scottish business elites are closely networked with each other and with other fractions of the ruling class–in particular with the political class and the intellectuals (including academics) in Scotland'.

The utilization of 'soft power', such as political values, culture and foreign policy relies on attraction and persuasion to change behaviour and influence international events, which protects the current liberal international order and generates Scotland's own future prosperity and security. Indeed, the British Council report, *Gauging International Perceptions: Scotland and Soft Power*, claims 'Scotland's most useful way to pursue objectives beyond its borders is to utilise the full spectrum of soft power'. Additionally, the British Council website states, 'in essence the UK "brand" is actually the compound of many different brands: regional, local, and even individual, which make the whole more than the sum of the parts. Scotland, Wales, Northern Ireland, the great municipalities of the Midlands and the North of England are all core parts of the UK's global appeal, as well as benefiting in turn from it'. Furthermore, particularly since the March 2021 public launch of the Alba Party – a new Scottish political party that failed to secure any seats in the 2021 Scottish Parliament election nor the 2022 Scottish Council elections – it is evident that the current Scottish political context is one that has changed a lot since the 2018 publishing of *No Problem Here: Understanding Racism in Scotland* (Davidson et al. 2018).

In the following chapter we examine the rise of the term 'New Scots' (Davidson and Virdee 2018) and what the messaging surrounding it suggests about matters concerning neoliberal multiculturalism, notions of belonging and history in Scotland, and the nation's positioning within British and international politics. In writing about these matters, we reflect on how 'newness' is being conceptualized and what it is being contrasted with (e.g. who are 'Old Scots'?). We also consider the comments of Maya Patel (1994: 10) whose work points out the 'distinction between a multicultural and an anti-racist approach', as well as the work of Mahn (2019: 8) who has written about 'the relationship between Scotland and England, and discussions of race in Scotland through recent iterations of an inclusive Scottish civic nationalism'. Additionally, our writing on such topics is guided by the work of Hesse (2000a) on *Un/Settled Multiculturalisms* which defines multiculturalism as referring 'to particular discourses or social forms which incorporate marked cultural differences and diverse ethnicities'.

In previous years, Scotland's lack of effective efforts to acknowledge its links to slavery has sometimes resulted in the nation being referred to as exhibiting 'amnesia' in relation to such an aspect of its history. Despite this, we maintain that the word 'denial' is much more appropriate than the problematic use of 'amnesia' and encompasses the intentional ways that some individuals and institutions seek to distance Scotland's present-day public image from this element of its past. As Scottish writer, broadcaster, and language activist Billy Kay states in an interview on 'Black Scotland' with Shelley Goffe-Caldeira, printed in the Black and Asian Studies Association Newsletter 47 (2007: 10):

> We Scots have been clever at playing the Scottish card when it suits us . . . and as far as the excesses of the British Empire's concerned, it is easier for us to plead not guilty and pretend we were not involved! We were as involved and as guilty as any other European people.

Geoffrey Palmer's extensive work on Scotland's long history of slavery has played a significant role in current and ongoing changes that have involved important discussion and action in Scotland to make visible the nation's racist past and how this has impacted racism that still occurs (t)here today. In addition, the crucial work of author, poet, and the founder of Edinburgh Caribbean Association, Lisa Williams, among other grassroots and community-led groups, has provided people with the chance to learn more about Scotland's history of slavery, such as via insightful walking tours in the capital city, Edinburgh. Other examples of vital work include walking tours in Glasgow which relate to CRER Scotland and deal with the city's mercantile past, which have previously been led by Adebusola Ramsay and Marenka Thompson-Odlum.

The significant work of Williams (2020) also includes 'Remaking our histories: Scotland, Slavery and Empire' which was published on the National Galleries of Scotland website and takes 'a selection of portraits of famous Scots' as its starting point as part of detailed discussion of Scotland's connections to the transatlantic slave trade. Williams (2020) outlines how the Acts of Union with England in 1707 bolstered Scotland's attempts to seek out profit from slavery. The writing of Williams (2020) presents a necessary challenge to what Davidson and Virdee (2018: 10) may refer to as being 'an unwillingness to confront the legacies of empire and racism in which Scotland is implicated'.

Another related example is the online abuse faced by Mercury Prize-winning Scottish band, Young Fathers, after band members Kayus Bankole and Alloysious Massaquoi appeared in a 2017 video commissioned by National Galleries of Scotland and the National Portrait Gallery, London. 'The video, which was a creative meditation on issues of inclusion, exclusion, race, Scotland's art scene and history, resulted in much reactionary and vitriolic racist online commentary. This is indicative of the need to unsettle ideas regarding who, and what perspectives, pictures, and politics, have a place in creative contexts in Scotland' (hill and Sobande 2019: 109), and to continue to disrupt the ways that the interdependent existence of colonialism and antiblackness in Scotland has been denied.

Notably, since the BLM protests that took place in Summer 2020, some changes have occurred within creative and cultural industries (CCI) discourse and activities that relate to inequalities in Scotland. Such changes include the creation and announcement of Creative Scotland's (2021) 'Equalities, Diversity & Inclusion Advisory Group' which was the result of 'an open recruitment process' that led to the appointment of 'an independent group of twelve individuals' until January 2023. As of 10 February 2021, Creative Scotland, which

21 The band Young Fathers performing in Sefton Park, Liverpool in July 2018. Photograph by Francesca Sobande.

is the public body that supports the arts, screen and creative industries across all parts of Scotland, stated that:

> EDI is a key priority for Creative Scotland. In addition to legislative responsibilities in tackling inequalities and eliminating discrimination, the prioritisation of EDI is crucial to the quality and richness of creative activity and ensuring that as many people as possible can access and participate in arts and culture across Scotland.

The rhetoric of EDI and the ways in which it can be interchanged with terms such as anti-racism or decolonization, not only allows individuals and institutions to claim to be responding to inequalities by adopting 'new approaches'. It can also obscure the specificness of antiblackness and stymy transformative changes. As academic and writer Rinaldo Walcott (2019: 399) asserts in relation to a North American context, particularly, Canada:

> To claim that we can diversify, achieve equity, indigenize, or decolonize without taking on the social, cultural, political, and economic arrangements of whiteness is to enter the terrain of lies. Such claims of indigenizing and decolonizing in that fashion are coterminous with the logic of 'putting history behind us.' Such claims leave intact institutions not built for us, never meaning to receive us, as

the ongoing regimen of our society. In essence, then, such appropriations of language invented to produce transformative change, work to keep white supremacy intact even if it is an understated white supremacy.

When considering such a perspective in relation to the setting of Scotland, we found ourselves ruminating on the increasing and, sometimes, tepid, use of terms such as 'anti-racism', 'decolonial', and 'intersectionality' by and within a range of Scottish institutions, including civic, educational, political, and third-sector organizations. Seldom do such organizations seem to entertain the possibility that part of such 'anti-racist', 'decolonial', and 'intersectional' work may result in their organization being dismantled, or the active redistribution of resources in ways that do not simply result in funds continuing to circulate among a select few who are arbitrarily deemed credentialized 'authorities' on these matters. There is a real risk that the mere rise of such rhetoric ('anti-racist', 'decolonial', and 'intersectionality') in Scotland is assumed to indicate a substantial shift in terms of actively addressing inequalities and the societal treatment of Black and other marginalized people.

Race, pennies, 'n' wirk: Racial capitalism, work, health, and the COVID-19 crisis

The term *racial capitalism* which encompasses the racist underpinnings of capitalism is synonymous with the work of Robinson (1983) on Black Marxism and Black radical thought. Thus, naturally, when thinking about how racial capitalism impacts Black people in Scotland, we turned to the words of Robinson (1983: 9) who analysed how '[t]he historical development of world capitalism was influenced in a most fundamental way by the particularistic forces of racism'. Robinson's (1983) vivid account of how racism was enshrined in capitalism since its inception enables us to understand how elements of the contemporary work, labour, and class position experiences of Black people in Scotland are shaped by longstanding racial hierarchies and structural racism that bolster modern day marketplace activity. Despite Scotland's history of being connected to the transatlantic slave trade, relatively rarely has research and scholarship on race and racism in Scotland explicitly explored how racial capitalism is implicated in the nation's contemporary context. In fact, sometimes issues pertaining to racism and classism in Scotland are treated as though they exist separately from

22 Members of the public walk past anti-racism graffiti at London Road on 10 June 2020 in Edinburgh. Photograph by Jeff J Mitchell/Getty Images.

one another which can result in research findings that obscure the different classed experiences or, more specifically, the material conditions, of Black people.

The words of several individuals who responded to our 2020–2021 survey on Black Lives in Scotland signpost some of the ways that Black people feel their lives are impacted by the intersections of racism, classism, and capitalism, including the expectation that Black people tolerate harassment and discrimination at work in Scotland:

> As is often the case for raising problems with racism with colleagues this [particular incident] was badly received. I was pushed into a position of leaving my job and friendships came to an end. The gaslighting and attacks on my character during this time as well as having to leave my workplace were damaging for my mental health. Other racism has been indirect just the usual microagressions etc.
>
> 12 December 2020 (36–45 years-old)

> I believe that the problematic of race is not related to one nation … this issue in Scotland, but rather to do with economic development, opportunities, class and culture clash.
>
> 10 December, 2020 (26–35 years-old)

Whilst working in an after-school club, I experienced racist behaviour from a few of the children, who had clearly picked this behaviour up from their parents or society. It left me feeling deflated, it affected my self-esteem and demonstrated how racism is passed on through the generations.

6 December 2020 (46–55 years-old)

As a teacher, I was called a fucking nigger by a pupil ... The policy [I would implement if I could] would be based upon protecting black educators across Scotland, whereby not gaslighting their experiences and adopting further strategies in schools/institutions to protect their health and wellbeing. Anti-Racist training should be given not just to adults but embedded in school curriculum from a young age.

27 October 2020 (26–35 years-old)

I have experienced many more instances of aggressive and direct racism whilst living in London, yet here it is the little ignorances that have affected me more [here in Scotland]. It was great to see so many people attend the protests but I feel that people are unwilling to put in the level of work to challenge anti-racism. My journey as a teacher, has been stunted due to a racist incident and I feel that there is a large majority of people who are tired of hearing about black lives matter. These voices are the ones that I'm most concerned with, as they are only interested in black people when they are being entertained but anyone who wants to voice an injustice or challenge an anti-racist attitude or behaviour is just seen as being 'angry' or 'playing victim'.

27 October 2020 (26–35 years-old)

It [racism] has had some impact on my career trajectory but my resilience and tenacity, patience and drive in surmounting structural and institutional barriers helps to keep things on the balance.

17 October 2020 (56–65 years-old)

[Policy changes should address ...] Recruitment of Black teachers in schools. Funding for Black students to study for undergraduate and postgraduate degrees. Slavery, racism and migration has impacted on the chances of social mobility. Black families are generally not wealthy enough to send a child to university for multiple degrees. The university staff is mainly white and this won't change until Black students get funding all the way to PhD level and at every stage.

10 October, 2020 (46–55 years-old)

Also, on the topic of Black experiences of work in Scotland, Jonathan Wilson said the following about these matters in previous decades:

I got jaw drop moments where I arrive for the interview – and this is before the internet as well – and they see a black man and literally the interview lasts 10/15 minutes and it's been a one and a half hour either way train ride and stuff. I applied for a bunch of jobs [in Scotland] and got nowhere, and with a chemistry degree and an MBA from Dundee, that's a joke. But London opens its arms to me and that's why I came down and stayed there ... I remember going back [to Dundee] for a graduation and you see families coming; I'm sure there are many other reasons. But it did feel like, okay you've got more people, but I don't know. I'd have to stay around longer ... I'm going back to Glasgow probably next month. You kind of feel like visitors or polite tourists or something. I don't know if I've seen the same swagger, where I'm looking for evidence of those young kids bossing it, in the shopping centre, on the street corner, or doing something in a cheeky way that says, I own this city, or I own this neighbourhood. I don't know if there is evidence of that yet, but I could be completely out of touch.

While the words of people who responded to the survey relate to a range of different material conditions that they have dealt with, and experiences of work and labour, a strong theme that was apparent across such responses was the forms of anti-Black racism and abuse that some Black people deal with when working as educators. Such views that were expressed often resonated with the perspective of Maya Patel (1994: 9) who, while working as a Children's Worker with Shakti Women's Aid in Scotland in the 1990s, wrote the following as part of a collection of writing on *Challenging Racism in the Early Years: The Role of Childcare Services in Scotland and Europe*:

Racism is very much present in Scotland, despite the myth that 'there's no problem here'. Why do we constantly get fed this line? Is it the belief that Scotland's own history of oppression and marginalisation has made it less prejudiced, more sympathetic to the struggles of black people? Or is it because of another belief, that Scotland's lower proportion of black people, compared to that of the rest of Britain, gives rise to less 'racial tensions' – that phrase which presupposes that the presence of black people anywhere equals problems. From a European perspective, the increased incidence of racism and fascism within certain parts of Europe has brought racism firmly onto the European agenda, whether we like it or not. The development of what many term 'Fortress Europe' will potentially deprive many black people within Europe of basic rights in relation to freedom of movement, and their entitlement to adequate pay, housing, education and childcare.

Many people who completed the survey expressed frustration regarding experiencing societal expectations that they tolerate discrimination at work because there was an anti-Black assumption that they should be so grateful for having a job that they put up with oppression in the workplace. Comments about experiencing oppression at work included the following:

> I have been confronted with; Racial discrimination, institutionalized racism and have challenged these for many years. Employability has improved but still more work to be done. Still there are no structural solutions in place to resolve institutionalised racism and the workplace has become more toxic for most black and ethnic minorities.
>
> 4 February 2021 (56–65 years-old)

> I've had positive experience living in Scotland. People are welcoming and I find that most people are interested in learning about my heritage however I feel the struggle is in finding office jobs – I have experienced low key discrimination.
>
> 24 January 2021 (36–45 years-old)

> I think we need to look seriously at the level of discrimination that still goes on in the work place and other institutions. I think that some sort of affirmative action or wide scale quota policy should be implemented across industries and public institutions.
>
> 13 January 2021 (26–35 years-old)

> When I moved to Bo'ness I was one of very few [Black] people and there was a feeling of not belonging. However, my biggest hurdle has been in my professional life where the microagressions are on a level that have led me to consider leaving Scotland. Once you call it out, you're then blamed, bullied, ignored, and gaslit. Most people think there is no problem with racism in Scotland because they compare themselves with say England – but my experience has shown me that Scotland's hidden race issue is in many ways worse than England.
>
> 17 March 2021 (26–35 years-old)

The same person also stated that racism has made them 'want to leave Scotland and the impact it has had on my mental health cannot be put into words. To be discriminated against because you're Black, is a pain I wouldn't wish on my worst enemy'. As hill (2019) has previously asserted when critically considering disparities between people's experiences of work, including forms of abuse they face there:

> As Western societies continue to experience social, environmental and economic crises, our ideas and beliefs on what constitutes work and what kinds of work are valued are ever changing: whether it be the ways care and sexual labour are regarded, the role of exploitation and criminalization, or imagining what a post-work terrain could look like.

To address underrepresentation in the workforce and reflect the make-up of the city, Glasgow City Council held its first BME Recruitment Event in 2019, 'to provide information on our current Catering, Cleaning and Home Care job opportunities'. For an industrial city such as Glasgow to hold its first BME recruitment event only in 2019 arguably exposes a perception that prior to this, Black workers have not been considered as permanent residents, able to take up (permanent) employment within the public sector.

Public sector jobs can offer additional security as they are often unionized, and include guaranteed pay rises and access to paid holidays and pension schemes. Despite these 'benefits', when the Black worker's economic value is realized, where their skill is considered to be located is determined to be low-paid, strenuous, and lacking in opportunities for progression. As Evans' (1995: 144) asserts, 'the low social status attributed to African people in European racist discourse has not escaped Scots and Scotland in spite of the anti-racist tradition upheld by the Scots'. Glasgow City Council's BME Recruitment Event would then appear to be encouraging Black workers to enter into work and roles which echo elements of those of enslaved women, described by Stella Dadzie (2020: 9), 'Away from the fields, some women can be seen dusting the silver or waiting at table with lowered eyes and pricked ears. Others are busy hauling produce to market or hiring out their skills as cooks, seamstresses, laundresses, nurses and midwives'. This would support Evans' (1995: 145) assertion that: 'Racism emanating from historical racial theories still plays an important role in determining the social status of African/Caribbean people in Scotland.'

As race, ethnicity, and health scholar Gwenetta Curry (2020) highlights, '[t]he insistence that the UK be framed as an egalitarian society where racism does not, can not, and should not, explain health disparities forces Black researchers to dismiss obvious trends in data as anomalies and contrary to fact'. Also, work and labour where Black people are over-represented, such as care work, has become more dangerous and demanding in the continuing COVID-19 pandemic landscape, so Black people's experiences of this crisis are impacted by issues concerning race and capitalism. Those who continue to work are faced with protecting themselves and those they live with from exposure to COVID-19, when travelling to work via public transport and working in conditions where there is a lack of safety measures, including the provision of Personal Protective Equipment (PPE).

As was indicated by interviewees for this book, stressful working and living environments impact significantly on well-being and mental health, particularly for those on low or no income and living in 'deprived' areas. A recent report,

23 Public seating area featuring 'Please keep your distance' sign. Photograph by Najma Abukar.

Racial Inequality and Mental Health in Scotland (Mental Welfare Commission for Scotland, 2021) looked at ethnicity and detention under the Mental Health Act; the views of people with lived experience of this; the experience and training of Scotland's mental health services workforce; racial equality in that workforce; and recording and reporting of ethnicity across mental health services; including in the Commission's own work. One of the key findings highlighted:

> ...there is a relationship between areas of socio-economic deprivation and detentions with higher proportions of detained people from the more deprived Scottish Index of Multiple Deprivation (SIMD) categories, however this relationship was more distinct in the black group where 58% who were detained were from the most deprived areas of Scotland compared to white Scottish people of whom 36% were from the most deprived areas.

It is also important to note that '[i]n Scotland, someone from a Black and minority ethnic (BME) background is around twice as likely to experience poverty as someone from a white Scottish/British background. There is a danger that, in 2020 and for years to come, the wide-ranging impacts of the Covid-19 pandemic will contribute to a rising tide of poverty amongst those on low incomes, including a disproportionate number of BME people' (CRER 2020b). For Black workers whose income is derived from the 'informal economy', such as sex work, access to waged work – and trade unions – is made impossible due to a range of factors such as lack of childcare, language barriers, societal stigmatization, anti-Black racism, or No Recourse to Public Funds (NRPF), enforced on those 'subject to immigration control'. The COVID-19 pandemic has brought changes to the way in which most of us access paid work. Increased focus and warnings to pay more attention to hand hygiene, has seen society move away from cash payments to 'contactless' payments. Though this may be considered safe and convenient for most, financial surveillance becomes an ever-present reality and crucially, access to 'informal economies', which are often reliant on cash, becomes even more difficult to navigate.

According to Arshad and McCrum (1989: 220), 'It is often ignored that black women like any other have always borne the multiplicity of roles, as carers, mothers, consumers, providers, objects of desire and abuse. They too tend to be at the bottom of the pay and power scales, employees not employers, and unpaid sowers, reapers and breadmakers, not recognized to be breadwinners.' Additionality, as reported by CRER – the Coalition for Racial Equality and Rights (2020), '[u]nemployment rates are higher for minority ethnic people in Scotland; in 2019, the gap in employment rates between minority ethnic people and white people in Scotland was over 16%. This gap is much wider for minority ethnic women at 22% compared to 9.5% for men. BME women in Scotland continue to face serious barriers in access to work, including racist and sexist attitudes and discrimination'. As society rebuilds from the pandemic, a focus on those who experience the violence of sexism, anti-Black racism, and class oppression produced by capitalism should be at the centre of transforming the way we live and work in the future.

Prison abolitionist and geographer Ruth Wilson Gilmore (2020) captures the racist roots of capitalism when stating that 'all capitalism is racialised from its beginning, and it will continue to depend on racial practice and hierarchy no matter what'. Additionally, Robinson refers (1983: 9) to the '[n]onobjective character of capitalist development' which articulates that capitalism is far from being neutral in any way. Rather than capitalism being a system devoid of racial hierarchies, the architecture of capitalism is built on inherently oppressive foundations that are scaffolded by racism, elitism, classism, and intersecting oppressions such as sexism, and misogyny. The effects of this include the normalization of discrimination and harassment in the workplace, where Black people are expected to tolerate abuse while in pursuit of paid work and social mobility opportunities.

The racism which Black people experience while at work and the (in)formal socialising (where relationships leading to work progression can be developed) which often accompanies it, is nuanced and experiences of this can drastically vary, dependent on factors such as skin colour, perceived religion, class position or gender identity and location. A dark-skinned Black person working in roles such as those within the National Health Service (NHS) or hospitality, might experience brazen racism and colourism from the public, as well as structural forms of such oppression from those with whom they work. Charmaine Blaize, who works as an IT Health Management professional for NHS Scotland, states:

> I have a right to be here, I have the right to live comfortably and be free. I have the right to apply for jobs and be seen for my ability and not seen for the other parts of me that doesn't belong to this landscape ... My Trinidadian accent, my Blackness. You know we talk about intersectionality now but when things happen for me in workspaces, people don't have that kind of awareness or sensitivity. You start to think about all the things that make you the 'Other'. Is it because I am a woman? Is it because I am Black? Is it because I have an accent? I'm in senior management and there is no-one else who looks like me in senior management. The other thing is, we don't supervise. You get professional roles where you work professionally on your own. You don't line manage. You don't get opportunities to line manage Scottish people.

Walcott (2019: 402) observes, 'value is always already linked to capital and its racial economy rather than ideas about human work'. Indeed, how and where Black people work is framed, at times, by the perceived usefulness of their Blackness to the employer, which often demands even more work. Also, as Arshad and McCrum (1989: 221) assert:

> Many employers can claim that black women have entered into semi-professional or professional jobs, such as the authors of this paper. On closer examination, these women have more often than not, ended up in race-related fields, such as multi-cultural education, community relations councils, or projects sponsored to work with multiracial communities. Women in this category are often used to provide antiracist training, and to lend credibility by acting as token blacks [sic] on committees and other forums. Their opinions are requested on draft policy papers, to assist in areas unrelated to their job descriptions, and many are over-worked and underpaid for the amount of work and advice offered.

Despite positive action strategies which employers utilize to demonstrate they encourage applications from 'under-represented groups', a Black person's suitability as an 'acceptable' employee, who won't 'cause trouble' or upset the status quo, can be determined by the posts they share online. Many employers now search the social media networks of prospective employees to ascertain their suitability to the role or organization. Though many social media profiles can be 'locked' or made private (to a certain extent), posts made from a person's profile elsewhere online can still be viewed and attributed to them.

For Black people who have found solidarity online and choose to share posts related to their experiences, doing so can hinder employment prospects. As the research of Simon Howard, Kalen Kennedy, and Francisco Tejeda (2020: 2) shows, 'Black job candidates who post about racism on their social media profiles will be evaluated less favorably (i.e., be viewed as less likable), less likely to be extended an interview, and less likely to be hired than Black candidates whose social media posts were race neutral'. Furthermore, some work, such as roles in the creative industries requires 'having presence' and networking to develop relationships in order to access work, with much of this now being done online. Maintaining online presence and relationships is additional labour and factors such as time, space, knowledge, and access to the equipment required to undertake this labour, can become additional barriers to Black people participating in such work and activities.

Informal online communities created by industry peers to offer support and increase work opportunities, can also be sites of anti-Black oppression and exclusion. Scotland based Nikko Dingani an entertainer who generously agreed to be interviewed for *Black Oot Here: Black Lives in Scotland*, describes his experience:

> I'm an entertainer, so I joined an online Scottish entertainment forum. The community has over 2000 people, members. It's not only Scottish entertainers, but every entertainer who has performed in Scotland, at the Edinburgh Festival for example. This means there are people from all over the world, but it's managed by Scottish entertainers. I remember one case, this old guy, he started attacking me. Racial abuse online about my creative stuff. The argument was like, I said there is racism in Scotland and in the entertainment industry. He said, prove it. I was like, there is no need for me to prove it, you are the evidence. I'm talking to you right now and look at the words you are using and the way you are speaking to me. I remember me and him arguing for four hours online, and other people start getting on and stuff. There are three things in this entertainment thing, the industry. There is bullying, jealousy and racism. Those things, I've experienced them, and I've seen them.

Furthermore, Evans (1995: 237) argues that 'positive actions' such as equal opportunities and ethnic monitoring policies function to disadvantage and exclude Black people from the workforce:

It is difficult for ethnic minorities, in general, and African-Caribbeans in, particular, to obtain main-stream employment even with major employers who claim to be an 'equal opportunities employer' or 'striving to be an equal opportunity employer' and 'do not discriminate according to race, creed, age, gender, sexual orientation, ethnic origin'. In England, Equal Opportunities policies work to a certain extent but in Scotland lip service is paid to these policies. Some employers have had these policies in operation for many years yet fail to employ or expand, on their numbers, or sometimes even to admit African/Caribbean or other ethnic minorities to their work force. In fact the prevailing view is that 'ethnic monitoring' on job application forms is being used by firms to weed out black applicants. Racism in employment seems to be the most effective Scottish way whether deliberate or otherwise of keeping the numbers of ethnic minorities small in Scotland even for those who were born here.

Such views were also expressed by those of many people who responded to our survey. However, other people expressed different perspectives:

[Racism in] Scotland is very subtle. it is not down and outright nasty. you don't get the job you applied for because 'somebody else was just better than you' but your interview and cv was perfect. Your son does not get invited to birthday parties. The women in your keep fit group go on night outs but you do not get invited. you live in a village but you are never invited to 'tea'. you constantly live on the peripherals of their society and never get invited in. but at the same time you can not accuse them of excluding you just 'omiting'.

17 February 2021 (56–65 years-old)

Very soul destroying, I lost all my confidence as the racism I experienced mainly at work. It took a lot for me to get better. Also my spiritual belief system and share grit has pushed me to continue to strive and hold my head up. I also got involved in activism and that helped.

10 February 2021 (46–55 years-old)

I haven't experienced any sort of negativity here and I can honestly say it's been welcoming. I have had a drunk guy attempt to reach out and touch my hair but I shut that down real quick. That was 2018 and it hasn't happened since. I recently moved from govanhill and I experienced some stares there from groups of men, but I think that would go for any woman walking alone.

22 January 2021 (36–45 years-old)

There are many people who have witnessed the violence of racism but they remain silent. Their silence is complicit. Regardless of how hard you work and how much you do in your community in the name of humanity somehow being

Black is a crime that you have to pay for on a daily basis. This has a significant impact on mental health. You try to speak up, seek therapy counselling etc. but in a space that is in constant denial of your experience then how can you fully heal?.

11 October 2020 (46–55 years-old)

I think racism is everywhere. I have had one instance of overt racism that shocked me, otherwise it's the little things and in that sense Scotland is no different. In terms of impact, I live with it. I seek out new groups to form new communities....it's just there always latent, a part of life and would be difficult to quantify ... To be honest, it's the same racism I've experienced my whole life. I think the racism I experience feeds into my imposter syndrome at work ... sometimes I'm worn down by racism, sometimes I'm angered by it. It's hard to say what exactly the effects have been on me, but they've certainly made life more challenging and hard work.

9 October 2020 (26–35 years-old)

Many people who completed the survey outlined incidents involving them being discriminated against and harassed by work colleagues. One person wrote the following:

...Incidents wise, there's too many to list but examples include security following me when shopping on my own, people assuming my daughter isn't mine as she is lighter than me with long straight hair, randoms shouting slurs, randoms trying to touch my hair, sexual harrassment [sic] from men of all creeds and white women. Events wise, if it's a gig it's usually some form of sexual harassment or me shouting at people who keep touching my hair. Was once at a work's night out where there was an act of three men in disco suits and big fake afros. One colleague tried to convince me to dance 'with the other afros' and when I declined 3 colleagues pushed me on to the stage. It felt very 'dance monkey, dance' and I left immediately.

3 February 2021 (26–35 years-old)

As Robinson (1983: 2) observes, '[t]he development, organization, and expansion of capitalist society pursued essentially racial directions' which involved the structural oppression of racialized people, including in the form of the enslavement of Black people who were treated in abhorrent ways. Examples of the lack of adequate acknowledgement of Scotland's involvement in the enslavement of Black people illustrate a denial of how aspects of its present-day economy have been made possible due to the profits of slavery that were pursued in the past.

Throughout history, there are myriad examples of Black people cruelly being treated as commodities and a means to aid commerce. Contemporary conversations about the perceived 'socio-economic value' of racialized migrants, which are dependent on a harmful socially constructed binary opposition of 'the good immigrant' who is worthy of societal acceptance, and 'the bad immigrant' who is an alleged drain on society (Cowan 2021; Shukla 2016), are connected to the currents of racial capitalism. Scotland does not have control over the entry of nationals from other countries independently from the UK. The Scottish Government (2020b) has called for the devolution of immigration powers with a stated objective to, 'grow our population to ensure Scotland has sustainable, vibrant, and resilient communities and drive improvements in inclusive growth'. As such, its primary goal is to attract migrants, 'who will raise families to grow the future working age population that will pay taxes to fund the essential public services that society – and especially an increasingly ageing society – demands' (Scottish Government 2018).

So-called 'inclusive' and 'progressive' discussion about 'welcoming refugees' and working to 'upskill' migrants in Scotland can quickly morph into discourse that is dependent on the racist, xenophobic, and capitalist idea that such people should only be welcome in different countries if they can prove their 'economic value'. Moreover, an emphasis on allegedly 'upskilling' migrants is also often based on the assumption that migrants need more skills to find work and puts the onus of responsibility on them to 'improve' themselves, as opposed to compelling institutions to address the structural and oppressive barriers that often prevent such individuals from securing sustained and safe employment. Such a focus on 'upskilling' feeds into what author of *Border Nation: A Story of Migration*, Leah Cowan (2021: 42), refers to as 'Meritocracy myths and the "resource drain" lie' which involves migrant communities commonly being 'forced into a position of defending their existence in the UK based on the fact they "contribute" to the economy' (Cowan 2021: 43).

Further still, as Nwonka (2020: 7) contends as part of the analysis of 'the black neoliberal aesthetic', 'neoliberalism's dominant hold of contemporary life now very much includes blackness, black cultural products and black representations'. Hence, the need to avoid mistaking the visibility of Black people for indication of societal changes that have addressed anti-Black racism and intersecting oppressions (Warner 2017). Racial capitalism is entangled with notions of nationhood, and by extension, ideas about who does and does not belong where, and who is and is not entitled to what (Robinson 1983). Therefore, within societies touched by racial capitalism, the concept of the stigmatized 'Other' often operates in harmful ways:

The Other is likely to be cast as needful of our society's resource and wealth; putting strain on already stretched services. The Other is likely to be feared; living lives which are incompatible with Western society. We've seen the Other manifested as LGBTQIA, as young, as Irish, as Muslim, as working class and poor, as living with disabilities and as Black. We seldom learn of the plundering from colonial and imperial rule or of the violence of detachment which capitalism dictates … The Black 'Other' is both hyper visible and invisible in Scotland. Census data documents those who can be documented, the undocumented are noticeable in other ways. Both however, remain noticeably absent in Scottish public life. Erasure of the existence of the Other happens at home without the need for physical borders.

hill 2018

The COVID-19 crisis, which is reflected upon throughout our book, has highlighted pre-existing failures by the state – including the healthcare system – to address institutional racism and antiblackness. The 'hostile environment' policy, interfered with the very foundation on which the NHS was built; healthcare for all, free at the point of delivery, based on clinical need not the ability to pay. Prior to the COVID-19 pandemic, inequalities faced by Black people navigating the healthcare system have been well documented. As Bryan, Dadzie and Scafe (1985: 89) state:

The creation of the NHS enabled the needs of capitalism to be reconciled, albeit temporarily, with the demands of the people, and the import of Black women's labour was the convenient short-term means by which this goal would be achieved. Since we were never identified as potential consumers of the service, our health needs did not enter the debate about the kind of health provision the country would establish. The NHS was geared, first and foremost, to meeting the needs of the white man as economic producer and – to a lesser extent – those of the white woman, as re-producer. These priorities have remained enshrined within the NHS ever since. They are reflected in every facet of the service, from the allocation of its resources to the structure of its workforce. As such, our treatment within the NHS is probably the most clear and damning indictment of our social and economic value to Britain.

A disturbing narrative emerged during and as we move through the ongoing pandemic, that of blaming Black communities for outbreaks, when they are often the ones putting their lives at risk to support the smooth functioning of society, through 'essential' and 'key worker' jobs. Nikko Dingani reflected on this and his experiences during the pandemic:

We should never forget is the beginning of the pandemic, the way they were labelling Black and Asians. We are likely to die from COVID, we are likely to catch it and spread it. It was a negativity the media put to us, so we would stay in the house. Because now they have turned around, oh Black people and Asians don't want to take vaccines. I never said I don't want to take it, all I said is I just want to know what is it? What is wrong with asking? The media is always twisting things. They are always going to make us fight. It's up to us as well, just ignore those kind of things cause otherwise it's just going to put fear and negativity.

At the beginning of the pandemic, it was difficult. It was tough, if you live yourself. I decided to rearrange my routine of doing life. It was difficult in the beginning. You don't have to meet people anymore. You can only go for a walk for a very short time and that's you. There is a positive on it because I started to learn new things. Because I knew if I have to stay in that corner of panic and worry, I won't get out of life. The other things I cut down was drinking alcohol. That's something people need to be careful – when you are put in a small space where no-one can save you, you need to avoid triggers. You need to avoid things that can make you weak for your own self. I've never talked so much with my families in Africa and that's because of the internet, I'm really thankful for that. I have time now and every time we are talking, we are sharing this same fear, I think the world was experiencing the same thing and people came together. Never mind what the government says about us.

An area of considerable concern in Black communities, like other communities under pressure from the economic impact of the crisis is the disturbing rise in domestic abuse. Concerns have been raised that people who do not speak English have been turned away from refuges, even when there are available places. Also troubling, are the huge changes to grieving, death, and bereavement rituals such as funerals that have been brought in by the government as a result of the pandemic. It is recognized that these restrictions are an issue for all, and more could be done to address the lack of opportunity for people to express grief and memorialize lives in communal ways.

How Black people have experienced – and continue to experience – the COVID-19 pandemic is varied and can be read in the words of respondents to our survey:

Variation of how seriously different teachers followed covid guidelines pressurised BAME teachers because it made us appear over cautious.

19 March 2021 (56–65 years-old)

Negatively. I have less income, less access to mental healthcare, and can't travel to see friend groups of women of colour across the UK. This is lonely.

13 January 2021 (26–35 years-old)

Extensive evidence indicates that Black people in Britain are among those who have been hardest hit by the COVID-19 pandemic (Curry 2020, 2021; Office for National Statistics 2020), including due to experiences of dealing with medical racism which can be part of their encounters with the NHS. In the words of race, ethnicity, and health scholar Gwenetta Curry (2021), for *The Scotsman*, the '[i]mpact of racism and discrimination on death rate cannot be ignored'. Curry's (2020) work highlights that '[p]revious studies have demonstrated that where we live can be a clear marker for life-expectancy and opportunities. In the UK, ethnic minorities are over-represented in overcrowded or deprived areas, and these conditions are linked to higher COVID-19 incidence and death'. Also, research by The Diaspora African Women's Support Network (DAWSUN) (2021) on 'The Social Economic Status of Africans in Scotland' suggests that 68% of their 'respondents have either lost their jobs, savings, are unable to pay their mortgages, cannot afford food, or have relied on friends and family to cover living expenses since the outbreak of the pandemic'.

As scholars Eve Hepburn, Michael Keating, and Nicola McEwen (2021: 22) state, 'the COVID-19 crisis, and the enormous health, economic and social challenges it has created for governments across the globe, also shapes the background against which any decision on Scotland's future would take place'. Therefore, this is a truly unique time for Scotland to demonstrate what an independent Scotland could be like, but at present, such a vision is unclear. Unsurprisingly, experiencing ongoing oppression and societal marginalization, both before and during the pandemic, can result in individuals identifying ways to work together to attempt to address the systems and structures that maintain the subjugation of people. As such, there is a strong history of activism and organizing in Scotland which we now turn our attention to and reflect on again in Chapters 3 and 4.

In it th'gither: Black activism in Scotland and ideas about Scottish Independence

Years of Black activism and organizing in Scotland preceded the media visibility of BLM protests and events in Scotland such as the Edinburgh in Solidarity for Black Lives Matter meet at Holyrood Park on 7 June 2020. Among the many Black groups, organizations, and spaces that predated 2020 are the African Caribbean Centre in Glasgow, the African & Caribbean Women's Association (ACWA), the African Women Group Scotland in Aberdeen, and Lothian Black Forum (LBF) which campaigned in 1989 to ensure that the murder of a 28-year-old Somali student Axmed Abuukar Sheekh, by white fascists in Edinburgh, was recognized as a racist crime (Smith 2020). Those involved in LBF included African Asian Scottish writer and performance poet Kokumo (Kumo) Rocks, as well as journalist, author, broadcaster, and academic Gary Younge, who was a student in Scotland at the time that LBF formed.

When interviewed by Ayeisha Thomas-Smith (2020) for a New Economics Foundation podcast recording on The Global Black Liberation Uprisings in 2020, Younge reflected on his involvement in LBF:

> I lived in Scotland as a student and there was a Lothian Black Forum which was created in protest at the racist murder of an asylum seeker ... the Black forum kind of existed for about three, four years, did wonderful work: organised marches, convened, got people together and then there was a kind of OK, let's almost form working groups, let's do our own thing.

In March 2021, Gary Younge kindly agreed to be interviewed as part of our research. Gary moved to Scotland in 1987 and was there until 1992, with a year out to France and Russia as part of the course that he was studying at the time. While living in Scotland Gary started working as a journalist, including for *The Scotsman* student supplement. In Gary's words, 'just to set the scene of when I was in Scotland ... it was all under the Tory government. I arrived just after they won the 1987 election and left shortly after they won ... surprise victory of the 1992 election ... the poll tax was introduced while I was there, and so there was a significant amount of repression ... of feeling repressed ... that Scottishness had not been given this space to bloom'.

Since leaving Scotland in the early 1990s, Gary has sometimes returned for various social occasions, to see friends, and when participating in events such as 'Telling our Own Stories: People of Colour in Scotland's Media' (Kinning Park Complex, 27 September 2019).

When reflecting on his time in Scotland in the late 80s and early 90s, Gary said the following:

> Some of the most intense racial experiences I've had in Britain have been in Scotland. The most intense being chased by two men with baseball bats down Lothian Road, shouting 'nigger', which was towards the middle of my second year. I hadn't been there very long ... a couple of years ... when there was a murder ... Axmed Sheekh. That was the dawning ... until then ... it seemed to me that this was a place that had not seen that many Black people, so I would be there and people would sort of point and ... in a way that I don't think they would now, I don't know. This is in Edinburgh it's not even in kind of small towns

24 Poster for 'Telling Our Own Stories: People of colour in Scotland's' Media event on Friday 27 September 2019. Photograph by Francesca Sobande

. . . and it took me awhile to kind of figure out . . . there was some confused sense of affinity about being Scottish and being Black . . . *not* from me but from other people . . . and so there were some people I met who came to issues of race through their Scottishness or through their sense of oppression or whatever, which was different because my entire experience up until that point had been in England. I was ignorant about Scotland as a separate place. I used to say to people . . . I used to confuse (not for very long because people soon put you straight!) Scotland and England . . . and then I got up to Scotland and thought 'okay . . . right . . . this is different'. It felt different in a range of ways . . . and there was this sense of identification possible . . . it was confused, like I say . . . but some notion of potential solidarity, and it did seem also that there was more space with *more* people for better racial conversations than in England. It seemed that way to me . . . *not* with everyone . . . but with *more* people . . . but there was also significant ignorance. Even the racist insults were kind of outdated.

Gary reflected on different examples of racism in Scotland and what the future of the Scottish political landscape may hold:

They would call me things like 'golliwog' or something. I'd be like . . . nobody has called anybody that since 1970, you need to up your racist game and kind of call me something a bit more modern . . . and my experience having been back [to Scotland since leaving] and particularly doing some reporting from there around knife crime and other things . . . was that the existence of the Scottish parliament and the possibility of an independent Scotland which, whether it's there or not . . . whether it exists there or not, is being prepared for in a range of ways, not least ideologically . . . people are thinking about 'what kind of country do we want to be?'. Even to have those thoughts about what kind of country are we was to break out of the kind of stale notion of we are an occupied territory in Britain and that kind of defines all our politics . . . To me, in England, when I go there [Scotland] it feels like a much more accessible political entity. That you might know some of the people who are your political representatives . . . that you might see some of them on a train. It's a political entity of a size that means you can pick up the phone to quite a lot of people and things might get done . . .

Gary referred to there being moments in Scotland in recent months and years that suggest there is a sense that some people believe that 'the role of race in whatever new country we are forming is in play'. Gary's perspective is consistent with the words of Jackson (2020: 2) who argues that '[e]ven without formal powers over migration and citizenship, which under devolution remain reserved at Westminster, Scotland has its own public political culture of race'.

As Gary pointed out, the potential for issues regarding race and racism to be addressed differently in an independent Scotland 'offers opportunity, but it also offers potential disaster'. The words of someone who responded to our survey seem to be very similar to these sentiments: '. . . I am wary that Scotland as a "new" nation would be used to obscure this country's violently racist and imperialist past. And as a consequence, it might become harder to address issues of racism that exist today . . .'. In agreement with such perspectives, we recognize the need to challenge any assumptions that an independent Scotland would be an inherently anti-racist Scotland.

When continuing to speak in detail about racism in Scotland in the late 1980s and early 1990s, Gary discussed the ways in which some people attempted to suggest that racism was an English import rather than something embedded in the foundations of Scotland itself:

When I was chased. I remember the guy who ran the SNP at university asking 'were they English?' which I thought was a weird question. Then I said 'you know . . . I didn't get a chance to find out . . . because they were chasing me with fucking baseball bats'. When Axmed Sheekh was killed there were kind of these fraught articles about whether Scotland was catching this English disease. There was this notion that somehow Scotland was pure, and this had been imported from somewhere else, whereas in the meantime, and this was the lens through which I kind of got a sense of people identifying with or against racism, was the sectarian divide.

When thinking about football match days back then, and the dangers for Black people in Scotland, Gary spoke about 'a group of men who started banging on my train window at Haymarket and shouting racist insults ... The really entrenched racism that one would see ... it was likely to be football related ... you're like a unicorn walking around in these places [at an Old Firm game] ... like an apparition ... people would say things like "Fucking hell ... it's Bob fucking Marley!".

While revisiting Gary's words in this interview we found ourselves reflecting on the questions John Horne (1995) was asking in *Racism, Sectarianism and Football in Scotland*:

> ... why are not more black players involved in Scottish football? Is it because they do not constitute a sufficiently large proportion of the Scottish population? Are there greater economic opportunities open to them in the Scottish labour market and hence are the restrictions that operate in England to channel young blacks [sic] into sport as a possible route of social esteem and mobility less in evidence? Or is it because of the perceived racism in the Scottish game? At present we can only pose these questions, not provide any clearcut answers.

When speaking to Gary Younge and learning about his time in Scotland, we also wondered what it might have been like to experience Scottish football, and

25 American WBC world heavyweight boxing champion Muhammad Ali is greeted by a traditional Scottish pipe band on his arrival at Glasgow Airport, 18 August 1965

indeed Scotland, when Gilbert Heron (father of poet Gil Scott-Heron), became the first Black football player to play for Celtic FC in 1951, or when heavyweight boxing champion Muhammad Ali touched down in Glasgow Airport in 1965.

As we listened to the words of Gary Younge, we also thought about how Scottish football has changed even since the early 2000s, which was a time long before witnessing some Scottish football players take the knee on the field as a symbol of support for the Black Lives Matter movement. A 2021 BBC documentary, *Mark Walters in the Footsteps of Andrew Watson* illuminated some related issues

26 'Safeway International Challenge Match: Scotland v Nigeria, Pittodrie Stadium Aberdeen 17 April 2002' wall hanging. Photograph by Francesca Sobande.

and featured former Rangers Football Club player Mark Walters, reflecting on the racism he faced while playing for the club. The documentary also highlights the career of Andrew Watson, a Black footballing pioneer who, in 1881, captained Scotland. Scoutable United (2021), a grassroots football club formed in 2019, is doing much to progress the careers of Black players in Scotland and build community links. The Scoutable United website states amongst the reasons for their existence is 'scouting bias – often unconscious – means many gifted footballers from diverse backgrounds go overlooked', indicating the questions John Horne was asking in 1995, remain relevant in Scottish football today.

When continuing to speak about Scotland in the late 1980s and early 1990s, Gary described the various ways that people in Scotland took notice of anti-Black racism, which included people acting as though 'however local it [anti-Black racism] was, it would always be foreign'. He continued to say 'it was a very, very uneven terrain. Some people were kind of ignorant but there were more people who were open. Some people were quite advanced. Other people were completely backward'. Gary referred to there, sometimes, being a 'sort of convivial ...a convivial embrace at arm's length. "You're different ... it's nice to see you ...". Not always that ... sometimes it was "you're different ... and fuck off!" but like ... actually more common would be a recognition of the difference and a ...a desire to kind of note the distance and then some kind of weird welcome'.

While discussing those times in the late 1980s and early 1990s in Scotland Gary also spoke about what felt like 'a nascent flourishing of Black Scottish activism':

> I don't know. I hadn't been there before so it could be that there was quite a lot of Black activism there that I didn't know about, but the Lothian Black Forum was relatively new and so this particular iteration anyway was quite new, and there were people who had been working on things for quite some time. Mukami McCrum sticks out but there were several and they, within the activist world, were incredibly welcoming and embracing. But then there was another world of professionalised anti-racism ... it was quite small and there were a handful of jobs around certain institutions, and there were some really good people there but also some bad faith actors trying to protect their turf really, who, because the community was so small, had a relationship to that activist group and may even have been in it, but they weren't the same thing *as* it.

Writing about her experience of LBF in *Grit and Diamonds: Women in Scotland Making History 1980–1990*, Kokumo Rocks (1990: 176) states:

> Finally, Black people are meeting together in various groups in Scotland. I joined the Lothian Black Forum in 1988. Now there is somewhere for our children to go

and discuss how they feel. One of the aims of the forum is to let our Black children talk to each other and share and grow, so they don't have to struggle alone.

As Gary Younge mentioned during his interview with us, people who have been doing work to address racism in Scotland for many years include Mukami McCrum, born in Kenya in the late 1940s but who has lived in Scotland for most of her life. McCrum has worked for the Scottish Government as the policy manager in Gender and LGBT Equality and Violence Against Women. She has been the chief executive of Central Scotland Racial Equality Council and was a founding member of Shakti Women's Aid, which helps BME women, children, and young people who are experiencing, or who have experienced, domestic abuse in Scotland.

McCrum was also a speaker at the first African Women Group Scotland conference, *Our Invisibility in Scotland,* held in Aberdeen in 1998, where she delivered a presentation on *African Women in Scotland: Living and Not Just Surviving.* Other speakers at this key conference included a range of Black women, living and working in Scotland; Myrtle Peterkin, then a Consultant Haematologist at the Glasgow and West of Scotland Blood Transfusion Service, who spoke on *Meeting The Challenges – The Medical Profession and the Black Woman,* Gillian Neish, a trainer and counsellor who specializes in anti-racist, anti-oppressive ways of working, who delivered a speech on *Being the Best we Can,* and June Evans, whose workshop, *The Presence of the African Women in Scotland* was presented as a play, formed from Evans' PhD thesis, *African/ Caribbeans in Scotland: A socio-geographical study.* Zeedah Meirghofer Mangel shared their experience of living and organizing as a Black woman in Switzerland, in *African Woman: Her Visibility and Invisibility in Scotland,* to demonstrate how Black women could also organize in Scotland. Amongst the recommendations made from the 1998 *Our Invisibility in Scotland* conference were:

> There is a need for African women to identify and support each other.
> There is a need to meet and discuss issues that affect us
> There is a need to get involved with communities services and demand our right for better services.
> More research should be done into the position of African Women in contemporary Scotland.
> There should be more conferences of this kind, where we can learn to articulate our issues.
> To raise awareness in issues that affect African Women across Europe
> Encourage African Women to write their stories for posterity.
> Encourage African Women to join voluntary organisations, community groups and professional bodies to raise their profile.

Increase access to information such as training education rights.

Raise awareness on how to acquire the skill of lobbying.

Establish links with other African groups in England and in Europe at large

If we have been here for over 400 years, our history should be in School Curriculum and more people should know about it too.

From the responses we received to the survey and interviews, as well as our own recent experiences of organizing in Scotland, it seems the recommendations made from the African Women Group Scotland conference, *Our Invisibility in Scotland* in 1998 are still as relevant today as they were then.

Other Black people who have been involved in crucial organizing work include Kubara Zamani, who was born in Edinburgh in 1965 and lived there until 1988. Kubara was involved in political action for the Edinburgh Youth Campaign for Nuclear Disarmament (CND), Anti-Apartheid, Edinburgh United Against Apartheid, anti-deportation campaigns and other solidarity groups. Kubara's extensive work also includes a self-published pamphlet in 1983. From 1985 to 1988 Kubara, who had a melodica as a child, played in two reggae bands based in Edinburgh. Part of Chapter 4 is based on an interview to which Kubara thoughtfully agreed.

To grasp the significance of Black activist efforts in Scotland in recent years it is important to consider the history of forms of collective resistant organizing,

27 'Nelson Mandela Place' in Glasgow. Photograph by Najma Abukar.

including by acknowledging the different ways that the term 'Black' has functioned as part of such grassroots work. Several examples of such collective organizing exist, amongst these is the Scottish Black Women's Group, which multicultural and anti-racist education scholar Rowena Arshad (1990: 119) describes as follows:

> Through our isolation and frustrations came together a group of Black* women who began meeting in Edinburgh in the winter of 1985. Our group was about creating a space which allowed us to be our own point of reference. It was time and space for our self expression, a forum to record our own lives, experiences and struggles for justice. We came from all backgrounds – some of us were mothers, all of us were daughters; some of us were young, others young at heart; some of us were in employment, others studying or still searching; some of us had begun the journey of emancipation, others were further ahead, but all of us had lived and felt the varying forms of oppression, particularly those of racism, sexism and class ... We hoped that a group such as ours would bring a much needed political dimension into an area plagued by pseudo-cultural and quasi-sociological interpretations that had led to inappropriate measures, like 'cultural evenings' for ethnic minorities, racism-awareness 'guilt-tripping' sessions which have done little to allow Black women and the Black community to define for ourselves a course of action.

Feelings of isolation are echoed in Meg Agbemetsi's (1990: 121) account on the formation of the African & Caribbean Women's Association in Glasgow (ACWA):

> I was invited by Strathclyde Community Relations Council in 1988 to help organise a one day conference for ethnic minority women in Glasgow. The aim of the conference was to encourage women to organise self-help and support groups within their own communities. I persuaded a few friends from the African & Caribbean community to attend. The conference was a success, and the African & Caribbean women were very impressed with the progress made by our Asian, Chinese and Jewish sisters to improve their lot. I dare say, 30th October was the 'day of awakening' for our African & Caribbean sisters. There was a common concern for the total isolation of African & Caribbean women and their families and the lack of any form of cohesion among the African & Caribbean living in Glasgow, or for that matter Strathclyde. The lack of representation and participation of African & Caribbean women in the decision-making processes within Strathclyde region had resulted in neglect and lack of political will by various agencies, including Strathclyde Regional Council, to meet our most basic social needs. It was evident that we would remain the minority of the ethnic minorities unless we sought to organise ourselves into an effective social group. On 13th November 1988, the first ever Pan-African women's group in Scotland was founded in Glasgow with eight members.

Agbemetsi (1990: 122) goes on to acknowledge the difficulties and constraints found in organizing, due to caring responsibilities, work and education commitments, but that in spite of there being very few African & Caribbean women living in Glasgow – 'exact number of women is not known' – the membership of the Association had grown from eight members in 1988 to 40 women in 1990.

'Black women and women of colour are often made invisible amidst data and discourse related to gender, race, and diversity in Scotland. It is all too common that discussion of gender and women in Scotland is synonymous with the perspectives of white women, and that conversations to do with race do not explore the

28 'Bird's eye' view of Black women and children at an event in Glasgow. Photograph by Najma Abukar

entanglements of racism and sexism' (hill and Sobande 2019: 108). As the inimitable work of Johnson (2020) emphasizes, normative notions of womanhood are intrinsically linked to whiteness, thus, much public discourse to do with women's rights does not meaningfully, if at all, engage with the lives of Black women.

The struggles faced by Black women, identified in the 1980s and 1990s by groups such as the Scottish Black Women's Group and African Women Group Scotland persist to the present day, however there has been mounting criticism of the homogenizing concept of political blackness . 'Black is an adopted category with essentialist undertones (color) but flexible boundaries (any color and ethnicity has been included in this particular context and location [Europe], from Irish to Chinese, Indian, and African)' (Essed 2009: xii).

Based on an account in the edited collection *Grit and Diamonds: Women in Scotland Making History 1980–1990*, the Scottish Black Women's Group, established in the 1980s and which lasted for a couple of years, was upfront regarding their use of the term 'Black' 'to refer to all people of colour who are discriminated against by racist structures and attitudes within Scottish/British white dominated society' (Arshad 1990: 120). In the context of the Scottish Black Women's Group the term 'Black' was used as 'a political rather than physiological expression to include Asians/Chinese, African & Caribbean, Arabs, Latin Americans etc.' (ibid.). Put briefly, the Scottish Black Women's Group did not solely consist of Black women of African descent.

As part of a crucial article in *Ethnic and Racial Studies* that examines the different ways that the term 'Black' is used in research and society in Britain, education scholar Uvanney Maylor (2009: 369) affirms that 'Black' is a contested term. Its usage has attracted much academic debate. Issues of terminology are important as they produce real consequences for the lives of those using and/or who are subsumed within particular definitions'. Maylor's research regarding this has examined 'the implications of employing collective terminology in arriving at shared meanings and understandings' (ibid.). Influenced by Maylor's work, in this section we consider critical developments in terms of how Black activism and collective organizing in Scotland has changed in the twenty-first century.

The notion of political blackness (although not always referred to as such) which was especially popular between the 1970s and 1980s, and undergirded groups such as the Scottish Black Women's Group, is dependent on the idea that people from a wide range of different racial and ethnic backgrounds can identify under the unified umbrella term 'Black' due to a perceived shared political commitment to addressing racism, capitalism, imperialism, and various structures that maintain forms of societal oppression. When writing about different understandings and uses of the term 'black' in Britain, Nwonka (2020: 5) reflects on 'the homogenising of ethnic difference under the unified category of 'black' as the natural defence mechanism against white racism'. Maylor (2016: 370) states, '[d]uring this time, a common identification with a 'black' identity was used positively by coalitions of African, African-Caribbean and South Asian organizations in their struggles against racial discrimination and quest for racial justice'.

Although there are examples of vital and transnational solidarities forged across racial and ethnic differences, the concept of political blackness has rightly received much criticism, including due to how the idea of political blackness can obscure specific forms of oppression faced by Black people of African descent, including antiblackness that is upheld by other racialized people. Researcher and writer on Islamophobia, trauma, and power, Maryam Jameela (2021: 59), asserts that '[c]ultural and racial specificity has been integral in moving away from catch-all terms like "politically Black"'. As Jameela (2021: 60) observes:

> . . . even the latter half of the 1990s saw, along with the advent of online social organizing, a kind of democratic platform availability which allowed individuals to intervene directly into the process of identity and race subject formation. The most pertinent strategies for organisation, then, have been the inclusion of platforms which allow for greater interaction with the social world on every level which have also allowed for individuals to inscribe their own bodies with their own racial subjectivities; this inscription no longer relies upon unity or solidarity built upon homogenous unity. In other words, a specificity which seeks to articulate differences amongst a range of racial identifiers.

The concept of political blackness has facilitated some of the collective organization of anti-racist activists and racialized people, particularly in the trade union movement. As Charmaine Blaize describes:

> When I started working, I decided to get connected with the [trade] union, as no support came to me, and I needed some kind of support mechanism or support group. The (trade) union was one of my avenues for getting connected with Black people and people who are interested in human rights and making people's lives better. Involvement in the union back home was a necessary evil – you have it as a back-up, as insurance. Here I realised that as one Black person you can't have a voice, you have to align yourself. That's how I got involved with the [trade] union.

Political blackness has contributed to some fruitful past trade union organizing efforts such as those described by campaigner for racial equality, Anita Shelton (2001: 51), 'the establishment of a Standing Committee of Black Workers in 1997 . . . Black female members have been integrally involved in the range of activities undertaken to mainstream racial equality, strengthen advocacy of black workers and promote trade unionism'. However, the considerable limitations and oppressive effects of the notion of political blackness are, arguably, undeniable. As Black Studies scholar Kehinde Andrews (2016: 2060) outlines, 'Political blackness is based on an inaccurate understanding of the relationship between multiculturalism and anti-racism; a misreading of the complex and global nature of racism and a non-strategic essentialism'.

Further still, the notion of political blackness can involve false equivalences being made between the lives and experiences of people with distinctly different racial and ethnic backgrounds, and in ways that, contrary to what the term may suggest, *do not* account for the particularities of anti-Black racism directed at Black people of African descent. In the poignant words of Jameela (2021: 60):

> The room for difference in social justice movements across communities of colour speaks to an evolving version of identity and race formation and central to this is activism that occurs without being beholden to or enamoured with whiteness. Political Blackness is a term which categorizes all people of colour as 'Black' and is often used as a catch-all for anyone that isn't white. The centring of whiteness at the heart of the term, whilst a draw among communities looking to understand and process race formation, is a centring which is, at best, a shaky foundation for anti-racist work.

Evans (1995) has convincingly argued that Black people have intentionally been made invisible in Scotland for centuries, 'to be taken note of as and when it is convenient to do so'. It is therefore pertinent to understand why the use of political blackness in Scotland can sometimes perform and reinforce anti-Blackness within organizing spaces. As Evans (1997: 117) describes in their foundational research:

> So pervasive was the invisibility of the African/Caribbean presence among service providers that African/Caribbeans were ignored even when they were part of community groups or committees. This omission was particularly evident when the proceedings was chaired by an African/Caribbean, whose presence in Scotland was totally ignored with members just pursuing matters concerning the 'majority' minorities. Avenues to Equality in the Arts (1989) a conference organised by the Scottish Arts Council and the Scottish Council for Racial Equality is one such example. Most speakers dealt solely with the 'majority' minority at the exclusion of both the Chinese and the African/Caribbean communities. Even the guest speaker from Strathclyde Regional Council Education Committee spoke only about the 'majority' minority until the marginalisation of the Chinese community was pointed out by a Chinese

participant. An African/Caribbean participant was not allowed a say on the exclusion of the African/Caribbean community as this session was quickly brought to a end because of the obvious dissatisfaction among delegates at the blatant omissions.

Thus, in *Black Oot Here: Black Lives in Scotland*, although we include recognition of the role of political blackness in past activism and some present-day organizing , we predominantly focus on examples of activist work led by Black people of African descent, and we address how political blackness can be very harmful to such people. An account of the evolution of Black activism in Scotland that evades acknowledgment of how political blackness has played a part in it would be an incomplete, if not downright inaccurate, account. However, reflecting on how political blackness has operated in Scotland should not be confused as either promoting its use or denying the importance of coalitional activist struggles. To date, various groups and third-sector organizations in Scotland continue to make use of political blackness, to varying degrees. What is of much more interest to us is examples of activism and organizing in Scotland that undoubtedly focus on the encounters of Black people of African descent.

Between us we have experience of being involved in several Black-led spaces and groups in Scotland over the last decade and have witnessed newfound interest in Black activism and collective organizing , including as expressed by organizations and corporations who try to rebrand themselves as 'allies' or 'anti-racist', despite sometimes having been part of the oppressive problems that Black organizers seek to address, or despite having consistently rejected funding applications by such organizers. Still, '[t]he neoliberal logics of diversity can consume the radical potential of collectives, who may become "flavour of the month" when funding opportunities arise and can quickly become caught up in the very "tick box" activity that they intended to dismantle in the first place' (hill and Sobande 2019: 113).

Nwonka (2020: 1) offers a conceptualization of 'the black neoliberal aesthetic' which 'describes the mediated outcomes of the commodification of black images and popular narratives for the purpose of both black social engagement and public voyeurism'. When considering how Black activism has developed in Scotland it is helpful to remain alert to the ways that neoliberal politics and the institutions that maintain such a position are implicated in some actions that may be framed as examples of Black activism. In other words, we are wary of moments when commercial and profit-making activities tethered to neoliberal market logics and forms of racial capitalism are presented as examples of radical Black activism. They are anything *but* that.

As we state throughout our book, the visibility of Black activism and collective organizing in Scotland has increased in recent years, partly aided by the rise of social media and online content-sharing platforms that enable some activists and organizers to reach many more people than they could in previous times (Jackson et al. 2020; Sobande 2020). Such visibility has not gone unnoticed by organizations in Scotland that are in constant search of new ways to improve their public image, including by performing their supposed interest in supporting Black people. When writing about 'the physiological work of black liberation', McKittrick (2021: 3) reflects on 'asking for a mode of recognition that does not itemize-commodify black liberation and black embodied knowledge'. While reading such words, we thought of the expanding ways that certain Scottish institutions have attempted to, arguably, itemize-commodify Black liberationist work as part of their public relations approaches which often involve a structurally white gaze that objectifies and dehumanizes Black people.

Responses to our 2020–2021 Black Lives in Scotland survey offer a range of explanations of perceptions of Black activism and organizing in Scotland, including the following comments:

I am aware of many [organisations or groups in Scotland that specifically focus on the lives of Black people there], in fact, I have contacted many of them

29 Peering through a publicly accessible telescope in Edinburgh, 2013. Photograph by Francesca Sobande

(regarding a project i am developing to benefit the community) to the point of giving up, because i noticed that they are not properly organised and run very badly. There is need of strong and informed leadership, organisations that are well structured and with a clear agenda, not populistic bandwagon-jumping individuals with lack of vision and direction. But this is a worldwide issue. . . .

10 December 2020 (26–35 years-old)

It was encouraging and inspiring to see young black and white people protesting in Glasgow during the BLM rally.

17 October 2020 (56–65 years-old)

I know that the BWC of the STUC wrote to First Minister and its concerns were being considered.

17 October 2020 (56–65 years-old)

There is definitely work to be done, in terms of documenting, archiving black history/presence of blackness within the Scottish fabric. We need space(s) to meet, create, share and celebrate Black Scottish identity.

14 October 2020 (46–55 years-old)

I will not raise my children here. Scotland lives in constant denial of its role in slavery and colonialism. A lot of white Scottish folks live in denial of their own alliance with white supremacy. They deny racism even when found to be perpetrators of violence. This extends to academic institutions, councils, workplaces. etc. In these spaces racism is accepted justified and protected. It's only now since the global impact of BLM that white young people are really working and redefining their behaviour and actions but truly will this change Scotland?.

11 October 2020 (26–35 years-old)

There are many still in shock and denial regarding BLM. There has been a lot of backlash towards Black Scots talking about their experiences. Nothing has changed just seems that we are being forced to accommodate denial. . . .

11 October 2020 (26–35 years-old)

There are a few [organisations or groups in Scotland that specifically focus on the lives of Black people there] but hardly receive funding or space. There are many active Black folks that have ideas and actions that are never really executed due to a lack of access to funding and space.

11 October 2020 (26–35 years-old)

The biggest change is currently happening, in the wake of George Floyd's murder. There seems to be a willingness, genuine or otherwise, to understand the perspectives of Black people.

9 October 2020 (26–35 years-old)

'We have attended numerous events where people have professed that Black communities in Scotland are "too difficult" to engage with' (hill and Sobande 2019: 118). BLM in some ways has accelerated a process which was subtly shaping the Black Scottish narrative within public spheres. Prior to BLM, these efforts and processes lacked substance and often evaded critique. These efforts now appear to be clumsy and reactionary. We have also watched as the same organizations who peddled this narrative post their carefully constructed statements in support of BLM in 2020, and beyond.

While we are heartened by the widening work to address antiblackness and racism in Scotland, including since the impact of BLM protests in 2020, we also hope that in engaging in such discussions and work, institutions will recognize the legacy and plurality of Black activism in Scotland which predates the twenty-first century. Further still, the huge amount of work and labour involved in Black activism can result in considerable strains on the health and wellbeing of organizers. As American activist and organizer Mariame Kaba (2021: 4) states

> Our imagination of what a different world can be is limited. We are deeply entangled in the very systems we are organizing to change. White supremacy, misogyny, ableism, classism, homophobia and transphobia exist everywhere. We have all so thoroughly internalized these logics of oppression that if oppression were to end tomorrow, we would be likely to reproduce previous structures ...

Organizing against oppressions and internalising these same oppressions daily, whilst attempting to offer and recreate alternative visions of how lives free of oppression could be, requires energy. Commitments to practices of care should be embedded into such organizing, not only to maintain wellbeing but build healthier structures to live by and within.

Those who responded to our survey include organizers who have been doing much work to tackle anti-Black racism and the issues that Black people in Scotland face:

> I have been organising with Black people who organised BLM protests in Scotland in June. We are working to create a cohesive Scottish BLM Group with unifying principles ... I was surprised to see how many people supported BLM in the summer, but I found it a bit exhausting (as an organiser) to be repeatedly asked the same (very basic) questions by white journalists.
>
> 13 January 2021 (26–35 years-old)

Some people who responded to our survey mentioned the backlash that has emerged in response to important BLM and decolonial work. In the words of one person, who also referred to the behaviour of transphobic self-proclaimed feminists who perpetuate harm but claim otherwise:

> It [Scotland] has changed since the 80s but seems to be returning to those bleaker times. Events like BLM and decolonisation of Scottish history seems to have unnerved numerous people. The most overt example being over Robert Burns and his links to the slave trade contradicting 'a man's a man or all that' etc. Also, like trans exclusionary feminists there seems to be a privileging of Scottish suffering in exclusion of other forms. Or, a kind of 'we can't be racist' lack of insight.
>
> 13 January 2021 (46–55 years-old)

Whilst recollecting Black organizing in Scotland and attempting to contextualize what and who drives it today, we should consider what has changed, what has been replaced and what is missing from our liberatory struggles. It is worth noting the words of writer and independent researcher, Annie Olaloku-Teriba (2018):

> The 1980s neoliberal backlash against the increasing political power of the Third World and its diasporas in the West has resulted in a chronically weak Left and a restructuring of the economic and social relations upon which communities were conceived. It is in this context that the #BlackLivesMatter movement and more academically-directed decolonisation movements such as Rhodes Must Fall have emerged and spread across the globe. Both movements, and their eponymous slogans, intervene in a historically unprecedented moment, where identity-based social justice politics have largely replaced class politics. While Union density in Europe and North America is waning and the language of class is increasingly scarce, a new brand of identity politics is on the ascendancy in many arenas, not least university campuses.

When asking Nikko Dingani who has been living in Scotland since 2007 to share his thoughts on Black activism and organizing in Scotland, he reflected:

> I don't know any Black groups to be honest. There are people fighting for refugees, but specific to Black people, I don't know any. If there was, I should be involved! I know some Black people in the Scottish Government, but I think they do it for their own business and it has nothing to do with us. You only hear about these 'Black groups' because elections are coming, then they start popping up and coming to the community saying they can do this for you. This is called self-serving, not groups. They do for themselves. The African and Caribbean Centre is an example, people use the words, 'African communities' for their own benefit. It's all about themselves and when it's done, its done. As Africans, as communities, we need to build our own strategy on how to get there – we need that.

How will Black and racial justice organizing in Scotland develop whilst facing some of the challenges that we have outlined? An anti-racist movement in Scotland that is not equally concerned with class struggles will likely be an anti-racist movement that simply serves a select few and fails to support the most marginalized, including Black working-class people. Therefore, we hope that the future of such organizing is one that takes seriously the interconnected nature of racism, classism, xenophobia, sexism, misogyny, homophobia, Islamaphobia, transphobia, and other interrelated forms of oppression.

Yin muckle fowk? The Scottish and British relationship

I don't like the idea.

19 April 2021 (36–45 years-old)

I think it has the potential to drive Scotland into far right or nationalism inspired extremism. However, I think it's important for Scotland to decide the future it wants for itself, and to be given the freedom to do this. Especially with England and issues like Brexit impacting Human Rights and equality.

17 March 2021 (26–35 years-old)

I'm for Scottish Independence, quite frankly, Westminster can get to fuck. Our country's votes mean very little and we have little say on what happens. Fuck the tories.

3 February 2021 (26–35 years-old)

An independent Scotland could change the experience of black people and POC here. It offers some opportunity to redefine what it means to be Scottish and to offer better systems than the racist systems and policies in place. but only if it is anti-racist independence, not just nationalist rhetoric for white people.

12 December 2020 (36–45 years-old)

Yes i am [aware of the movement for Scottish Independence], I think that every nation has the right to be free. Scotland has a strong unique identity and if the wish of the majority is to be independent, this should be respected.

10 December 2020 (26–35 years-old)

No [I don't think that an independent Scotland would change my experience as a Black person] in Scotland I think people would still hold the same views/ values. I think a racist will still be a racist.

8 December 2020 (26–35 years-old)

Yes. I am in favour of it. I think that Scotland should be in charge of their own policy decisions. Scotland could be a world leader in tackling issues such as racism ... Without policy changes that tackle racism or discrimination, such as the aforementioned ones, then there would be little change to my experience as a black person in Scotland.

6 December 2020 (46–55 years-old)

I am. I support it. Anything the English touch turns to ashes to be honest. Let the Scots be free of this tyranny ... I do. I experienced the hostility of the Home Office immigration first hand. I know Scots are still white, but from everything I've witnessed (anecdotal I know) I feel like their immigration policies would be humane in comparison.

25 November 2020 (36–45 years-old)

Brexit has been adopted against Scotland's will. Independence is the only solution.

11 October, 2020 (26–35 years-old)

The Scottish and British relationship is a thorny one which has been laid bare by campaigns and conversations concerning Scottish independence that have emerged since the '"devolutionary" period of time' (Jackson 2020: 4) in Scotland that has been identified as 'spanning the referendum of 1979 to the early years of the Scottish Parliament' (ibid.). Although the outcome of the Scottish Independence Referendum in 2014 suggests that, at that time, most people in Scotland did not want the nation to become independent, in the years since a majority (55%) voted to stay in the UK, a chorus of calls for independence have continued and new pro-independence political activity in Scotland includes the establishment of the Alba Party. In addition, parties and institutions who have previously been pro-union, or have not taken a position on the constitutional question, are now talking about not standing in the way of Scotland's 'right to self-determination'.

It is helpful to consider some of the reporting surrounding the last Scottish Census (2011) when dealing with the topic of Scottishness and the diverse ways that people define their national identity (if they identify with a sense of nationhood at all). The 2011 Scottish Census indicated that '62% of the total population stated their identity was "Scottish only". That proportion varied from 71% for 10 to 14-year-olds to 57% for 30 to 34 year-olds'. The 2011 Scottish Census reporting on national identity also suggested that: 'The second most common response was "Scottish and British identities only", at 18%. This was highest in the 65 to 74 age group, at 25%.'

Such reporting outlines that 'British identity only' was chosen by 8% of the population who responded to the census. The highest proportion stating this identity was the 50 to 64 age group (10%). Such Census information may represent strong generational differences in terms of how people define their national identity in Scotland. Also, it is useful to note that the 2011 Scottish Census reporting highlights that 34% of all minority ethnic groups felt they had some Scottish identity either on its own or in combination with another identity. The figure ranged from 60% for people from a mixed background and 50% for those from a Pakistani ethnic group, to 21% for those from an African ethnic group. This compared to 83% for all people in Scotland.

Moreover, in the words of Jackson (2020: 4), '[a]ny unitary narrative of "Britishness" cannot be politically anodyne in a historical period marked by ongoing constitutional challenges to the integrity, and even the continuity, of the Union'. The apolitical and non-partisan edited collection *Dearest Scotland: Letters Written to the Future of a Nation* features many people's words which 'provide a snapshot of the nation in the six-month period prior to and after the Independence Referendum' (Snook 2015). As is outlined on the book's back cover, '... the Dearest Scotland team travelled across the country asking what might Scottish educational facilities, high streets and landscapes look and feel like twenty, thirty or fifty years from 2014'. Among the many perspectives expressed in the book are those of people who hope that the future of Scotland will include its independence from the United Kingdom.

The same year as the Scottish Independence referendum, race, identity and citizenship scholar Nasar Meer (2015: 1480) suggested that 'it remains to be ascertained as to where ethnic and racial minorities, sometimes dubbed the "new Scots", might come to rest in debates about nationalist politics, identity and contemporary nationhood more broadly'. Since then, there has been much more public and political discussion of such matters, including as a result of some small yet gradual changes that have resulted in the increasing presence of Black, Asian, and racialized people in Scottish political parties. An example of this is Kaukab Stewart (Scottish National Party – SNP) representing Glasgow Kelvin becoming the first woman of colour to be elected as an MSP in the Scottish Parliament election in 2021. On the same day as the election results, the leader of the SNP and current First Minister of Scotland, Nicola Sturgeon, publicly spoke about the fact that 'for the first time foreign nationals and refugees could vote in the election' and referred to this as being 'a tangible symbol of the inclusive country that we are'.

As is indicated by the survey responses that feature at the start of this section of this chapter, the thoughts of Black people in, from, and connected to Scotland, on the topic of Scottish Independence, vary. For that reason, we avoid making strong claims about whether most Black people do or do not support efforts to pursue Scottish Independence. Instead, we reflect on responses to the following question that we asked in our survey: 'Are you aware of the movement for Scottish Independence and, if so, what are your thoughts on it?':

I am aware. I might be for it if it means going back into the EU.

4 May 2021 (36–45 years-old)

Yes, caution is counselled. Scoxiteers should avoid Brexiteers' traps by articulating reasoned post-Scoxit best and worst case scenarios and ways of leveraging/ mitigating each. Data and history, not emotion and hyperbole, should ultimately inform any decision to leave.

2 May 2021 (56–65 years old)

Yes. Scottish are more open and receptive to our experiences because they experienced the clearances – especially in the Highlands where people were stopped from speaking their own language.

19 March 2021 (56–65 years-old)

I support Scottish independence. I support re-application to EU.

12 March 2021 (aged 36–45 years-old)

negative the most vocal supporters think that this a green light to stop immigration or integration of people of colour.

17 February 2021 (aged 56–65 years-old)

yes, scotland will become more inward focused and not open to diversity.

17 February, 2021 (aged 56–65 years-old)

Pretty relaxed about it. I was born in England so I don't have the emotional attachment to Scottish independence, but neither do I to Britishness or Englishness I suppose. I think there should be a 2nd referendum because of the dramatic changes that have happened against Scotland's will since the last one, as well as the consistent polling in favour of Yes. But I don't know whether I would personally vote in that referendum.

5 February 2021 (aged 26–35 years-old)

yes yes yes … this nation is not very diverse and nationalism can sometimes exclude so voices from diaspora need to be louder in yes movement.

10 November 2020 (aged 26–35 years-old)

Also, when asked 'Do you think an independent Scotland would change your experience as a Black person in Scotland? Please explain', one person stated, 'I don't know about my personal experience, but I think the Scottish gov is much more open to discuss equality/diversity than the Conservatives'. As the words of people who completed the survey suggest, concepts, terms, and nationality categories such as 'Scottish', 'British', and 'English' are ones that some Black people may have a connection and emotional attachment to, while others do not. Some of the comments of people who responded to our survey included insightful reflections on related topics such as 'English accentness' in Scotland:

> When I first got here I barely saw black folx. I would get a lot more questions, comments and curiosity. Found it super difficult to access foods, hair stuff, make up, basically all the things a lot of my peers took for granted. Like, I had to save up and fork out to go down to London to get my hair done, etc. It was also really difficult to find community – many of the people I did meet were recent migrants from abroad but never really met black scots or folks who grew up here. I'd get comments, often masked as compliments, on my hair, skin, etc. And I was ALWAYS the only black person and black womxn in the room. It's changed a lot, perhaps because I've been here so long. I'm still the only black person in the room, often in professional settings but not in private or recreational. I also find folks less interested in why i'm here now, I get less questions though my English accent did also place me in a weird position because people constantly ask where my accent is from and it used to be hard to tell if people were asking me where I'm from based on my blackness or my English accentness. Probably both ... becomes clear when I say from here or from the UK and folks ask for more clarity.
>
> 20 November 2020 (26–35 years-old)

On the topic of the relationship between Scottishness and Britishness, when reflecting on Black writing in Scotland, Jackson (2020: 3) claims that 'blackness in Scottish writing is not simply a subset of blackness in British writing. Just as contemporary Scottish literature has never translated cleanly into a shared "British" literature, the late-twentieth-century prominence of "writing blackness" in a Scottish national frame troubles a unitary "black Britishness". Jackson (2020: 4) goes on to state:

> 'Black Britain' is an uneasy component of a state-nation still deeply inscribed with structural racism: racially discriminative public policies on immigration and policing, a national economy leveraging neo-colonial economic and cultural relationships, and a British national narrative still oscillating between postcolonial melancholy and periodic celebrations of the benevolence of Empire. The critical and interrogative national dimension of black Scotland, meanwhile, stands against any attempt to deploy a unitary and undifferentiated black Britain

in defence of the Union. Instead, literary attempts to imagine a black Scotland demand a reconceptualisation, or even the complete 'break-up', of black Britain.

Just as Jackson (2020) makes the case for not simplistically equating Black Scottish writing with Black British writing, in *Black Oot Here: Black Lives in Scotland* we argue for more specificity when referring to and seeking to archive the lives and experiences of Black people in Scotland. Put differently, we push against claims that to be a Black person in Scotland is to *always* also be Black British or is to always be Black Scottish for that matter.

We acknowledge our own personal position concerning matters to do with nationalism, the prospect of Scottish Independence, and being Black in Scotland (we want independence for Scotland but are not supporters of any political party, and, typically, we both identify as Scottish, among other things), while affirming critiques of nationalism and the relationship between nationalism and Scottish Independence efforts. In other words, while we both support the call for Scottish Independence, we remain critical of investments in nationalism and utopian claims about what an independent Scotland may be. Like Millar (2010: 133), we recognise, 'neoliberalism is alive and well in Scotland and has progressed via some of the same mechanisms as in England and indeed the world'. Furthermore, we often ponder the possibilities of Scottish Independence without party politics and an independent Scotland free of neoliberalism.

Jackson (2020: 5) argues that '[d]espite attempts by pro-Union commentators to cast the Scottish National Party as a collection of anti-English racists, nationalist party politics in Scotland remain mostly civic and civil'. However, Scottish party politics activities, including the actions of some who are aligned

30 An Indy Ref march, Calton Hill Edinburgh, September 2013. Photograph by Francesca Sobande

with the SNP, are far from being completely removed from racism and other forms of oppression, such as transphobia. We are acutely aware that Scotland's own racist and colonial legacy, which contrary to what some people may claim, would not miraculously disappear were the nation to become independent. Racism in Scotland cannot be dismissed as simply being a result of Scotland's inclusion in the United Kingdom. Also, in the words of three people who responded to our Black Lives in Scotland survey:

> I'm not sure independence would change things on its own.
>
> 4 May 2021 (36–45 years-old)

> Yes I am aware of the Scottish Independence, it could be a good option for Scotland but the last referendum amplified racism.
>
> 4 February 2021 (56–65 years-old)

> I support independence, but there is definitely racism within the movement. The SNP definitely has a misogyny and transphobia, and from things I've heard, I would say they are not doing enough to address racism within their party and the wider independence movement.
>
> 13 January 2021 (26–35 years-old)

Another perspective regarding the prospect of Independence is offered by John R who we interviewed:

> Personally, I don't think that we're going to get to independence. I think we will get to a referendum, and we have to get to a referendum, that is the manifestation, a culmination of a political dialogue that we thought had been settled with the last one. But for folks like [Boris] Johnson to say, 'it's a once in a generation' thing, like Brexit didn't happen, when more people voted to remain in the Union, obviously a 2:1 split in Scotland, but that was a larger margin to remain in the Union than the English got to take us out of the EU. It's just amazing that he would try and discount the relevance of the will of the Scottish people.

Any meaningful moves towards an independent Scotland must involve explicitly acknowledging and addressing the fact that structural racism, xenophobia and interconnected oppressions are part of the nation and are *not* an English import, despite what is sometimes suggested by individuals who assume that Scottish independence will automatically result in a more just society for *all*. In the words of Gary Younge who reflected on his time in Scotland in the late 1980s and early 1990s:

> There was a notion that if it [racism] came it was foreign and felt kind of uncomfortable. The presence of England and the manifestations of Englishness as being kind of imperial and colonial and all of that . . . gave an out for Scotland

quite often that they didn't deserve [laughs]. You know, Scotland was involved in all of that shit and you didn't have to be a bloody genius to work it out, and this continues even now ... there was a notion of 'we don't really have that problem and we don't really have those people' and so forth. Black people are the most visible invisible people you can find in Scotland ... because anti-Black racism in Scotland, while it was rife in the culture, not rampant but evident ... it didn't feel like it had a sufficient time to be codified within the institutions. There seemed to be space ... in a way that ... if you were in London or elsewhere in England, they [non-Black people] would think they knew ... 'oh, here's this Black guy. This is what I know about him ...'. Whereas in Scotland, I got a sense that they were kind of ... whatever they knew seemed very foreign, so while they may have been racist, they didn't know exactly what to do with it, so it seemed like there could be more space at times. I don't know whether or not that's true but that's what it felt like sometimes.

Black people living in Scotland, may have experience or knowledge of pro-independence and anti-colonial struggles gained from countries where they were born, or have an ancestral connection to. As Trinidadian-born, Charmaine Blaize shared in her interview, 'When the British left, they left. They left with our water systems – they even left with the plans. There were lots of gaps in knowledge'. This may influence how Black people view Scotland as both colonized and colonizer and indeed, calls for Scottish self-determination. Charmaine continues:

I remember for the Commonwealth Games, we went and made a Trinidad and Tobago presentation at my children's school – because Trinidad and Tobago is one of the Commonwealth countries. And I remember one of the boys asking, how did we get independence, if there was no war. And I found that interesting because there is always a fight, there is always a sacrifice to get what you want. So, for Scottish Independence, I think Scotland will be fine if we become independent. Of course, there will be a settling in phase, but I think we will be fine. Things like No Recourse to Public Funds, you know just some of the really hostile and racist immigration policies. I think that we have the opportunity to change that if we have independence. When the independence question came up and I read the manifesto and how it would work, I was like yeah, wow, I love this. But then right after that an incident happened and I changed my mind about it. My only concern is the nationalism. Nationalism can sometimes be extreme, and you know, Scotland for white Scottish people as opposed to Scotland for all of us. So, that's my concern with independence. If the ideology that is put forward for independence, if it's from the manifesto, if that's true and that's the political will and spirit of the people then yes, I support it. But we are living in a world which is quite extreme now.

Speaking at the second anniversary of the New Race Today in 1976, John La Rose, a West Indian publisher and political activist connects nationalist struggles in the Caribbean to those in Scotland:

> When Edward Short, the British Government Minister responsible for Devolution, made the announcement recently about the proposed constitutional changes for Scotland and Wales, it was like hearing and seeing a faded replay of a scene in the deadly, colonial, constitutional game. Political life in the Caribbean had become pretty familiar with scenes like these, for most of this century. What is happening in the last of England's remaining colonies – in Scotland, Ireland and Wales – will therefore not be new to the worker emigrants from the Caribbean and more so to those sections who were active in the anti-colonial and anti-imperialist, nationalist struggles in the 1940's and 1950's.

La Rose refers to Scotland as England's colony and for many years, Scotland as a colonized nation has been contested as much as Scotland has as a colonizer. As debates on Scotland's right to self-determination continue to be had, so do those in which Scotland needs to decolonize from English imperialism. In some of these debates, Scotland is positioned as an innocent *Gàidhlig* society, 'civilized' to become an unthreatening nation within the Union. We remain cautious of the use of decolonization language and reference to indigeneity in the foregrounding of these debates, which often erase the indigenous leadership and activism of decoloniality as it is defined and understood by those who have been undertaking this work in settler colonial nations. As discussed earlier in this chapter, white Scottish people have benefitted from their whiteness and continue to do so, particularly in settler colonial nations.

Scotland's quest for independence should recognize and learn from similar struggles for self-determination and indeed seek international support, which may well be found in the countries of origin of Black supporters of Scottish Independence. However, as sociologist Sivamohan Valluvan (2019: 59) writes, 'these twentieth-century decolonialization contexts boasted a much more fully formed radical political agenda in waging their respective national liberation campaigns'. Whilst Scotland is making attempts to reconcile with its colonial history, whilst simultaneously determining who exactly are today's 'New' and 'Old' Scots and continuing to erase the historic and present-day lives of Black people, we are wary of the ways in which Black people's knowledge and experiences – including those of anti-Black racism – could be framed in the ongoing campaign for Scottish Independence, or indeed in the event of independence having been achieved. As Valluvan (2019:60) further asserts:

To somehow suggest therefore that recent Scottish and other similar separatist nationalism from within Europe, of all places, would chart a different path seems to hinge on an act of faith that we ought to be cautious about. Important here is the observation that the emergent national spirits, upon having acquired a state and its own numerical majority, struggles to retain the former political centre as its primary negative object, that object being Westminister, Madrid, Moscow, and so forth. The newly minted nation-states can no longer orient their primary nationalist energies against the unit that was previously the potent foil against which the nation cause was asserted. Once this external unit is relinquished/vanquished, the political gaze, if it is to remain a politics of nation, must look elsewhere to locate its sources of negational definition, anxiety, threat and decay. The likely terrain that will prove conducive for any post-independence national project seems obvious.

Examples of such framings which could be used to increase support for Scottish Independence and a referendum can be seen in the weeks of, and which followed, the Scottish Parliament 2021 elections. Nicola Sturgeon branded a right-wing candidate, Jayda Fransen – the former deputy leader of the alt-right Britain First organization – a 'fascist and a racist', '. . . not welcome in Glasgow south side, or anywhere in Scotland' when confronted by her outside of a polling station on election day. Across social media and mainstream press, the First Minister's actions were congratulated and commended from supporters and non-supporters of the SNP and Scottish Independence alike:

> Nicola Sturgeon and I are on different sides in this seat, but we are all united when it comes to standing against intolerance, bigotry & hatred. I know the people of Southside will – once again – tell the far right where to go.
>
> @AnasSarwar. 7 May,2021

> Massive kudos to @NicolaSturgeon for facing down these far right thugs.
>
> @OwenJones84. 6 May 2021

Another example follows from protests which took place on Kenmure Street in Glasgow in May 2021, against an immigration law enforcement attempt by the Home Office to detain and deport two residents of the area, on the day Eid al-Fitr was being observed. As discussed earlier, immigration is not devolved to Scotland; policing, however *is*, and as the protest grew in size, so did the attendance of Police Scotland. Though the heavy policing of the non-violent protest was criticized by some individuals and groups on social media, such as:

> Huge police presence in Pollokshields supporting the work of Home Office as locals resist the eviction and detention of members of their community.
>
> @HumzaYousaf @NicolaSturgeon

What you doing about this? Why does Police Scotland support the forced detainment of our communities?

@NotOneRogueCop. 13 May 2021

Commentary by politicians from across political spectrums and what followed in mainstream press did not focus on the policing of the protest and instead, framed Glasgow and Scotland, it's political ideology and institutions and its people, as being fundamentally different to Britain and therefore England.

The front pages of newspapers the following day included headlines such as, 'Glasgow 1, Team UK 0. People Power stops detention as despicable Home Office is forced to backtrack' (The National 2021) and 'Welcome to Scotland. Think Again, Home Office. Glaswegians turn out in force to block raid and force UK Government into a humiliating climbdown as First Minister hits out at Tories' vile immigration policy' (Daily Record 2021). The Home Office's actions were positioned as English and British, rooted in imperialism and racism, whereas the people of Glasgow – with its long history of activism – and Scotland, were positioned as anti-racist and pro-immigration.

As Evans (1995: 216) writes, 'Scottish nationalism differs from English nationalism. Scottish nationalism is aimed at throwing off the yoke of the English oppressor. English nationalism, on the other hand, has a shortage of oppressors thus the conspicuous darkskinned members of society become targets unlike their counterparts in Scotland who are ignored'. Evans' (1995) writing supports Valluvan's (2019: 66) assertions of what a post-independence nation state is likely to become, 'any consolidation of contemporary populist canards, is likely to take shape within a nationalistic embrace – likely, in turn, to yield one prevailing political command: to make war on the negative object that is *a priori* the nation's definitional Others, these being the various constitutive Others already within the nation-state's confines or those from outside who threaten these 'Other' communities'.

Many of the protests, demonstrations and indeed, celebrations which have taken place in Scotland since 2020, have drawn large numbers of people, despite the threat of a virus. It is then worth considering, if the Kenmure Street protest would have taken place outside of the pandemic. With fewer people in work due to precarious work, increasing unemployment and the furlough scheme, as well as fewer workplaces able to become unionized, is class consciousness and struggle manifesting and masking itself through other lenses of oppression, such as race? As Isoke (2013: 114) puts it:

Activists and opinion leaders often make issues political by designating them to a particular level of scale (neighbourhood, local, urban, national, international, or global). In the twentieth century, key civil rights issues were made legible by framing these issues within national discourses. Women's rights, gay rights, and citizenship rights for African-Americans were made by making identity-based claims to the federal (national) government. As a result, our understanding of gender, race, and sexuality have often been understood as 'single issue' politics that are based upon groups that are often wrongly imagined as homogenous and mutually exclusive. Under neoliberalism of the twenty-fist century, struggles around identity and against marginality are also always contestations about scale.

To reiterate our previous question, is class consciousness and struggle manifesting and masking itself through other lenses of oppression, such as race? Or are the intersections between class and race finally being realized in ways which may well build 'new' collective movements in Scotland, which understand the connections between struggles, locally and internationally, and are genuinely united against all oppressions to both make and demand change? If, however, these collective actions and movements are only mobilized by (in)actions of the state, then they are at risk of only achieving reform, not abolition or at the very least, an imagining of life without state involvement. As justice and social inquiry scholar HLT Quan (2017: 178) asserts:

> Rather than imagining the future in terms of democratic living, sensibilities, and formations of justice, state addicts leave us dependent on the state for means of expressions and terms of engagements. Their imaginary domains are thus entirely dependent on the state's projections. The state's memory becomes our own memory.

Though we recognize the importance of political leaders publicly denouncing fascism and racism in all its forms, sincere efforts should be made to ensure the present-day and future Black population in Scotland become a part of the political fabric of society. This should include a radical rethinking of immigration systems – should Scotland become independent, or immigration becomes a devolved matter – and going beyond soundbites in order to mobilize Black people's vote, and the votes of those who believe only words (and demonstrations) are an adequate reflection of Scotland being a progressive and anti-racist nation.

At this point, it is worth again considering the words of Black people who when responding to our survey reflected on what life has been like for them in Scotland:

> It has generally been excellent. I see Scotland is much more diverse now than when I was younger in 80's/90's.

> 19 April 2021 (36–45 years-old)

When I moved to Scotland I was quite aware of racial issues and I have Jamaican heritage which I only found out a few years earlier was Scottish-influenced. I have experienced Scotland as incredibly white but have never had negative experiences based on my ethnicity. That said I live in a privileged, cosmopolitan area where most people are very open to 'exotic' diversity and I have the privilege of skills and experience that have been fairly easy to utilise in Scotland.

12 March 2021 (36–45 years-old)

Felt like a holiday at first as I came to study. Then decide stay on a Fresh talent visa. Life was good until I started looking for decent professional work to suit my skills and abilities and I found myself starting over in many ways. Today 14 years later I am professional one level above what I did back home. I have reconstructed my entire life physically, emotionally, psychologically through my myriad of experience both fantastic and abysmal. Scotland has definitely become more diverse I am seeing a mix of people in my town whereas 5 or 6 yrs ago it was predominantly white scottish. Due to the political environment Scotland has become more divisive however at a national level there is a political will to make things better and to have a freer fairer society.

10 February 2021 (aged 45–55 years-old)

When I arrived in Scotland in 2004 it was a complete different country to what it is now. The population of black Africans has increased significantly. What has not changed much during my time is the issue of racist incident.

7 February 2021 (aged 46 –55 years-old)

There have been many experiences of racism in Glasgow, which have not vastly differed from those I've experienced in the US and in Sweden. The impact on my life primarily includes caution in interacting with unfamiliar white and BME people of non-African descent in employment, civic involvement, and life, in general.

6 February 2021 (aged 77+ years-old)

I came into contact with few Black people during my early years in Glasgow. This changed significantly in the late '90s when many asylum-seeking families became resident in Glasgow. At present, the city's population is far more diverse with a greater international perspective.

6 February 2021 (aged 77+ years-old)

I think living in Scotland has made me think about what it means to be Black more so than ever before in my life. This is partly because my work forces me to study things related to my own identity. But also because you're made to feel Black in Scotland by the comparative lack of Black people here. I grew up in Manchester and was rooted in a Caribbean community, where you didn't have to think as much about your wider Blackness. Scotland doesn't seem to have that to the same extent, so it forces a kind of reckoning with yourself.

5 February 2021 (aged 26–35 years-old)

Many people who completed our survey wrote at length about their experiences of racism in Scotland:

> I never really labelled myself as 'Black' until I moved here. I knew that I was African and raised with a rich sense of culture/identity and knowledge of self. But 'black' in Scotland was different. Scotland is racist. The air and heinous nature of apartheid is quite prevalent. As Black people we are constantly held and seen as inferior. I have experienced heinous racial violence and emotional abuse in every city that I have lived in. In every educational institution, every work environment and in every social setting. This trauma is an open secret for many. To say I'm Black and Scottish is not something that is well received because Scotland's children have been raised and taught that Blacks [sic] are inferior and have never been native to Scotland despite significant records in history. It's an aging population that has never really advanced in recognizing it's faults.... It's acceptable to be Asian and Scottish but to be Black and Scottish is still a new concept despite significant evidence of Black people in Scotland 100+ years ago. Scotland has taught me that I will never belong. This hurts because it's my home. It's children will never want me. It's offensive to be Black and Scottish. Not to me, but to Scotland's people. This is the general consensus. Yes there are some people that are accepting and open etc. But the majority are not. Black Scots are foreigners in their own land.

11 October 2020 (26–35 years-old)

When writing *Black Oot Here: Black Lives in Scotland* we did so with an understanding of the different ways that the lives of some Black people in Scotland are shaped by feeling part of a Black African diasporic experience, or not feeling part of one at all. Anthropology scholar Jacqueline Nassy Brown's (2009: 201) insightful writing on 'Black Europe and the African Diaspora: A Discourse on Location' includes comments such as the following ones:

> The most abused term in the study of Black folks here and there is the very term that describes them: diaspora. The term's ostensible inclusiveness is the source of its potential to negate. The association of diaspora with worldwide black kinship, as it were, can actually render certain kinds of Black subjects, experiences, histories, and identities invisible.

Brown (2009: 201) goes on to state that:

> Rather than assuming that we know what the nature and basis of the connections and/or differences between Black Europe and the larger diasporic world are,

students of Black Europe might adopt a diasporic approach focused on the situated encounters in which people actually express some form of desire for connection. Presumably, desire for such would not exist were it not for the recognition of an operative and meaningful – even if perceived – difference.

When reading the work of Brown (2009) we were reminded of the need to be attuned to differences, as well as similarities between Black people in, from, and connected to Scotland. We were also reminded of the importance of not assuming that a sense of kinship underpins all interactions and relationships between such Black people. As the mechanics of Black capitalism and 'The colonial roots of class formation' (Brown 2009: 203) reveal, matters regarding class, commerce, and the potential to pursue socio-economic mobility can involve some Black people, namely, those who are middle–to upper-class, treating other Black people in oppressive and exploitative ways.

Here, it is beneficial to engage with the scholarship of S. Sayyid (2000: 41–42), whose words on diaspora and nationalism shed light on related issues:

> Earlier I made the point that diasporas are dependent upon the discourse of nationalism. Without a form of nationalism it would be difficult to construct a diaspora. The idea that diaspora is a nationalist phenomenon is, however, not the only way in which this phenomenon has been described. Diasporas have also been considered as *anti*-national phenomena. Unlike the nation with its homogeneity and boundedness, diaspora suggests heterogeneity and porousness. Nations define 'home', whereas diaspora is a condition of homelessness; in the nation the territory and people are fused, whereas in a diaspora the two are dis-articulated. The diaspora is not the other of the nation simply because it is constructed from the antithetical elements of a nation, it is, rather an anti-nation since it interrupts the closure of the nation, since a diaspora is by definition located within another nation.

Influenced by the work of Hesse (2000a, 2000b) and Black cultural studies, Black digital studies, and research on Black geographies, in parts of both Chapters 3 and 4 we spend some time critically considering the relationship between perceptions and experiences of Black Britishness and contemporary media and cultural production in Britain. In turn, we ponder over Jackson's (2020: 4) perspective that 'The ready-made concept "black British" has been co-opted into the larger cultural refurbishment of Britishness that has accompanied the constitutional and legislative reforms of devolution and political multiculturalism'.

We engage with Hesse's (2000b) account of 'Diasporicity: Black Britain's Post-Colonial Formations' and Brown's (2009) work on Black 'Europe and the African

Diaspora: A Discourse on Location' to consider how understandings and media and cultural representations of Black Britain have changed over the last two decades and in recent years. Since Hesse (2000b: 97) reflected on how 'Black Britishness is a discourse whose increasing currency has yet to be conceptualized seriously', studies and theorising regarding Black Britishness have considerably expanded. However, there is still a dearth of work that attends to the regional and local nature of Black experiences in Britain, particularly beyond England. Thus, in conversation with work such as Hesse's (2000a, 2000b) and Brown's (2009), in Chapters 3 and 4 we delve into some of the regional details of Black media and cultural production in Britain. As such, we continue to reflect on how differences between Britain's constitutive nations and the dynamic between them shape the lives and media and cultural representation of Black people (t)here, as well as the various words and terms that are used in reference to them.

31 'Vote Yes' Next Time or Leave our Land graffiti, Glasgow, July 2020. Photograph by layla-roxanne hill

Yin o' us?: Multiculturalism, 'New Scots', and Black women's lives

Despite the wide range of identities and experiences that are part of people's lives and who they are, societal conversations about race, racism, and Black people, often involve the use of binaries that obscure nuanced differences *and* similarities between such individuals. Here, we are grateful for the illuminating words of Azeezat Johnson (2019: 92) from the crucial article 'Throwing our bodies against the white background of academia':

> Although the Self/Other binary is useful in illustrating the distance that is assumed through our positioning as not (white, liberal, male), it also ends up homogenising several experiences of Othering into one category. This can risk re-centring normative whiteness instead of centring the voices and experiences of racialised persons ... I must therefore avoid falling into the trap of fixing processes of Othering onto the body: there has to be room to examine how our identity performances shift across different social situations and spaces, and how our beings are more than just oppositional to a white Self.

Johnson's (2019) poignant words encompass the importance of attempting to understand and articulate the fullness of Black people's experiences, rather than depending on oppositional binaries such as 'Self/Other' which are limited in their capacity to capture differences between people who are described using such terms. Shaped by the scholarship and change-making of Johnson, in this chapter we critically discuss different words and categories that have commonly been used as part of public and political conversations concerning Black people in Scotland.

In addressing this topic, we return to reflecting on terms such as 'women of colour' (WOC), 'people of colour' (POC), 'Black, indigenous, and people of colour' (BIPOC), 'Black, Asian, and minority ethnic' (BAME), 'mixed-race', and 'political blackness'. This chapter is not intended to be some sort of superficial glossary. Rather, our aim is to further contextualize and critically comment on the different ways that such terms have developed, while considering to what extent these terms and their use are helpful to efforts to address antiblackness and support Black people in Scotland.

As part of this discussion, we call for more connections to be made between analysis of matters regarding race and analysis of matters regarding class in Scotland. Influenced by Johnson's (2019) work, as well as the research and writing of others on Black geographies and locatedness (Brown 2009; Jones 2019), we consider how the contours of societal Othering are shaped by anti-blackness and the material conditions (class position) that different people deal with. Thus, we too try to 'avoid falling into the trap of fixing processes of Othering onto the body' (Johnson 2019: 92), including by thinking about the context-dependent nature of moments in time when people are Othered. For example, what does it mean when many public and political conversations concerning the Othered experiences of Black people in Scotland foreground the perspectives of Black middle-class people, who undoubtedly have access to resources and forms of power that Black working-class people do not? In what way does any concept of being Othered which fails to account for issues concerning race, class, *and* various intersecting oppressions quickly come undone?

In addition to critically thinking about how the term 'Othered' is used and who it is used by and in relation to, in this chapter we also spend time mulling over binary oppositions such as Margins/Centre, to unpack the tensions at play when Black people in public positions of power and authority may claim to speak from the margins, but without recognizing that, at times, they also operate from somewhat of an exclusionary and powerful centre.

Throughout this chapter and reflecting on the words of Otele (2020: 7) who writes about how '[q]uestions of inclusion and acceptance are also linked to issues of citizenship and integration models for minority groups in Europe', we analyse the different meanings that may be ascribed to the notion of 'New Scots' which has become embedded in current political discourse in Scotland. Such scrutiny of the term and strategy surrounding 'New Scots' is influenced by our understanding of how '[t]he multicultural is a signifier of the unsettled meanings of cultural differences in relation to multiculturalism as the signified of attempts to fix their meaning in national imaginaries' (Hesse 2000a: 2).

Put differently, we pay close attention to how the concept of 'New Scots' can be interpreted as being, at least partly, a by-product of the relationship between the management of multiculturalism and notions of national identity and communities. Drawing on other explanations offered by Hesse (2000a: 2), we account for how '*diaspora formations* which as transnational processes deeply unsettle the idea of self-contained, culturally inward-looking nationalist identities' relate to or differ from the 'New Scot' experiences that are referred to in *The New Scots Refugee Integration Strategy 2018–2022*. To be precise, we are interested in how Black diasporic experiences trouble some of the perspectives put forward as part of 'New Scots' discourse.

As we indicated earlier on in our book, it is now that we ponder over the question of who are 'Old Scots' in relation to those who are positioned as 'New', and what might such distinctions reveal about perceptions of Scotland, identity, belonging, and permanence? In this chapter, we think about what messages are mobilized to frame Scotland as 'a rich and diverse country which sees many different cultures from across the world living in harmony together' (Scotland is Now 2021). We also connect to the crucial work of Lewis (2019a, 2019b 2020) which provides a critical intervention into research related to mixedness. As Lewis (2019b) states in an E-International Relations interview:

> Much of the previous literature on mixedness has focused on (mixed) racialised identities and how race and race thinking has affected lived experiences. I'm attempting to move beyond conceptualising mixedness by attending to experiences of racialisation and racism in relation to place, space and family formations. This is a further contribution to the scholarship on mixedness that has sought to challenge frequently binarised portrayals of Black mixed-race families within public life. Through ethnographic observations and conversation between family members, I stress that the emphasis on place, space and the family unit help to confront the doxa around 'progressive' and 'problematic' representations of Black mixed-race populations.

Informed by such insights, this chapter includes discussion of some of the specifics of the experiences of Black mixed-race people in Scotland, and the importance of recognizing forms of oppression that some of such people do not encounter but which other Black people do face.

Wurds dae mean something: 'BAME', 'New Scots', and 'raceless multiculturalism'

Growing up in Aberdeen during the mid 90s/early 2000s, I didn't really know or see a lot of other Black people. My mum is white, and any other Black kids I knew tended to have two Black parents. I experienced some incidents of racism at school from a young age. This was usually in the form of name calling. Although this happened, I wouldn't say it was constant or marked a significant part of my school experience (though it was present from as young as 5). I feel like the level of everyday racism I experience hasn't really changed that much. I think that the level of micro aggressions has probably stayed around the same. I still hear people use the word coloured, people still touch my hair without consent, I'm still asked where I'm really from. It doesn't happen every day, and I would say that people's understanding of racism has increased, but people still don't get why certain things are upsetting.

13 January 2021 (26–35 years-old)

In the opening chapter of *Writing Black Scotland: Race, Nation, and the Devolution of Black Britain*, Jackson (2020: 1) poses the question 'What does it mean to speak of a "black Scotland"? One definition might draw on the significant presence of black people in Scottish history'. Building upon such a perspective, we emphasize the need to acknowledge the contemporary experiences of Black people in Scotland as part of efforts to articulate and understand what may be perceived of as a 'black Scotland' (Jackson 2020: 3) which 'encompasses the ongoing critical and representational practices that take as their object a national history of race, racism and racialised experience' (ibid.). While Jackson (2020: 1) understandably asserts that 'the notion of a black Scotland demands more than a record of individual black lives', we also stress the importance of not erasing the individual lives of Black people (particularly those not deemed 'exceptional') as part of work intended to shed light on what life has been like for Black people in Scotland.

There are lots of words that are used by non-Black individuals when referring to Black people in Scotland, and as is alluded to in the survey comment at the start of this section, some of which are very offensive. Moreover, much recent political and media discourse on race and racism in Britain has focused on terms that have been used to describe Black people. While we understand and unequivocally support efforts to challenge the use of racist words and reductive labels used in relation to Black people, we also take note of how some institutions eagerly attempt to frame their decision to stop using catch-all terms such as 'BAME' (Black, Asian, and minority ethnic) as a revolutionary act that can help to eradicate racism.

In late March 2021 there was a deluge of media coverage of the Commission on Race and Ethnic Disparities report on racial disparity which had suggested the term 'BAME' should be scrapped (White 2021). The swell of discussions surrounding this report recommendation included perspectives that praised the suggestion and called for more specificity regarding words used to describe Black people, including by moving away from referring to racialized people as 'minorities' as they actually are part of a 'global majority'. Contrasting viewpoints challenged the assumption that *all* Black people want to be visible to/recognized by the state, while articulating a concern regarding the potential for a focus on terminology to detract from substantially working towards tackling relentless anti-Black violence. In the words of Nadine White (2021), Race Correspondent for *The Independent*: 'News that the public sector may scrap the generalised label which refers to Black, Asian and minority ethnic (Bame) people has been widely welcomed, albeit with a dose of scepticism.'

Scrapping the use of the term 'BAME', which often functions in ways that dismiss significant differences between the identities and lives of the people who the term is used to describe will not bring about an end to racism, nor will it be what catalyses the dismantling of white supremacy. However, as has been expressed to us by several Black people in Scotland who choose to remain anonymous, a range of third-sector organizations that profess to offer funds in support of the work of Black people often do so in ways that require such individuals to identify as 'BAME' and actively avoid referring to 'Black' or 'anti-Black' anything. In other words, institutional gatekeeping behaviour that is part of some third-sector work in Scotland includes the way that organizations refuse to recognize the specific experiences and needs of Black people, and only tentatively express a willingness to support if the particularities of Black people's lives are disappeared by them being solely regarded as 'BAME'.

This presents a problem for Black people seeking funds in support of work (e.g. arts, creative, educational, community-orientated) to solely focus on Black people and/or to address anti-Black racism, as the funding application process and the cultural norms of the funding organization may be predicated on the notion that all Black, Asian, or 'minority ethnic' people are the same, or, at least, similar enough to not need to self-define or do work that attends to particular forms of racism and oppression such as antiblackness.

Some of the responses to our survey and interview questions may be interpreted as exemplifying why it is helpful to be specific when articulating the different racial and ethnic identities and experiences of people. For example, often, those who responded to our survey and were interviewed reflected on the presence or representation of other racialized people in Scotland in ways that elucidate different demographic changes over the decades. A case in point is the following comment made by Kubara Zamani:

> I was born in Edinburgh and went to school and college there. From around eight-years-old I became aware of racial discrimination and so became heavily interested in the cultures and countries of the world and the different ways that

people were treated. At school, which I attended with 3–4 sisters, I faced minor racism. I have been racially abused while walking around the city and have been chased by racists on a few occasions. We knew Afrikan families in various parts of the city but we were the only Afrikan family in my primary and in my secondary school there was only about 12 people of Afrikan descent, a few more Asians and a handful of people from Latin America.

Also, survey responses such as the following specifically distinguish between some of the experiences of, and societal ideas about, Black people and non-Black people:

> Trauma. Even talking about it with non-Black people is a crime because Scotland is comfortable with denial. There are many people who have witnessed the violence of racism but they remain silent. Their silence is complicit. Regardless of how hard you work and how much you do in your community in the name of humanity somehow being Black is a crime that you have to pay for on a daily basis. This has a significant impact on mental health. You try to speak up, seek therapy counselling etc. but in a space that is in constant denial of your experience then how can you fully heal?.
>
> 11 October 2020 (26–35 years-old)

Without terms such as 'BAME' being located within discussions that also include a good amount of attention to the detailed and different experiences of the many people that are referred to as such, use of the term can contribute to homogenizing claims and essentializing ideas about people from a wide range of different racial, ethnic, and class backgrounds.

In the words of Otele (2020: 3) whose research 'traces a long African European heritage through the lives of individuals both ordinary and extraordinary', 'naming played a crucial role in the process of erasure'. Indeed, contemporary conversations about the inadequacy of the term 'BAME' often involve claims about the potential for the term to erase the experiences of Black people, including by obfuscating the precise nature of antiblackness. We have made such similar claims, when contesting others' use of the term 'BAME'. Although we still support many of the arguments made in objection of the prevalent use of the term 'BAME' in Britain, our own understandings of oppression and the lives of Black people have evolved in ways that have led us to question the benefits of Black people's visibility and recognition in various contexts.

When and why is erasure, or to be exact, lack of visibility and an absence of acknowledgment by the state, perhaps desired and in the interest of Black people? What do Black people stand to gain, if anything at all, by being referred to in ways that differ to 'BAME'? How do the power dynamics and political underpinnings of institutional processes of naming impact Black people in harmful ways, regardless of what terms are being used to describe and discuss them as part of data collecting efforts? In what ways do Black people attempt to subvert the gaze of the state and state actors' strategies to socially discern, discipline, degrade, and discard Black people? You do not have to say the word 'BAME' many times before the silliness of it surfaces. Who the 'minority ethnic' part of the acronym refers to is often left a mystery and is moulded by predatory institutions that decide who is or is not a 'minority' by determining who they do or do not want to support at any given moment.

Relatedly, the notion of 'New Scots' must be understood as emerging within a particular politics and politicizing of multiculturalism influenced by 'the competing ways in which the legacy of Scotland's place in the British Empire is appropriated by actors of different political hues, and so assumes a multiform role' (Meer 2015: 1477). Here, it is imperative to explore the knowledge articulated and shared in *Un/settled Multiculturalisms: Diasporas, Transruptions* edited by Barnore Hesse (2000a), and which includes discussion of how national imagined communities contribute to how multiculturalism is understood. The collection of critical contributions to contemporary conceptualizations of multiculturalism deals with the ways 'that questions of inequality and power in Britain and beyond are constitutive of the western formations in which cultural differences, particularly structures around race, ethnicity and gender, are *recurrently politicized*' (Hesse 2000a: n.p.n.).

In examining associated topics and themes, the edited collection substantially engages with, and contributes to, Black British Cultural Studies (e.g. Hesse 2000b; Noble 2000). Although *Unsettled Multiculturalisms* does not focus on a Scottish context, much that is outlined in the critical collection sheds light on some of what has contributed to current conversations and constellations concerning multiculturalism, migration, and the perceived newness of racialized people in Scotland. After all, regardless of the extent to which Scotland differs to Britain's other constitutive nations, it remains a part of Britain, including its racist and colonial legacy.

The many insights in *Un/settled Multiculturalisms* include considerations of 'the difficulty of trying to settle the meaning of western multiculturalism within a national vortex of *unsettled* and *unsettling* diverse accounts of its implications, values and trajectories' (Hesse 2000a: ix). We view such an ongoing 'national vortex of *unsettled* and *unsettling* diverse accounts' (ibid.) as being fashioned by the myth of Scottish exceptionalism and the interconnected particularities of both Scotland's nation-brand and that of Britain. Put simply, both imagined and experienced multiculturalisms in Scotland are influenced by intra-national and regional relations in Britain, such as dynamics between Scottish political powers and those of Westminster in England.

The 'New Scots' narrative that is considered in our book may be regarded as both *unsettled* and *unsettling* in the sense that there is a lack of clarity in terms of exactly who 'New Scots' are and what labelling them as such does to/for them, and to/for Scottish multiculturalisms and political entities. Questions that remain include the following: When does a 'New Scot' become an 'Old Scot', how and why? What is the descriptor 'new' intended to suggest? What is the relationship between racial politics and perceptions of who 'New Scots' are? Partial answers to questions such as these may be pieced together by closely analysing the content of documents such as *The New Scots Refugee Integration Strategy 2018–2022* (Scottish Government 2018) which is the second of these strategies.

The New Scots Refugee Integration Strategy 2018–2022 (Scottish Government 2018: 4) opens with the words of Gonzalo Vargas Llosa, UNHCR Representative to the UK, which emphatically imply that Scots are welcoming people who 'have really opened their hearts to refugees' (Llosa 2018: 4). Interestingly, the opening words appear to be premised on the idea that Scots and refugees are two entirely separate groups of people which, arguably, contrasts with the concept of 'New Scots' which is intended to challenge the idea that experiences of being a Scot and a refugee are mutually exclusive. That said, the views of individuals we interviewed, such as John R, reflect that work in Scotland to support refugees extends far beyond the introduction of the term 'New Scots':

> Nicola [Sturgeon] has done a brilliant job and not just in, as we would say in the States, 'talking the talk' but 'walking the walk', of putting the Scottish Government squarely in the column of supporting refugees into Scotland, and understanding that it's not just a moral imperative but an existential imperative for Scotland . . .

The New Scots Refugee Integration Strategy 2018–2022 (Scottish Government 2018) document cover features silhouettes of people in different colours (e.g. purple, blue, green) which resemble various media and marketing messages that are part of depictions and discourses of multiculturalism that have been referred to as mosaic, prideful, and celebratory in nature. Typically, such depictions and discourses of multiculturalism hint at racial and cultural differences without explicitly articulating them or forms of racism and xenophobia. *The New Scots Refugee Integration Strategy 2018–2022* (Scottish Government 2018) document might be interpreted as reflecting a perspective that contrasts with what Hesse (2000a: 15) refers to as being 'the racially exclusive narcissism of the nation' when writing about Britain.

The New Scots Refugee Integration Strategy 2018–2022 can also be interpreted as evidence of what race, identity, and citizenship scholar Nasar Meer (2015: 1477) has described as being 'an aspirational pluralism, in so far as political elites are less inclined – in contrast to counterparts in some other minority nations – to place ethnically determined barriers on membership of Scottish nationhood'. More recently, Jackson (2020: 5) stated that '[p]owers over immigration and equal opportunities legislation are reserved to Westminster, but the Scottish Government retains devolved powers that make up a larger politics of race, such as education and policing, and conducts promotional campaigns such as the "One Scotland" initiative'.

As is indicated by the document's table of contents, *The New Scots Refugee Integration Strategy 2018–2022* (Scottish Government 2018), appears to focus more so on terms/ideals such as 'social connections', 'employability', and 'language' than referring to pervasive forms of racism and xenophobia that are part of the realities faced by many asylum seekers, racialized people, and refugees in Scotland. Furthermore, the document's inclusion of terms and statements such as 'strong, inclusive and resilient communities' (Scottish Government 2018: 8) may be perceived as muting calls for the dismantling of societal power regimes that harm the most marginalized people, by promoting the neoliberal notion that individuals and communities must merely develop 'resilience' in response to structural inequalities and oppression.

An uncritical and un-reflexive emphasis on a politics of 'integration' and 'inclusion' rather than anti-racism, racial justice, and sustained efforts to address xenophobia seems to be an inadequate response to the concerns and experiences of individuals such as the following person who responded to our Black Lives in Scotland survey question, 'Have there been any events which have happened in Scotland which have affected you as a Black person living in Scotland? Please describe/explain':

> Yes, the stabbing at a hotel, deportations by home office, women and children being removed from their accommodation in the heart of a pandemic, home office refusal to stay has kept some of us scared to our bones and makes life meaningless. Having fled your home for safety only to experience rejection. Sometimes I desire to just go to the forest and start a life of my own where I won't live in fear of political leaders or immigration process.
>
> 29 January 2021 (36–45 years old)

The same person who responded to our survey expanded on related issues when answering the question 'If you could implement a new policy in Scotland to address issues faced by Black people there, what would the policy be and why?':

> Acceptance and equal opportunities. Simplify the process of integration. Get them involved in decision making. Accept that Scotland is our new home and therefore we can be represented in Parliament to be part of the decisions that affect our people as well.

Another person who responded to the same survey question stated:

> I think we need something for black people by black people, who can address issues on a higher level. It feels like despite us making people aware of racist attacks and discrimination, the white majority don't care.
>
> 3 February 2021 (26–35 years-old)

The New Scots Refugee Integration Strategy 2018–2022 (Scottish Government 2018: 11) is intended 'to support refugees and asylum seekers in Scotland's communities. This includes people who have been granted refugee status or another form of humanitarian protection; people seeking asylum; and those refused, but who remain in Scotland'. What does *The New Scots Refugee Integration Strategy 2018–2022* (Scottish Government 2018) mean for Black people? When attempting to answer that question it is useful to reflect on the fact that the word 'Black' does not feature even once in the 81-page report, the word 'racism' only features four times, and the words 'xenophobia' and 'Africa' do not feature at all.

While it is understandable that *The New Scots Refugee Integration Strategy 2018–2022* (Scottish Government 2018) does not solely focus on the experiences of Black people, it is both bizarre and telling that the document scarcely names 'racism' and, in turn, at least to some extent, appears to decouple the experiences of racialized people from those of refugees and asylum seekers. If a Black person is no longer considered a refugee or asylum seeker, are they a 'New Scot', Black, or both?

It is important to consider the words of Nikko Dingani who details his experience of navigating the asylum system and becoming a 'New Black Scot':

> My problem with the Home Office started in 2010, so I was moved to detention. Then after that, without explanation, I was moved to Glasgow. That's where they put all asylum seekers and refugees. At that time, because I had already been in Glasgow, I didn't fear much. The only thing I was fearing was the Home Office itself, instead of the people. Glasgow has been nice to me, I think. I like it. If I go

to Edinburgh, everybody I knew in Edinburgh have all left. I've become a tourist, like I'm just coming to see the city. Glasgow, the main thing for me is the African communities. When people were helping me with asylum stuff, that was the focus, not being Black or African. When that help stopped, people didn't want to know about the racism, the things I was facing. So, I started to hold back actually talking about racism because I was thinking maybe things will change. But some things have happened to me, so many times and I start thinking this is no good. This is no good, we need to start talking about, or fighting it. I dunno. There is a difference being a victim and being a fearful person, like every time you look at your skin you start being scared. I don't want that. I want to look at my skin and be proud. And know that is the way it is. But we are put in this situation where, as Black people here and now, even if you look at yourself in the mirror, you think, no, I'm not going outside. I think the racism has grown up, since the pandemic it has been really … people are frustrated, I think. So many incidents.

Despite *The New Scots Refugee Integration Strategy 2018–2022* being an opportunity to outline the Scottish Government's efforts to address racism and xenophobia as part of their aim 'to support refugees and asylum seekers in Scotland's communities' (Scottish Government 2018: 11), the document instead seems to emphasize ambitions related to 'inclusion', 'cohesive' communities, and 'integration', which is captured in the aspirational statement 'Integration From Day one' (Scottish Government 2018: 11). Thus, the strategy may be viewed by some as an example of 'state-sponsored integrationism' (Hesse 2000a: 7) that has 'illiberally posited the "common sense" of the good (white) British society' (ibid.) as being superior to the 'cultural orientations and decisions' (ibid.) of those who are identified as 'New Scots'.

What mode of multiculturalism might *The New Scots Refugee Integration Strategy 2018–2022* (Scottish Government 2018) be understood as upholding or challenging, and why is it helpful to grasp this as part of efforts to support Black people in Scotland? In what way does the strategy relate to how multiculturalism has previously been interpreted as having 'become a contested frame of reference for thinking about the quotidian cohesion of western civil societies uncertain about their national and ethnic futures' (Hesse 2000a: n.p.n.)?

The New Scots Refugee Integration Strategy 2018–2022 appears to differ from assimilationist discourse and strategies that have 'utopianized the prospect of a British national identity preserved through the eventual cultural acceptance of the migrants into the putative British way of life, in exchange for generational dissipation of ethnically marked cultural differences' (Hesse 2000a: 6). However, despite this and a lack of explicit discussion of racism in some related documents, the strategy has the potential to be perceived as being part of a history of strategies and 'policy interventions designed to support and encourage the ideal of the "non-white immigrant" disappearing into the norms and habits of (white) British culture' (Hesse 2000a: 6), or to be specific, (white) Scottish politics.

Previously, Hesse (2000a: 8) wrote about changed perspectives regarding multiculturalism which involved moves away 'from routinely tolerating the temporary social persistence of minority ethnic cultural differences to actively valorizing their aesthetic permanence in the national way of life …'. When elaborating on this, Hesse (2000a: 8) outlined how this also meant that 'racism went unconceptualized and racial antagonisms were perceived as merely resulting from ignorance, personal prejudice or mutual difficulties of cultural adjustment between majority and minority cultures' (ibid). Some of the terms and statements at the core of *The New Scots Refugee Integration Strategy 2018–2022*, and the scarcity of others (e.g. racism, xenophobia), are potentially demonstrative of how racism is unconceptualized as part of such an integrationist orientated approach.

In the foreword for *Black Europe and the African Diaspora* edited by Darlene Clark Hine, Trica Danielle Keaton, and Stephen Small, scholar Philomena Essed (2009: n.p.n) writes about racism at that time:

> Over the past decades, there has been ample finger wagging among European Union members about the spread of racism in Europe. But when it comes to accountability, each and every member state looks the other way: racism might be out *there,* somewhere else, but never *here,* not in our own country.

Over a decade later, such sentiments still resonate. The 'out *there,* somewhere else, but never *here*' (Essed 2019: n.p.n) mentality regarding racism has permeated much political and public discourse in Scotland, particularly prior to the momentum of Black Lives Matter and liberationist organizing from 2020 onwards.

'The racialized reconstruction of Britain as an imagined community in the initial post-war period (1945–1962) is partly characterized by developments in public culture which attempt to turn the common sense of Britain away from an imperial cosmopolitanism towards a nationalist parochialism' (Hesse 2000a: 5). Although the Brexit referendum outcome means that Britain (including Scotland) is no longer part of the European Union (EU), such a departure does not amount to the nation's distance from the type of pervasive racism that Essed (2009) articulates. After all, 'Europe created "Other" in order to find a common identity' (Essed 2009: xii), and as Younge (2018) has asserted, '[f]or while the Brexit vote was certainly underpinned by a melancholic longing for a glorious past, the era it sought to relive was less the second world war than the longer, less distinguished or openly celebrated period of empire'.

The scholarship of Michaela Benson and Chantelle Lewis (2019: 2211), 'focusing on the testimonies of British People of Colour living in the EU-27 offers a unique lens into how Brexit is caught up in everyday racism, personal experiences of racialization and racial violence, and longer European histories of racialization and racism'. As Benson and Lewis (2019: 2211) highlight, '[i] importantly, these experiences precede and succeed Brexit, taking place in both Britain and other European Union countries'. Similarly, as Gary Younge (2018) states, 'Britain's imperial fantasies have given us Brexit'. Thus, while Britain's exit from the EU marks some very clear ends, and may contribute to the ongoing 'branding of British identity' (Hesse 2000a: 27), Brexit certainly does not mark any end to racism in Britain, and Britain's constitutive nations continue to be unmistakably shaped by 'European histories of racism and racialization and the routine racial exclusion at the core of collective imaginings of who is British and who is European' (Benson and Lewis 2019: 2211).

Jackson (2020: 5) asserts that 'the ethnic dimensions of Scotland came into sharper focus as a consequence of new conditions for a national politics and culture after the referendums in both 1979 and 1997, new conditions which found an acute registration in the literature of the period'. Now, we find it helpful to revisit the notion of 'New Scots' which seems to be premised on a binary of 'New' and 'Old' that is at risk of being framed in ahistorical and ethnonationalist terms that seek to deny the fact that people of many different racial, ethnic, and cultural identities have lived in Scotland for centuries.

While the notion of 'newness' that is alluded to via the term 'New Scots' may be one that is intended to acknowledge, and even welcome, the recent arrival of people, the pairing of this newness with a word undeniably tied to national identity seems especially jarring when accounting for the relentless ways that people who are not deemed to be Scottish are constantly reminded of this by others and institutions who treat them as anything but local, a neighbour, a Scot. A response to our survey reflects this:

> Immigration laws and visa fees have me in debt still. Prior to fulltime work I had
> to go to food banks and could barely pay my rent but nrpf near left me destitute.
> Thank God i am working fulltime and can see about myself and family now.
> 10 February 2021 (46–55 years-old)

As Meer (2015: 1482) has stated as part of work on multiculturalism and Scotland, '[w]e should be cautious, however, lest we assume that national identities in Scotland are able to be marshalled in a purely party political fashion'. Much like Britain's departure from the EU does not indicate its complete detachment from Europe and its racist and colonialist legacies, the symbolic work that the term 'New Scots' does is not enough to mask nor untether itself from the forms of xenophobia, racism, and interrelated oppressions that refugees may encounter when arriving and living in Scotland. We do not note this to disregard the importance of efforts to support such individuals. Rather, we state this to bring attention to the constrained potential of initiatives such as *The New Scots Refugee Integration Strategy* (2018–2022) which appears to place an emphasis on 'two-way integration processes', portraying Scotland as a welcoming place, but scarcely explicitly naming racism and xenophobia, or how they will be addressed in Scotland in the long-term.

There is a risk that the focus on a 'two-way process' (Scottish Government 2021) of integration absolves the Scottish government of its responsibility to do more to tackle the structural inequalities and abuse that 'New Scots' may face, by implying that such people, alone, have the agency and power to overcome them by 'integrating'. Individuals cannot 'integrate' themselves out of oppression, a point that seems to have been missed in some of the 'New Scots' literature that pushes for 'positive change in both individuals and host communities' (Scottish Government 2021).

The very use of the term 'host communities' also calls into question the extent to which those referred to as New Scots may be embraced as Scots as opposed to treated as temporary and transient additions to the nation. In our opinion, work such as *The New Scots Refugee Integration Strategy (2018–2022)* is another example of 'how elite political actors are positioning minorities within projects of nation-building' (Meer 2015: 1477) and are doing so in ways that neutralize, or at least diverge from, discussions of xenophobia and racism.

In 2014, Meer (2015: 1480) observed the following:

> At a time when all the political parties of Scotland are trying to establish a persuasive vision of the nation, inquiry into where ethnic and racial minorities fit into these debates provides one understudied means of bridging literatures on multinationalism and multiculturalism.

Although public and political conversations concerning race and ethnicity in Scotland have expanded in the years since Meer's (2015) publication on 'Looking up in Scotland? Multinationalism, multiculturalism and political elites', there persists much discourse on multiculturalism that does not even name, let alone deal with, racism.

When reflecting on the ways that reference to race and racism seldom substantially crops up in various discussions and publications regarding multiculturalism in Scotland, it seems fair to suggest that this signals the persistence of a seemingly 'raceless'/'post-racial' form of multiculturalism in Scotland. Jackson (2020: 5) suggests that '[a]ny vision of Scotland's "post-ethnic potential" must simultaneously guard against the depoliticising, celebratory multiculturalism often instrumentalized by the British state, and a complacent return to egalitarian exceptionalism'. Expanding on this, we seek to push against the pursuit of a 'post-ethnic' Scotland which would likely result in the same sort of denial of racism and xenophobia that is a key feature of post-racial and so-called 'colour-blind' perspectives.

Meer's (2015: 1477) work 'illustrates how elite political actors can play a vital role in ensuring that appeals to nationhood in Scotland can be meaningfully calibrated to include minorities too'. Drawing on such research is very helpful when attempting to make sense of the many meanings and messages that may be associated with the 'New Scots' work, and which is of course shaped by different vantage points. When ruminating on the issues and questions posed in Meer's (2015) writing, as well as those articulated in the 'New Scots' literature, we find ourselves scrutinizing what notion of minorities is alluded to in the Strategy, particularly due to its infrequent or absent engagement with words and terms such as racism, xenophobia, and white supremacy. The 'New Scots' integrationist approach may, to some, symbolize a disquieting emphasis on nationhood and integration at the core of many political efforts to support refugees in ways that veer into the type of paternalism and patriotism that are sometimes the bedrock of the structural inequalities that such people encounter.

The prior work of Meer (2015: 1480) 'elaborates on the ways in which ideas of a Scottish nationhood are being configured according to specific agendas of equality and non-discrimination, existing church settlements, prevailing notions of "civic" participation and inclusion, and implicit norms of "legitimate" and "illegitimate" minority claims-making, among other things'. Since then, and sparked particularly by the increased visibility of Black Lives Matter and Black liberationist organizing in Scotland since 2020, the terms 'anti-racist' and 'anti-racism' have inched closer to becoming part of mainstream political discourse in Scotland, but racism remains.

Part of the significant impact of racism on Black people in Scotland is perhaps encompassed by the words of someone who responded to our Black Lives in Scotland survey who described the impact of this on their life in the following way:

Feeling hurt and afraid. Feeling like an outsider. Feeling isolated – like my friends aren't really my friends. Feeling anger and rage. Often feel defeated, like what's the point in trying because white people just see me as lesser. Feel afraid for my children. Feel focussed [sic] and like there's work to be done.

> 24 January 2021 (36–45 years-old)

Groups, organizations, and events including, but not limited to, the African Women Group, the Muirhouse Anti-Racism Campaign, UncoverED, Project Myopia, and Resisting Whiteness have highlighted and addressed various issues regarding racism which relate to Scotland and elsewhere. Although discourse on anti-racism has expanded in Scotland, the words of Hesse (2000a: 9) from more than a decade ago still summarize some of what is occurring today: 'in the transition from the late 1980s to the early 1990s, from the Thatcher years of populism to the Major years of depression, public espousal of anti-racism was attacked across the political spectrum'. Hesse (2000a: 9) goes on to write:

Despite the best efforts of local community organizations in highlighting the rise in racist attacks, continuing deaths of Black people in police custody and punitively unjust asylum and refugee laws, racism had become a non-issue in the public sphere. It had been folded back into the unsayable, unplayable 'race card'.

When thinking about such a statement in connection to Scotland we find ourselves reflecting on which issues concerning racism and the lives of Black people are especially absent from certain political and public spheres.

Whaur is th' justice? Dispersing and policing (New) Black Scots

As outlined earlier, recent endeavours to acknowledge Scotland's role in the building of the British Empire and the transatlantic slave trade – though necessary – sometimes occur in ways that detract from the recent histories and present realities experienced by Black people in Scotland and elsewhere. If these narratives focus only on the story of African countries at the point of colonization with no reference to the often-communalistic societies of traditional African life – as told by the people who live(d) there – then this history becomes whitewashed. Scotland's need to preserve an image of progressiveness can be seen in the *Refugees are Welcome Here* and *New Scots* narratives.

This does little to speak to Scotland's *Contribution to International Development* (Scottish Government 2021), which includes 'work by Police Scotland on gender-based violence', allegedly 'improving child protection and supporting governance in Malawi and Zambia', nor the economic interest Scotland has in neo-colonial ventures which often create the conditions for (im)migration in the first place, and the vast profits which are made from those forced to seek refuge and asylum. Tony Blair's UK Labour Government combined liberal multi-culturalism, which, as Hall (2019: 96) puts it, sought to 'integrate the different cultural groups as fast as possible into the "mainstream"', whilst continuing to reinforce the harsh immigration policies of Thatcherism. The impact of such a time is still felt in present-day Scotland.

The 'No-choice' Refugee Dispersal System implemented in 2000, saw Glasgow City Council become the first Scottish authority to sign a contract (worth £101 million) with the National Asylum Support Service (NASS) to accommodate asylum seekers. The 'No-choice' dispersal policy had significant implications for people's subsequent experiences of destitution. For example, when compared with other cities within the UK, Glasgow had fewer existing Black communities in many of the areas where people were dispersed. This decreased the informal support networks available, including access to language and translation services and local knowledge they can provide ('What's going on?' 2005).

As of 2019, Glasgow remains Scotland's only dispersal area, described as 'proving to be one of the most dangerous areas for dispersed asylum seekers', with those dispersed often being placed in areas which have been decimated by the Thatcher government, such as Sighthill. As 'there was no development work prior to refugees being sent to Sighthill and the council did not use the financial support it received from NASS for the benefit of the whole community' (CARF 2001), racial tensions were perhaps inevitable.

Furthermore, many narratives concerning 'New Scots' and multiculturalism fail to acknowledge the ways that, depending on their use, labels such as refugee, (im) migrant, and asylum seeker, can serve to erase Black identity which, much like the 'No-choice' refugee dispersal system, alienates people from Black Scots and seeks to prevent claims to being Black and Scottish/Black in Scotland. Even when asylum is no longer being sought, leave to remain has been granted and naturalization as British citizenship has occurred – or, like the Windrush Generation, people *are* citizens – being Black and subject to antiblackness is a reality (Cowan 2021).

In addition, some discourse(s) in relation to recent Black Lives Matter organizing in Scotland can seem disconnected from xenophobia and struggles related to socio-economic status and migration, further alienating some Black people in Scotland. As Black feminist theorist, urban ethnographer, and political storyteller Zenzele Isoke (2013: 48) asserts in *Urban Black Women and the Politics of Resistance*, in reference to activism in the US:

> ...most of the organized opposition to unfair public policies was initiated by Newark's small, yet burgeoning black middle class. This resistance was fueled by complex motivations, including a desire for opportunities to enhance its own visibility, establish rapport with the larger white political community, and ensure a better quality of life for their offspring.

These motivations might explain why, Jessica McGraa, a Black woman who had moved to the UK from Nigeria and was killed whilst working as a sex worker in Aberdeen in 2017 (Miren 2017), receives little mention in relation to much Black and racial justice organizing in Scotland. Despite efforts by some politicians and activists to decriminalize sex work in Scotland, it remains a contentious aspect of the political community. As Juno Mac and Molly Smith (2018: 10) assert, 'attitudes towards prostitution have always been strongly tied to questions of race, borders, migration, and national identity in ways which are sometimes overt but often hidden. Sex work is the vault in which society stores some of its keenest fears and anxieties'.

Were Black feminist politics more prominent in Scotland, perhaps there would have been much more of an outcry about what happened to Jessica McGraa. As Isoke (2013: 118) has noted:

> despite the relevance of these early and sustained arguments about the importance of intersectional politics by black feminists, their insights have been evaded, ignored, misappropriated, and maligned in the black community, among white queer activists and social theorists, and even by 'progressive' observers of contemporary black politics. The refusal to see how class inequality, race, and sexuality are co-constitutive forces should also be viewed as a refusal to acknowledge and apply 40 years of social justice theorising produced by black women.

The death of Badreddin Abadlla Adam, an asylum-seeker from Sudan, shot dead by police in Glasgow (Scotland Against Criminalising Communities – SACC 2020), weeks after BLM protests – which had seen thousands of people in attendance in 2020 – is another death that is seldom acknowledged within BLM framings in media and public discourse in Scotland. Badreddin Abadlla Adam had seriously injured people who were staying alongside him at the Park Inn Hotel, having been forcibly transferred to stay there in March 2020, by Home Office contractor Mears, in response to the pandemic. Concerns surrounding poor conditions, loss of liberty, No Access to Public Recourse, and mental health issues had been raised by many of those who had been housed in hotels across the city (SACC 2020).

Sheku Bayoh's name is often, rightly, made visible in relation to BLM, and it could be argued that this is due to the circumstances and ongoing investigation into his death whilst in police custody, which directly connect to BLM demands against police brutality. Indeed, one of the purposes of the ongoing public inquiry is to establish whether race was a factor in Sheku Bayoh's death and the investigation which followed. However, Badreddin Abadlla Adam was, without any doubt, killed by Police Scotland yet his name is scarcely mentioned amid Black and racial justice discourse. All Black lives (and deaths) matter, as does any violence towards Black people, and those which have happened through or by the state must be challenged and should always be brought to light. Campaign group, Refugees for Justice (2021) have called for the incident to be fully and independently investigated and for the failures of the system to be exposed and justice done.

Recent data from the *Scottish Prison Population Statistics 2019–2020* (Scottish Government 2020c), report confirms, 'the absolute number of prisoners identifying as "Mixed or Multiple" or "Other ethnic group" have increased in the last 10 years'. Furthermore, in the periods 2011–2012 and 2019–2020, 'the incarceration rate for people who identify as African, Caribbean or Black, or from Other ethnic groups, remains significantly higher than for people who identify as White'. Then again, '[e]thnic groupings have been aggregated in this report, which is likely to mask variations within each group. Disaggregation of prisoner ethnicity data is currently being pursued for future analyses'. Despite the relatively small population of Black people, levels of incarceration – particularly within younger age groups – and detention under the mental health act, are disproportionate. Mimicking the disproportionate numbers of Black people within prisons in England and Wales where, by the end of June 2021, Black people made up 13% of the prison population, despite representing only 3% of the population as a whole (House of Commons Library 2021).

Also, in 2020, ten police officers lost their battle to prevent Police Scotland taking disciplinary action against them. The Police Scotland officers were accused of sharing via Whatsapp, messages which were, 'sexist and degrading, racist, anti-Semitic, homophobic, mocking of disability and included a flagrant disregard for police procedures by posting crime scene photos of current investigations' (Scottish Courts and Tribunals Service 2020). The messages were initially discovered after an investigation into another officer who was alleged to have committed a sexual offence.

Recently, the Independent Review of Complaints Handling, Investigations and Misconduct Issues in Relation to Policing (Scottish Government 2020) in Scotland, found that Black and ethnic minority officers regularly encountered racist attitudes while carrying out their duties. Some of those who contributed to the independent review said they thought racism was 'more prevalent within the service than within the community'. In addition to difficulties with retention – despite EDI-driven recruitment campaigns – there are no Black or ethnic minority people within the senior management structures of Police Scotland. It was also felt that when Black and minority ethnic employees complained of internal racism, the finding is always 'not found' and support from the Scottish Police Federation was not forthcoming.

We do not include aspects of this report to support or defend the harmful – and in some cases deadly – work of Police Scotland, nor to suggest an EDI approach could resolve these structural issues. Informed by abolitionist perspectives, the inclusion of our reflections on this report serves to highlight the existence of institutional racism within Police Scotland, and how policing and the way that Black people are policed, is inherently bound into the capitalist economic system which involves the structural oppression of Black people, irrespective of their 'inclusion' in structures.

Making sense o' 'mixedness': 'Mixed' Black people and notions of national identity

As was reflected in some survey responses, while mixed-race Black people in Scotland face anti-Black racism, and can be victims of police violence, the pervasiveness of colourism and white supremacy means that Black light-skinned mixed-race people whose embodied proximity to whiteness is visible do *not* deal with the same forms of oppression as all Black people, including the specific iterations of misogynoir directed at dark-skinned Black women and non-binary people. As one person who responded to our survey mentioned when writing about their thoughts on the media representation of Black people in Scotland, 'They usually use light-skinned black people'. The person who wrote this elaborated on their comment when stating: 'Companies think if they use black people in advertisements that they don't have to do anything else about racism. The media is extremely stigmatizing of black people.'

As we mentioned earlier, the work of Lewis (2019a, 2019b 2020) emphasizes the need for mixed-race people to be 'attentive to intersectional specificities' and 'entangled proximities to whiteness'. Some mixed-race Black people, particularly those who are light-skinned and benefit from their proximity to whiteness, can be complicit in structural antiblackness and efforts to deny the prevalence of white supremacy. Furthermore, the embodied racial identities of some, but not all, mixed-race Black people, may be perceived by others as ambiguous in ways that sometimes result in such individuals not being identified as mixed-race *or* Black. As one Black Muslim person of mixed heritage put it:

> ... because when I went to Central Asia, when I went to Kazakhstan, just because of frequency and who I'm hanging around with, they assumed that I was Arab. So, one of the things that got me thinking about Islam was that I was mistaken for an Arab and someone waved a pig's foot at me, and when I asked the translator what was going on she said, 'she's making fun of you, because she said that you're an Arab'. And I'd never been mistaken for an Arab before. So, part of that journey was to find out about more cultures and also just to explore identity/race/ ethnicity ...

As the above words allude to, the embodied identities of some mixed-race Black people are associated with racial ambiguity or a fluidity which results in them being perceived and identified in a range of ways that may be shaped by ideas/ assumptions about Blackness, as well as the racial histories and landscapes of the place(s) they are situated in and move through. Of course, such experiences starkly contrast with those of many Black people who have never, and *will never*, be racially identified as anything other than Black. When accounting for this and the pervasiveness of colourism which shapes many facets of Black people's lives, including the likelihood of dark-skinned Black men being criminalized and incarcerated (Foy, Ray and Hummel 2017; Monk 2015), it is clear that just as it is a mistake to perceive the experience of any one individual as representing the experiences of *all* Black people, the experiences of mixed-race Black individuals should not be regarded as being reflective of those of every Black person.

Future research related to the lives of Black mixed-race people in Scotland may benefit from examining the ways that such individuals are opportunistically framed as being evidence of the allegedly 'racially progressive' nature of places. It is worth noting though that while some Black mixed-race people have benefitted from their proximity, or perceived proximity, to whiteness, their own claims to Scottishness can sometimes still remain elusive. As Evans (1995: 130) asserts:

> Afro-Scots of mixed ancestry (white Scot/British and African origin or descent), even though born and bred in Scotland, are not perceived generally as Scottish. The 'mixed race' question in Britain, or more specifically in Scotland, is not unique and as recently as the mid 20th century such children in Britain have been overlooked in terms of Scottishness, Englishness or Welshness and the assumption made that all 'coloured' people are recent immigrants.

If Black (including Black mixed-race) people's 'Scottishness' is to be claimed, in order to promote 'diversity' and notions of 'New Scots', this should be interrogated alongside 'how present-day African & Caribbean celebrities in Britain such as Naomi Campbell, Bernie Grant, Moira Stuart and Trevor McDonald came by their distinctive Scottish surnames' (Evans 1995: 73). The historical practice of changing African people's names, acknowledges, including in violent ways, their connection to 'Scottishness', yet may render parts of their present lives and histories as invisible, as we have discovered in our research for this book. As Evans (1995: 73) notes, 'the effect of this name change is still being felt in contemporary Scotland where even though African/Caribbean people are physically visible their social presence is not'.

Further still, the 2011 Scottish Census reporting suggested that '34% of all minority ethnic groups felt they had some Scottish identity either on its own or in combination with another identity. The figure ranged from 60% for people from a mixed background and 50% for those from a Pakistani ethnic group, to 21% for those from an African ethnic group'. Thus, there is scope for more research related to the relationship between 'mixedness' and feeling a sense of Scottishness, as well as more work on how the perspectives of people from mixed backgrounds may be increasingly promoted by individuals and institutions that are keen to claim that 'minority ethnic' groups feel Scottish.

In keeping with our scrutiny of narratives and notions of Scottishness, as well as our concern with the interconnectedness of structural oppressions, we now turn our attention to the experiences of Black women in Scotland.

Yon Black lassies urnae fae aroon here: Black women in Scotland

For National Girlfriend Day 2016, the *Daily Record* ran '10 reasons why Scottish girlfriends are the best', (Glencorse 2016), which featured a list and images of famous Scottish women including, comedienne Elaine C. Smith and actresses Kelly Macdonald, Isla Fisher, and Rose Leslie. Amongst the reasons why Scottish girlfriends are the best were:

> Their accent will make your heart melt. Whether they're declaring their undying love for you or telling you to take the bins out, their voice will always sound like it's being accompanied by a heavenly choir.

Their flaming red hair is to die for. Despite what people say about gingers, there's nothing more mystifying than seeing those long, fiery locks blowing in the wind.

They have breathtaking natural beauty. No make-up and no filters needed. Scottish women have a fair, natural beauty from their striking eyes to their rosy cheeks.

Though this article can – and will – be read as light-hearted clickbait material, it is often these seemingly 'just a bit of fun' types of narratives, which help to reinforce and define who and what, is a 'Scottish woman'. Scotland and Scottishness is often coded as white, which means that ideas about Scottish women are also often read as such, actively making invisible those who do not fit into such codings.

Such definitions or stereotypes of Scottish women exclude Black women from being seen as Scottish. In addition, Black women must also navigate often inaccurate depictions and understandings of who is a Black woman. Factors such as age, accent, class, religion, skin colour, status as a Scottish or British national and expressions of gender and sexual identities, further define and deny who a Black woman is, and most importantly, *can be* in Scotland. As the writing, research and activism of Moya Bailey (2021: 18–19) highlights, including in *Misogynoir Transformed: Black Women's Digital Resistance*:

> The term 'Black women' is often assumed to mean straight and cis, with queer and trans Black women identified explicitly because of this normative assumption. Additionally, the term 'Black women' is not inclusive of nonbinary, agender, and gender-variant Black folks whose experiences of misogynoir are intimately connected with a misgendering of them. I struggled to reconcile my use of a term that is central to my definition of misogynoir yet excludes some of the people most invested in its transformation. For those of us on the margins of Black womanhood, 'woman' is not what we name ourselves even as misogynoir colors our experiences of the world'.

As we have shown throughout *Black Oot Here: Black Lives in Scotland*, despite attempts to obscure their multi-faceted lives, Black women *are here*. The lack of Black women in Scottish public life is painfully obvious in politics, mainstream media and the arts. Jackie Kay, who was Scotland's Makar from 2016–2021, was – and remains – Scotland's most prominent Black woman in public life. Kay, born to a Black Nigerian father and white Scottish mother, was raised by her white adoptive parents just outside of Glasgow. Upon Kay's appointment as Makar by the Scottish Government in 2016, First Minister Nicola Sturgeon (Office of the First Minister 2016) stated:

Jackie Kay's poems sometimes deal with challenging subjects, taken from her own life experiences, and she has a particular Scottish brand of gallus humour. She is hugely respected, is known for her poignant and honest words, and is a role model for many, and I am delighted to name her as the new National Poet for Scotland.

Though the words of Nicola Sturgeon speak to Kay's particular 'life experiences', it is Kay's Scottishness which is explicitly highlighted not her specifically being Black *and* Scottish. This is despite Kay often acknowledging the fact she is both Black and Scottish, which she has recognised Black feminist and writer Audre Lorde as having helped her to embrace (Spowart 2019).

As Black feminist author and cultural critic Michelle Wallace (2016: 214) asserts, 'Black women writers and critics are routinely kept from having an impact on how the fields of literature and literary criticism are defined and applied. Meanwhile, the highly visible success of a few black women writers serves to completely obscure the profound nature of the challenge black feminist creativity might pose to white cultural hegemony'. We are encouraged by the creative works of many, including Kokumo Rocks and Shola Von Reinhold, which subverts existing definitions of what it means to be a Scottish woman, who Black women are, and indeed, offer new understandings of what it is to be Black and Scottish, or a Black woman in Scotland.

Even within organizations whose purposes include representing all workers and promoting equality and social justice in Scotland, like the Scottish Trade Union Congress (STUC), Black women are seldom made visible. Despite the STUC representing 'over 300,000 trade union women' (2013: 65), in the STUC Women's Committee 2013 publication, *Inspiring Women*, references to Black and non-white women are made in an international context, where the Women's Committee and wider trade union movement support are in solidarity with such women, engaged in struggle across the world. Black women are seen as being elsewhere, and not here. As Arshad and McCrum (1989: 208–209) state:

> when we use the term 'Scottish', to whom are we referring – a white Scotland or multi-racial Scotland? It is a matter of the speaker's perception of what is the norm. Who do we therefore mean when we use the term 'woman'? Today, the political struggle for equality in Scotland has produced women's committees, women-only events, women officers within trade unions, women representatives on committees and so on, but how many of these represent the voices of black Scottish women?

The terms BAME, intersectionality and women of colour are often used interchangeably within public discourse in Scotland to claim representation and diversity, but this can allow for the continued erasure and invisibility of Black women to persist. Following the recent Scottish Parliament 2021 elections, many commentators rushed to praise the new-look Scottish Parliament, which saw an increase of representatives from minority ethnic backgrounds, including two 'women of colour'. Black people, however, remain notably absent.

Furthermore, calls to address 'pale, male and stale' organizational leadership and management, have often seen white women replacing white men in such positions, with claims of diversity and equality having been achieved. What often constitutes inclusion and representation, is limited when race and ethnicity is sidestepped by gender parity being framed as diversity. As Walcott (2019: 397) asserts in relation to North America:

> Logics of POC and diversity lack specificity and therefore can continue to do the work of whiteness. The invocation of diversity is meant to suggest that the work of 'race equity' is being done and that representation is being worked for, but such assumptions can obscure exactly who is being included and represented.

Such words, we argue, are highly applicable to the Scottish context as well, where expanding discussions of diversity and intersectionality should not be assumed to indicate substantial changes in terms of the societal treatment of Black women, many of whom are often absent from such discourse and excluded from the spaces that it circulates within. In addition to this, the writing of Lauren Michele Jackson (2021) on 'the illusions of corporate identity politics' is also relevant to activities and interactions in Scotland that symbolize the commercialization of rhetoric and representations associated with identity-based liberationist struggles.

Narratives espoused by non-governmental organizations (NGOs), third sector and other groups who are reliant on the Scottish government for the bulk of their income, or indeed journalists who are reliant on access to people involved with such organizations and politicians for comment or news stories, also make use of the language of EDI and appropriate terms such as women of colour, and intersectionality to project an illusion of equality and diversity. As intersectionality continues to be invoked as 'a corporate marketing strategy' (Rosa-Salas and Sobande 2022) in Western consumerist contexts, will we see more evidence of its capitalist capturing in Scotland?

The pervasive ways in which patriarchal and heteronormative structures shape our lives, can often mean the experiences and knowledge of Black straight, cis men (and occasionally) women are centred in public discourse, or Blackness is rendered as genderless. Black women and trans people as genderless beings in modern understandings of sex and gender, is rooted in the founding of American gynaecology, where enslaved Black people were used as a living laboratory for experimentation. As C. Riley Snorton (2017: 20) explains, 'captive and divided flesh functions as malleable matter for mediating and remaking sex and gender as matters of human categorization and personal definition'. Snorton (2017: 53) goes on, 'the existence (and persistence) of flesh gives rise to how sex and gender have been expressed and arranged according to the logics that sustained racial slavery' and where, 'captives were rendered as raw materials for the making of the field of "women's medicine", from which they were excluded as women according to the attenuating frame of plantation medicine's sexual economies'.

Due to intersecting oppressions, just *being* a Black woman, can place significant stress and strain on health, and challenging perceptions and the treatment(s) which arise from those misconceptions, can often have long-lasting detrimental effects. In 1985, Beverley Bryan, Stella Dadzie and Suzanne Scafe wrote of the dangers of the Mental Health Act in their book *The Heart of The Race: Black Women's Lives in Britain* (Bryan et al. 1985: 120):

> Section 136 of the Mental Health Act gives police and social workers all the authority they need to section us for disruptive or unsocial behaviour. Once in a place of safety – usually a police cell, in the first instance – we can be held without charge for up to forty-eight hours. Other sections of the act can then be used to detain us further, giving police doctors and psychiatrists total power to recommend drugs, electric shock treatment or solitary confinement, and to use any amount of 'reasonable' force which circumstances warrant. The majority of Black women who receive psychiatric treatment do so as a result of being sectioned under this act, often by people who have no expertise or training in the field of mental health.

For Black women living in Scotland today, this remains a cause of concern. As the recent *Racial Inequality and Mental Health in Scotland* (Mental Welfare Commission for Scotland, 2021) report highlights, there are differences in how the Mental Health Act is applied across communities in Scotland and who is determined to be more at risk to oneself and/or to others, and the criteria that must be met for authorizing involuntary treatment:

> … more people who were black or of mixed or multiple ethnicity were perceived as a greater risk to themselves and others, whereas all categories of white people were more often perceived as a risk to themselves. Gender exerts a role on risk perception. The greatest difference was between black women, 48.4% of whom were perceived as of risk to themselves and others, and white Scottish women, of whom 33.8% were considered to be both a risk to themselves and to others.

In addition to focusing on such report findings, we thought about the way in which the term Black woman is evaded, avoided, obscured, or appropriated within academia, policy, media and public life in Scotland. When thinking about this, we pondered if this had any influence on the reluctance of some Black women in Scotland to explicitly name themselves as Black feminists, even if they view themselves as such.

Writing in 2001, trade unionist, educator and activist Anita Shelton (2001: 47) describes Black feminism in Scotland:

> In discussions with black ethnic minority women in preparation for this chapter, the question of whether or not there is a black feminist movement in Scotland was answered with a decided 'no!' Population size and fragmentation, along with funding difficulties, were reason usually provided for this negative response. Other factors cited were opportunism among individual women and a generalised political apathy.

Even in today's Scottish organizing landscape, Black feminism is not explicitly mentioned/claimed by many groups. In her interview for *Black Oot Here: Black Lives in Scotland*, Charmaine Blaize discussed the naming of Women of Colour Scotland:

> We had to come up with a name or something to associate it with it and that's how we came up with Women of Colour Scotland. Because you have to name your clan, you have to name what you are about. We were reflecting with women of colour – we didn't want to say Black women, we didn't want to say African women and we didn't want to say Caribbean women. Sometimes the phrase Women of Colour is a very contested phrase within the UK and especially we realised it's a contested phrase for people who English is a second language. They think when you say women of colour you are saying coloured women and its two different things, two different viewpoints. We wanted it to be as inclusive as possible especially for people who come from mixed ethnicities because if for example you have a white Scottish mum and you identify that and you love your mum – that's part of you, that's in your blood, that's in your dna. Then you might have a west African or Caribbean parent of African heritage, of Asian heritage and you want to embrace that as well but there is no box you can tick to fit in there. Even though it is pre-dominantly African women and African Caribbean women, we wanted to have it like that, and its grown organically.

While listening to the reflective words of Charmaine we thought about contrasting times when Black women are active in their own silencing, including by thinking about Sylvia Wynter's (1990: 365) crucial words, 'What is the systemic function of her own silencing, both as women and, more totally, as "native" women? Of what mode of speech is that absence of speech both as women (masculinist discourse) and as "native" women (feminist discourse) as imperative function?'. Our inclusion of such a quote should not be mistaken for us inferring that Wynter's work advocates for Black feminism. Rather, we view the words of Wynter as emphasizing the many power dynamics that shape discourse, such as discourses of, and about, Black women, including simultaneous and conflicting societal expectations that Black women speak up and stay silent.

Our discussion of Black feminism and Black women's lives in Scotland undoubtedly draws on the work of Black women and feminists from elsewhere. Still, this should not be confused with us 'importing' an analytical lens that misunderstands the specifics of Scotland, which is a place with racial histories that are notably entangled with those of other countries. Throughout *Black Oot Here: Black Lives in Scotland*, we cite and think through the words of Black women and Black feminists connected to Scotland and international solidarities, who have been involved in Black feminist, and other activist work, for decades. The promotion of a purist perspective of what constitutes effective Black Scottish analytical frameworks can result in reinforcing ethnonationalist ideas and overlooking the multicultural nature of knowledge and experiences in Scotland and beyond, so, it is with an awareness of this that in *Black Oot Here* we embrace the knowledge of Black people across different parts of the world.

Put briefly, although mainstream media, public, and political discourse on Black feminism and the work of women of colour, remains more peripheral in nature than not, Black feminist and coalitional activist struggles in Scotland and further afield are far from being something entirely new. Hence, to refute the relevance of reflecting on Black feminism in Scotland is to misunderstand Scottish history, and, especially, Black Scottish history and women's history. For these reasons, we now spend more time considering various components of contemporary ideas about Black feminism, postfeminism, and their (dis) connections.

Mair than jist aboot yersel': Beyond Black (post)feminist possibilities

In the words of sociologist Ros Gill (2007: 147), '[t]he notion of postfeminism has become one of the most important and contested terms in the lexicon of feminist cultural analysis. In recent years, debates about everything from the history of exclusions of feminism to the gender consciousness (or otherwise) of young women and the ideological nature of contemporary media, have crystalized in disagreements about postfeminism'. It can be helpful to acknowledge that, at times, there may be some overlap or, at least, a relationship between strands of certain postfeminist and Black feminist perspectives. Still, such acknowledgment should *not* be confused for mistaking postfeminism with Black feminism, but such acknowledgement does open up questions about the possibilities and potential presence of a distinctly Black postfeminist position, including in Scotland.

'Although famous Black women such as Beyoncé have been at the root of conversations concerning neoliberalism, postfeminism and Black women, Black post-feminist visibilities amidst television remain comparatively under-explored' (Sobande 2019: 447). In the years since those words were written, the volume of work that seeks to examine and address dynamics between neoliberalism, postfeminism, media, aesthetics, and Black women has substantially expanded, and includes Simidele Dosekun's (2020) book, *Fashioning Postfeminism: Spectacular Femininity and Transnational Culture*. Therefore, in this section of Chapter 3 we think about matters concerning Black feminism, postfeminism and neoliberalism, in addition to connected issues pertaining to Black capitalism and individualistic self-empowerment that is (re)presented as being Black liberationism.

Uncertainty often accompanies definitions and explanations of what constitutes postfeminism; similarly, a degree of malleability frequently forms part of how Black feminism is understood and articulated. Put briefly, despite there being a wide range of definitions of both postfeminism and Black feminism, there is sometimes a lack of clarity concerning exactly what *is* and *is not* postfeminist and Black feminist, as well as who and what determines this. In our effort to observe some of the ways that a postfeminist position is sometimes perceived as a Black feminist one, we do not seek to present a purist perspective of Black feminism that denies the many different experiences and expressions of Black feminism that exist. Furthermore, as Lola Olufemi (2020: 1) states, '[f]eminist histories are unwieldy; they cannot and should not be neatly presented'.

We regard the parameters of different feminist positions as ever-changing, context dependent, continually contested and porous. That said, it is important to account for there being some relatively clear and core principles and values that bolster different feminist positions, as well as ideological approaches to life that are devoid of any feminist inclination. In other words, while we recognize the fluidity of interpretations and experiences of feminism(s), we also affirm the existence of longstanding social and political tenets that buttress postfeminism and Black feminism, including contemporary forms of such feminism(s).

Thus, in this section on Black (post)feminism and conflating individualistic 'self-empowerment' with Black liberationism, we consider the capacity for Black neoliberalism and Black capitalism in Scotland, and beyond, to be strategically reframed as radical and revolutionary in ways that reflect: (1) the commodification of Black activist ideas and images; (2) respectability politics; (3) the reductive idea that anything a Black person does for themselves and to pursue their personal desires is inherently Black liberationist in nature; and (4) individual and institutional impulses to (re)present the careers and consumer choices of specific Black individuals as indication of collective Black consciousness-raising and socio-economic advancement that benefits *all* Black people. Such writing of ours is shaped by the extensive work of Black feminist writer and organizer Lola Olufemi (2020: 3) who has written about 'a divide playing out in the mainstream. The emergence of neo-liberal feminism or "boss girl feminism", driving many contemporary discussions, clashes with a radical and critical vision of feminism'.

Through this section we seek to reflect on some of the differences between Black feminist radical self-care (which by nature, is connected to collective struggles) and contrasting forms of self-work and consumption-orientated choices that centre some Black women's wants and desires but lack a Black feminist foundation. Echoing the words of digital alchemist and scholar Moya Bailey (2021: 18), we contend that 'Black Women ≠ Black Feminists'. Not all Black women are Black feminists, but some Scottish institutions attempt to suggest otherwise, in their rush to be associated with Black feminism, intersectionality, and marketable notions of resistance and activism that can be alluded to via the tokenizing and instrumentalizing of individual Black women.

'Arguments about postfeminism are debates about nothing less than the transformations in feminisms and transformations in media culture – and their mutual relationship' (Gill 2007: 147). Aware of this, we argue that '[t]heorising post-feminism in this contemporary context necessitates discussion of post-feminism's (dis)connection to and from Black feminism and the politics of intersectionality' (Sobande 2019: 435). What we mean by this is that when writing and reflecting on postfeminism, particularly in relation to the experiences and perspectives of Black women, it is imperative to explore the extent to which postfeminism is in conversation, or at odds, with Black feminism. Can Black feminism ever be 'post-' in nature?

The term postfeminism is one that can conjure up many different ideas regarding feminism and, particularly, the lives of women. Arguably, 'postfeminism is commonly linked with the idea that women have achieved equality, which contrasts with Black feminism's emphasis on intersecting inequalities' (Sobande 2019: 436). Moreover, postfeminism is frequently associated with neoliberalism (Gill 2016; Hamad 2018; Tasker and Negra 2007) which includes 'individualistic notions of agency, choice and socio-economic self-empowerment, in contrast with Black feminist critiques of White supremacist capitalism, anti-Blackness and the pervasiveness of oppression' (Sobande 2019: 436). Although we do not define postfeminism and Black feminism as two halves of the one oppositional binary, we do assert that their distinct differences should not be overlooked and collapsed in the way that sometimes occurs when the individualistic, neoliberal, and capitalist-orientated actions of Black women are identified as being innately Black feminist.

We do not imply that any iota of self-interest expressed by a Black woman should be construed as the absence of a Black feminist point of view. Nor do we imply that any Black woman can simply choose to transcend capitalism. Rather, we seek to stay alert to when individualistic actions and choices, particularly those that uphold the oppression of other Black marginalized people, are (re)presented as being Black feminist for no reason other than such actions and choices benefit the one Black woman, or few Black women, making them. Indeed, the personal is political, but that does not mean that the personal (e.g. career goals and consumer purchases) is always radical and Black feminist. Such a point is particularly apparent when recognizing the pervasiveness of 'market logics propelled by gendered racial capitalism and the commercialization of identity' (Rosa-Salas and Sobande 2022).

Critiquing claims that uncritically equate all Black women's choices with expressions of Black feminism, or at the least, expressions of feminism, is not the same as being dismissive of the role of, and space for, Black women's autonomy, agency, desires, and self-care in Black feminism. In fact, our understanding of Black feminism is one that maintains the necessity and importance of radical forms of self-care and collective care which need not be mutually exclusive. However, the language and idea of self-care has become meaningless on many occasions in present-day society, including due to the term's embracement by and within consumer culture which seeks to sell people the pathway to their liberation (Barber 2021; Rosa-Salas and Sobande 2022) and (re)present brands as caring (Sobande 2022).

Also, there is no social movement or shared struggle without a strong sense of collectiveness. Collectiveness undoubtedly takes many different shapes and forms, but it is *never* just about the self-orientated actions of individuals. Ergo, the need to locate a link to a broader collectiveness and/or sense of shared community when attempting to ascribe Black feminist qualities to the self-work and individual choices and actions of any one Black woman. Here, we are not suggesting that Black women need or should sacrifice all their personal interests and desires to contribute to and support Black feminist collective struggles. Instead, we are highlighting the potentially problematic nature of assuming that a Black woman's interest and investment in themselves is a mark of their Black feminist tendencies. Making this point is prudent, especially when accounting for how brands can be quick to tap into discourses of 'Black joy' as part of their efforts to promote products, services, and structures that are part of the maintenance of the oppression of Black and other marginalized people.

'Black feminist aims, visions and methods are distinctly different to postfeminist perspectives; the latter of which often upholds individualistic notions of self-work and self-transformation in the pursuit of personal and professional desires' (Sobande 2019: 21). Of course, such work and pursuits can be a part of the lives of many people, not only postfeminists, and including Black feminists. Regardless, what is crucial to note here is that individualism and shallow neoliberal conceptualizations of 'self-transformation' are fundamentally in opposition to many Black feminist and wider Black liberationist approaches which emphasize the collective nature of struggles towards freedom, and the fact that Black women cannot 'self-actualize' and 'Black boss girl' themselves out of oppression.

A person's sense of self, self-interests, and aspirations need not be completely invisibilized or abandoned by embracing Black feminism. On the contrary, Black feminist thought and praxis can play a key part in meaningful and sustaining forms of self-work, *but* without any connection to collectively shared visions and community-orientated responses, the Black feminist credentials of Black women's 'individualistic notions of self-work and self-transformation in the pursuit of personal and professional desires' (Sobande 2019: 21) are undeniably opaque, if at all apparent.

In their impactful Black Feminist Statement, which indicates that '[a] combined antiracist and antisexist position drew us together initially, and as we developed politically we addressed ourselves to hetero-sexism too and economic oppression under capitalism', the Combahee River Collective (1978: 212) reflect on their being 'an undeniably personal genesis for Black feminism, that is, the political realization that comes from the seemingly personal experiences of individual Black women's lives' (1978: 211). Throughout the statement there is ample acknowledgement of how the personal experiences of individuals can connect to Black feminist politics, but the Combahee River Collective (1978: 211–212) also emphatically outline the collective nature of Black feminism:

> The fact that racial politics and indeed racism are pervasive factors in our lives did not allow us, and still does not allow most Black women, to look more into our own experiences and, from that sharing and growing consciousness, to build a politics that will change our lives and inevitably end our oppression.

Prior work has sought to analyse the ways that 'friction is involved in the coexistence of post-feminist and Black feminist sentiments in media and popular culture' (Sobande 2019: 436), including by exploring media depictions of 'millennial' Black women, and the different responses of Black women to them. Perhaps, 'as images of Black women increase in various media spheres, before claiming that such content conveys Black feminist sentiments, there is a need to account for the politics underpinning related cultural production processes, as well as the intentions of the creators of such media' (Sobande 2019: 446), and a host of different matters that may shape whether a media depiction is identified as being Black feminist, allegedly 'intersectional', or not.

As we observe the changes in the Scottish media landscape, we keep coming back to questions to do with this topic, including when trying to identify what meanings and messages institutions are attempting to construct and communicate in ways that are dependent on images of Black women and/or content created by them. Following on from the next and final section of this chapter, in Chapter 4 we continue our discussion on Black media, by highlighting more of the words of people who we interviewed and who responded to our survey.

Dinnae jist write it doon, ye hiv tae keep it nice: Black living archives

Portrayals of Black people's lives in Scotland are too often shaped by what has happened to us and not, what we have done, and this is reflected in what is archived. Furthermore, archives as they are presently, are often the product of the ideologies that make them. Work which challenges structures of oppression or offers an alternative vision, can often be appropriated, misconstrued, or made invisible.

When researching *Black Oot Here: Black Lives in Scotland*, many of the individuals, groups, and organizations who we discovered had contributed to Black Scottish history over the years could not be found easily, if at all. Even locating information on fairly recent activities such as those undertaken by, @

frican Media Group (African Media Group), founded in 2005 as a new pan-African organization, the African and Caribbean Network; a voluntary sector organization active in 2005 and which had 40 organizations affiliated to it in 2014 and ROSA!!, (Race on the Scottish Agenda), was difficult.

Though the pandemic limited our ability to visit libraries and archives as planned, this also highlighted the need for resources to be archived in ways which are widely available and easily accessible, including, but not limited to, online. For example, we were keen to access the Scottish Black Women's Issue of the Edinburgh Women's Liberation Newsletter, published in 1986, but, at that point in our project, we were unable to access the archive at the Glasgow Women's Library and the items were not digitized to access online.

Even with the increasing shift to digital, an online presence should not be indicative of all experiences of Black people in Scotland, particularly when what is online and indeed, *how* it is, can be subject to the demands of neoliberalism. As Nwonka (2020: 9) asserts, 'while amazingly integrated, black cultural value cannot be conceived as just an economic virtue for neoliberalism; it is also seen as a positive force both in its responsiveness to contemporary black moral crises and the visage of proactivity against the charge of under-representation'.

What contributions can be found are sometimes located within institutions, such as June Evans' PhD thesis, *African/Caribbeans in Scotland: A socio-geographical study*. Institutions which are obliged to keep our work, though who can also act as gatekeepers – ensuring the work cannot be accessed, or that Black Scottish narratives never surface, as brilliantly fictionalized in Black Scottish writer Shola Von Reinhold's novel, *Lote*. Indeed, the Glasgow Anti-Racist Alliance (GARA) which now operates as CRER – a Scottish strategic racial equality charity – produced and developed several items, including the Race and Regeneration Conference 2006 and a newsletter called Black Perspectives. However, currently, there is no reference or access to these materials on the CRER website.

We were able to find some of the work and experiences of people involved with the Lothian Black Forum and the Scottish Black Women's group in *Grit and Diamonds: Women in Scotland Making History: 1980–1990* and supplemented this knowledge through our discussions with Gary Younge. Many societies and cultures have relied on the telling of stories orally, and though there are critiques of the use of oral history, perhaps the rise in popularity of voice notes and podcasts has highlighted a desire to listen, and be heard, which could form 'new' archives. Furthermore, in the words of Kalinga (2021:10) on a decolonizing framework:

Decolonising is a framework contingent upon recognising knowledge productions within systems that often will never make their way into archival records. It centres the recognition and legitimization of the ways in which African people have collected and shared their histories. The knowledge we learn from these systems allows us to reckon with both the silence of archives and the fallacies of myth-making about African people.

When writing about 'Constituting an Archive', sociologist, cultural theorist, and political activist Stuart Hall (2001: 89) stated that '[n]o archive arises out of thin air. Each archive has a "pre-history", in the sense of prior conditions of existence'. Hall (2001) describes the significance of constituting an archive and refers to an archive as occurring 'at that moment when a relatively random collection of works, whose movement appears simply to be propelled from one creative production to the next, is at the point of becoming something more ordered and considered: an object of reflection and debate'.

Relatedly, in 2020 an enlivening Instagram Live conversation between Krys Osei (beauty geographer and scholar in Transatlantic Ghanaian aesthetics, cultural studies, and fashion media production) and Tosin Adeosun (curator, researcher, and founder of African Style Archive) highlighted the 'everydayness' of archives and the crucial role of oral histories and personal albums and ephemera in the formation of African diasporic archives. Inspired by such insights, this section of *Black Oot Here: Black Lives in Scotland* reflects on material accessed from archives, as well as the detailed personal reflections and ephemera that people kindly shared as part of research interviews that informed this book, and which we believe are examples of a 'living archive of the diaspora' (Hall 2000: 89). Even though we had not spoken to many such people prior to embarking on this project, there were clear moments of relatability when listening to them share their thoughts and experiences during their interviews, including the words of Kubara Zamani.

Kubara Zamani was born in Edinburgh in 1965 and lived there until 1988 with his parents (mum who was a nurse and dad who was an industrial welder), sisters, aunt, and gran. Kubara attended school and college there and from 1980 was involved in political actions for Edinburgh Youth CND, Anti-Apartheid, Edinburgh United Against Apartheid, anti-deportation campaigns and other solidarity groups. Kubara self-published one pamphlet of writings in 1983. Between 1985–1988 Kubara played in two reggae bands based in Edinburgh. The second of these, the Afrikan Ambassadors, was among the main unsigned bands in Scotland at the time.

Since 1981 Kubara has regularly attended the Edinburgh Festival for poets, theatre, musicians, comedy, books, and art exhibitions, and has previously attended the Africa in Motion film festival in Scotland. One of Kubara's sisters was Sandra George, a photo-journalist and community activist who worked in Wester Hailes and Craigmillar, in Edinburgh, and whose extensive work includes a photo archive of around 40,000 prints from the late 1970s–2013 which is now with Craigmillar. Kubara said:

> I would like to mention my sister Sandra George [who has passed away] she worked at Craigmillar and Wester Hailes. She was a photographer, community activist, she set up some Niddrie youth organisation ... there are two pieces of artwork of theirs ... one is in a place called the White House in Niddrie and that's like a painting, 3 by 2, the other one is a 10 foot 5 foot image of her made by bottle tops and it was on display in Craigmillar library ... she was one of the few Black photographers, Black artists around in Scotland at the time ... very influential among the people who met her ... I can't not mention her.

Another of Kubara's sisters has been an actress, singer and music teacher in the city since 1980, appearing in the Festival and on TV shows. Our interview with Kubara was a reminder of the importance of Black oral histories when archiving the experiences of Black people in Scotland. When first starting to reflect on life in Scotland, including, growing up in Southwest Edinburgh, Kubara said the following:

> ... We were the only Black family there. Other Black people around ... most of them around that time, my family knew, so there was one person who had come with the tree fellers in the second world war from Belize Honduras ... he was one of my dad's friends ... my mum knew other families who were involved in nursing, medicine, health ... for twenty years my mum was a hospital nurse and then for twenty years she was a district nurse operating so she travelled all around going to people's houses. I went to primary school with 3 or 4 of my sisters. Secondary school ... quite similar again. As far as my experiences ... most of the people around us when we were growing up were ok.
>
> We did have probably ... in the mid 70s ... a couple of times we had those deportation letters put through our letterbox ... the fake ones from the National Front, but there wasn't anything major ... most people knew our family and liked them. When I got to 15/16 [years-old] obviously ... well in fact younger, 12/13/14, I started kind of becoming aware of things for myself ... for me I was the only Black boy over that side of town and in my house as well ... so I started having to kind of be aware for myself of what was going on. I was very interested

anyway in different cultures and reading ... I was doing that from primary school age so it kind of made me aware of issues that were going on.

Kubara spoke at length about the significant and inspiring ways that his sister Sandra George influenced his life, including his political consciousness raising:

> She was 8 years older than me ... she was very influential on me and my political development because she was interested in Black issues. She was the first person I knew who had the Black book which was the book of all the photographs and that, and then, she went and did community work at Wester Hailes and Craigmillar ... I stayed with her when I was about 18 and there, I read a lot of Steve Biko books and things like that which was very important because I make a differentiation between what I was interested in before when I was about 15/16 and when I got interested in anti-nuclear issues, anti-apartheid issues ... anti-deportation issues ... I was very involved in those kind of campaigns but that was obviously ... being in Edinburgh ... white majority organising and I never really felt at ease ... even though from 17–18 I was always involved in doing newsletters for people making the leaflets going to the printers and the membership secretary so this was for CND (Campaign for Nuclear Disarmament) ... I did that and any local group I was in I was always involved in that side of things ... and so that got me to travel around Edinburgh a lot and meet different organisations ...

Kubara spoke about many different activist spaces and organizations that were around during the 1980s in Edinburgh and work by those involved in Teachers Against Racism at Drummond School there. As Kubara said, 'we also used to use the Workers Education Association'. When continuing to reflect on being involved in activism and organizing during the 1980s, Kubara remarked:

> I used to go round those different organisations as well quite often and so we're now in this ... I would say 1981/82/83 kind of period and for that first part I was actively involved in local politics, organising ... we would organise bus coaches to London for CND rallies ... we were all late teens ... early twenties so that was just us organising on our own ... and we'd also help do that for anti-deportations campaigns in 1985 cause we did the walk from Manchester to London the ... it was a big anti-deportation walk and we stopped off at all the towns going all the way down ... we got put up in mosques or youth clubs so we stopped in places like Leicester ... Rugby ... meeting lots of different people ... that would be in 1985 ... I was also involved in Fight Racism! Fight Imperialism! ... that was what they were called ... the Revolutionary Communist Group ... and they were involved in what was called the non-stop picket of the South African embassy in

87 and 88 so we would be up and down from Scotland going to there as well ...
but I fell out with them cause of in 1986 I said to them that Malcolm X was going
to be big ...

What Kubara said next encompasses some of the challenges that Black people
face when working with and/or within predominantly white organizing spaces
in Scotland and elsewhere:

> I remember this ... Cause they had this thing for ... they're white people ...
> Marxists ... so you have to learn your Marxist theory ... you have to do your
> Irish solidarity work ... which I'm all happy to do ... but whenever it was Black
> people it was 'oh Marcus Garvey ... he's a bourgeois Nationalist ...' Malcolm X
> was 'a religious something something' ... and I said to them in 1986 'Malcolm X
> is really big ... you need to have a better position on Malcolm X because the way
> that he's going to be so big ... your position of just dismissing the Black leaders
> as 'they're just this ...' and 'you need your white people at front' ... that's just not
> going to work!' So I left that organisation and then 5 years later Malcolm X was
> like the biggest thing in the whole world and for a lot of white organisations, they
> never really had a proper position on Malcolm X even at that time so things like
> that, I moved away from a lot of white led organisations and that was part of the
> reason why I left Edinburgh because at that time there wasn't that many Black
> people there ... I would say there was probably in the 80s ... maybe 500 ...
> maybe by the late 80s 1000 [Black people] and like you know, there wasn't one
> area that everybody lived or anything like that ... there was just people sprinkled
> around and for me I got fed up cause I was learning more and I was learning
> about African issues and sometimes I feel like sometimes you're talking to people
> and they've got their own conception of what they should or how they should
> talk about Black people and what they should say and how they should talk to
> me, and I wasn't very happy with the quality of some of the conversations that I
> was having ...

When speaking to Kubara, we reflected on the significance of Black people's self-
published work and personal and living archives. We affirm the words of Hall
(2000: 89) who stated that '"Living' means present, on-going, continuing, unfinished,
open-ended". Kubara generously shared a lot of knowledge and spoke in detail
about self-published work from the 1980s which we were excited to learn about:

> ... at the same time that I was doing political things I was doing my own writing
> and my own self-publishing ... so I first published one pamphlet called 'lost
> sense of balance! in 1983 that was just articles about what I thought, cause people
> said to me "you"re very quiet you don't say much' so I'm like ok ... and then
> someone said to me if people aren't interested in what you think then they're not

interested in you ... so I thought, you know what, I'm going to write this pamphlet over the summer of 83 ... and cause I already knew places to go get things printed and duplicated I just photocopied them ran them off and handed them out ... walk around and sell them for 10p ... if someone gives you 20p your lucky ... so I just went around ... then when people started reading this although these are people ... some knew me from school ... they were like 'oh we never knew you thought like that ...' 'I'm like how did you expect me to think as a Black man ... hearing everything that's going on in the world you know ...' I'm reasonably intelligent ... I was top in my primary school for English, maths, spelling and arithmetic ... I'm not a dunce ... what would you expect me to think looking at the world and the way it is ... and that kind of showed me that even though I was sitting in a room full of people ... the way that I was looking at the world ... they weren't there ... there weren't many people who I could communicate what I was thinking about Black politics, Black aesthetics, a Black history, everything like that ... then someone said to me you should do poetry, so I thought ok I'll do that ... so I started writing poetry ... I didn't publish the poetry until I moved to London, but I started writing.

Kubara, who moved to London in 1988, pursued journalism and self-published three further pamphlets of poetry, short stories, and arts reviews. In addition he was a presenter-producer on various radio stations between 1996–2010 and is currently putting videos of interviews with Afrikan political and cultural activists up on YouTube at Nubiart Archive.

Having listened back to all the in-depth interviews that have shaped our book, we spent time thinking about the different ways that notions and experiences of diaspora were discussed. Hall (2000: 90) articulates the complexity of diaspora when describing it in the following way:

> ... like so many similar terms, it is operating 'under erasure', it too cannot be deployed without a certain deconstructive operation being performed. Of course, 'diaspora' recognises the specific place and subject matter involved, but it must also acknowledge the peculiar status of an archive situated, as C L R James once put it, 'in but not of Europe': located in that disjunctive, unsettled space between metropolis and periphery, 'coloniser' and 'colonised'. The closed conception of diaspora rests on a binary conception of difference and identity. It stands in the relation of 'copy' to that 'original' culture from which it is endlessly doomed to be separated.

Our research interview with John R involved some detailed discussion that relates to the concept of 'diaspora', including Black diasporic experiences in Scotland:

32 'No Sympathy! Three Short Stories by Kubara Zamani'. (1996) Cover design by Motilewa / Kuba-Ra Graphics. Kubara '83 photograph by Lawrie Nowosad. Published by Afrikan Scientists of Truth (AST)

... I've come to Scotland, and actually, Scotland came to me first, rather circuitously. My mom was born not too far from where I sit in Lanark and met my dad during the war. He hailed from Jamaica and came to Britain to help make the world safe from the Nazis ... met my mom at the Airforce base down in the Midlands and offered her an opportunity to experience paradise ... not that he was a great salesperson but all you have to do is show a picture of Jamaica to a Scot, and so they came back to Jamaica and a brood of us grew up in Jamaica,

AFRIKAN SCIENCE
for the MASSIVE
MEDITATIONS ON THE THREE R'S - RACE, RELIGION & RELATIONSHIPS

Published by Afrikan Scientists of Truth (AST)   £3

33 'Afrikan Science for the Massive: Meditations on the Three R's – Race, Religion & Relationships'. (1995–1996) Cover design with Kwele mask by Kuba-Ra Graphics. Published by Afrikan Scientists of Truth (AST)

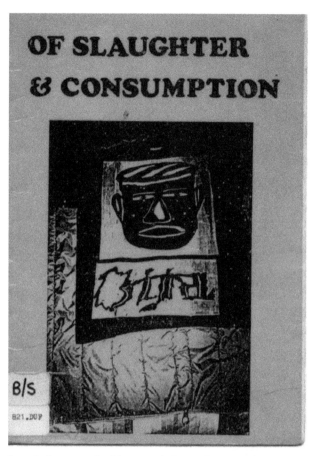

34 'Of Slaughter & Consumption'. (1991–92) Cover design and screenprinting by Kuba-Ra Graphics. Published by KARL / Leviticus 19 Productions

born in Kingston ... moved to the States and met my wife while there ... who also happens to have been born not too far from here in Scotland ... and started a family in the [US West Coast location] area ... but really have made Scotland my home for a variety of reasons ... first of all which happened to do with my mother-in-law not being very well ... so we decided to move the family over ... shortly after Trump's inauguration which was another reason. It also gave me an opportunity to requite, if you will, a yearning that I had long had to at least get in touch for a moment with the Scottish side of my existence. Growing up in Jamaica ... and I love Jamaica and I *am* Jamaican, and I will never be anything but *unapologetically* Jamaican to my core as my Kingstonian bredren would say, but Jamaica is ... like all societies that are very strongly majoritarian culture ... just gargantuan! So, I identified solely as Jamaican ... solely as African Jamaican

...and when I came to the States...when I moved to the States after high-school ...I had become more keenly than ever aware of race and the role of race in society...so we made the decision as a family to come back to [Scotland]...to come back to the question 'what it's like to be Black living in Scotland?'...I would say not that much different to my Black experience in the United States on one level, but I'm here in part because I believe in the *relative* progressivism of Scottish society...as my wife and I observe all the time...I feel a lot more comfortable, or a lot *less* uncomfortable, having him [son] walk the streets of Glasgow or Edinburgh with his buddies than I do having that happen on the streets of the United States, particularly given where we are now...so I have a bit of a different take on the question...it's what my experience is like relative to having lived in Jamaica and in the United States...a lot more comfortable thus far in our four years of having been here in Scotland, particularly from the perspective of a dad raising a teenage son of colour.

The same week that we interviewed John who spoke about 'the *relative* progressivism of Scottish society', which was also the week after the 2021 Scottish Parliament election, as we noted earlier, the world witnessed people take to the streets of Pollokshields in Glasgow to successfully resist an abhorrent immigration raid. Early on the morning of Thursday 13 May 2021, which was the same day that Eid al-Fitr was being observed and celebrated, a van with the Home Office insignia emblazoned on it appeared on Kenmure street in Pollokshields where there is a significant Muslim and migrant community, South Asian population, and presence of people of colour.

The raid involved two men from India forcibly being removed from their homes and made to enter the immigration van where they remained until their release was sparked by steadfast collective resistance embodied by neighbours and crowds of people who blocked the van from moving. Such effective, sustained, and organically community-coordinated action may be regarded as exemplifying 'the *relative* progressivism', or to be precise, relatively radical grassroots action, that is part of aspects of Scottish society. Furthermore, the swift and impactful reach of photos, videos, and updates that were posted on social media by all who were involved, perhaps, demonstrates how the rise of social media and its use by people in Scotland is shaping both national and global media coverage/framing of the nation and its socio-political sphere.

The significance of what happened on 13 May 2021 in Pollokshields in Glasgow should not be overlooked. Neither should the different and sometimes conflicting ways that such action has been interpreted and narrativized. To some, the eventual release of the two men who had been detained on 13 May 2021, and the collective action that catalysed it, indicates stark differences between the UK Government and the SNP's vision of a future independent Scotland. To others, what unfolded that day in Pollokshields specifically reflects Glasgow's rich history of anti-racist activism and working-class solidarity, rather than sentiments that are shared throughout the whole of Scotland. That said, similar action occurred in Edinburgh a year later (in May 2022) which signals that such activism, at least, spans more than one region of Scotland.

In response to what took place in May 2021, First Minister of Scotland Nicola Sturgeon posted on Twitter: '@ukhomeoffice action today is creating a dangerous and unacceptable situation in Pollokshields. As local MSP, I am also seeking urgent answers from them – they must resolve this situation ASAP'. The fact that the two men were released that day is, unfortunately, the exception, rather than the norm. Thus, their release, alone, should not be viewed as substantial evidence of Scotland being a welcoming place to all or a nation that is inherently unified in its aim to dismantle the Hostile Environment that the UK government has fostered, and which has been experienced by migrants, asylum-seekers, and refugees in Scotland, not just elsewhere in Britain. Nevertheless, while it is imperative to stay alert to how the events of 13 May 2021 have been framed in different ways that support a range of political perspectives, the momentous nature of the collective action that took place that day should not be denied.

Ongoing efforts to archive Scottish life, including Black history, will continue to be shaped by oral histories and interviews, such as those that are included in this book. Also, in recent decades archiving has increasingly involved digital efforts that entail care-full engagement with digital artifacts, social media activity, and information and content that is shared across a wide range of online platforms. We imagine that digital material and ephemeral engagement with the internet will continue to play a significant role in the future of archiving Black history in Scotland and the experiences of people of colour. This is especially apparent when reflecting on how social media use helped to facilitate Black Lives Matter action in Scotland in 2020 and resulted in global media coverage of what happened on 13 May 2021 in Pollokshields in Glasgow. In addition to social media impacting the future of archiving Black history in Scotland, Scottish media more generally may play a part in this too. Therefore, we now turn our attention to Black Scotland in the media and public life.

'No like us, a wee bit different, them pure exotic fowk': Black Scotland in the Media and Public Life

... I want to see Black Scottish people / Black people living in Scotland on TV and on Radio talking about things that aren't always about racism, or even race. While also beginning to analyse the complexity of structural racism and colonial legacies.

5 February 2021 (26–35 years-old)

We have both been personally and professionally interested in the media experiences and depictions of Black people in Scotland for a long time, and our first public discussion with each other was at an event on *Black Women and the Media*[1] which layla-roxanne organized with the National Union of Journalists (NUJ), and which took place in Glasgow on 6 October in 2016. In the days, weeks, months, and years that followed the event we found ourselves talking, laughing, commiserating, creating, researching, and writing together in ways that have culminated in our book *Black Oot Here: Black Lives in Scotland*.

We have both worked in a range of media, arts, and third and public sector settings that have undeniably influenced some of our thinking surrounding depictions and discussions of Black people in Scotland in the media and public life. Between us we have an infinite number of anecdotes about experiencing oppression in workplace environments and receiving responses that range from lukewarm to dismissive when challenging Scottish institutions that exclude and oppress Black people. We have also experienced high-profile Scottish media organizations asking to 'pick our brains' and seeking informal and unpaid consultation from us as part of their efforts to 'represent Black people', especially since 2017. However, this chapter is not based on our own encounters. Still, we acknowledge that many of the words and experiences of others who are quoted in the paragraphs that follow resonate with ours. Although this chapter focuses on Black people's experiences of and representation in media and public life in Scotland, we also reflect on connected commentaries concerning how public discourse on intersectionality in Scotland has developed.

On screens, stages, and side-lined: Black Scottishness, (re)presented

In the 2011 Census Black people made up approximately 1% of the total population of Scotland (Scotland's Census 2011) and approximately 21% of African census respondents 'felt they had some Scottish identity either on its own or in combination with another identity' (ibid). Relatedly, in recent years, a BBC (2019a, 2019b) documentary 'Black and Scottish' by Stewart Kyasimire focused on the experiences of 'prominent black Scots from three generations'. The documentary includes interviews with various people, such as Scotland's first Rasta councillor Graham Campbell (Scottish National Party – SNP), TV presenter Jean Johansson, and actor Ncuti Gatwa of the hit Netflix Series *Sex Education* (and soon, *Doctor Who*). The documentary was highlighted by someone who responded to our survey with words of praise about such media:

> I feel Stuart Kysamire did well with the Black and Scottish documentary, so far that's the only accurate representation of black Scots. The media industry seem to forget we exist, which has turned us into racial unicorns for Americans and mainland Europe.
>
> 3 February 2021 (26–35 years-old)

Other examples of twenty-first century media and creative and cultural productions about Black people in Scotland include '1745: An Untold Story of Slavery', written by and starring Morayo Akandé, and developed by and starring Moyo Akandé. Among recent creative work on Black lives in Scotland is also 'Scenes for Survival: Black Scots. An Extract from First Snow/*Première neige*' by Philippe Ducros, Linda McLean and Davey Anderson and directed by Niloo-Far Khan, with original composition by Patricia Panther. 'Scenes for Survival' was made available as a video on the National Theatre of Scotland's website on 14 July 2020. Starring Thierry Mabonga, the extract focuses on a young man recalling 'escaping the horrors of civil war in Congo as a child, to seek asylum in Glasgow with his mother. He finds surprising parallels between the barbarity and exploitation at the heart of that conflict and the shocking revelations of murder and profiteering painted away beneath the surface of his new homeland's history' (National Theatre of Scotland 2020).

Going further back, the BBC sitcom *Porridge* (1974–1977), set in the fictional HM Prison Slade, offered one of the earliest mainstream TV depictions of a mixed-race Scottish character of African descent. Portrayed by actor Tony Osoba, the character of Jim 'Jock' McLaren who is depicted as being an adoptee, faces racist abuse upon his arrival at Slade Prison. Although the sitcom was intended to be comedic in nature, some of what Jim 'Jock' McLaren deals with and depicts may also be seen as capturing institutionalized forms of hardship and harm that can face Black men from Scotland, including the prospect of criminalization and incarceration, and particular aspects of the experiences of mixed-race people who are often the most represented in Britain's 'care system'. Therefore, what the character of Jim 'Jock' McLaren symbolizes is much more than just a joke.

When considering and commenting on issues to do with the media and public life representation of Black people in Scotland we do so in a way that involves being mindful of distinct differences between the experiences of people in various regions of Scotland, and how being one of few Black people in parts of Scotland can sometimes result in experiences such as the following, which we previously referenced in Chapter 2, and was shared by Jonathan Wilson:

> So, Scotland was good to me, in that I think I became quite conscious of my black identity, being one of the only ... there were very few black kids in Dundee; you could count them on one hand. I ended up getting spotted at a gig and doing the voices and writing some rap songs for the Grand Theft Auto videogames, and so it worked out in my favour, being the only black rapper in Dundee, that they then thought, cool, we need him to be in our Grand Theft Auto videogame.

On the topic of different experiences of Black media and public life across various regions of Scotland, the following words of Gary Younge emphasize the importance of recognizing that Scotland consists of more than just the Central Belt:

> In the same way that when people talk about Britain, they are often talking about England ... quite often it has always felt that way to me when people are talking about Scotland. When *I'm* talking about Scotland, I mean Edinburgh and Glasgow *and* stuff in between ... Scotland would be a really weird idea if that [the Central Belt] was all it was.

We are cognizant of the fact that much mainstream media stemming from Scotland originates in large cities such as Glasgow and Edinburgh. Furthermore, perceived gains in terms of the representation of Black people in public life in one part of Scotland should not be assumed to indicate that such gains have occurred elsewhere in the nation.

35 Dundee in the distance, as it is approached by train on the bridge, 2018. Photograph by Francesca Sobande

36 BBC Scotland across the water in Glasgow, 2018. Photograph by Francesca Sobande

In the words of several individuals who responded to our survey and referred to the visibility of Black people amid media, politics, and public life in Scotland:

> . . . black people and by that I mean people of African and Caribbean backgrounds are barely represented if ever represented in Scottish Media. I work in and deal with the media and it's horrible. I always wonder what young black scots have in terms of role models or people that they can see themselves in. There's more south Asian representation but still even that is limited.
>
> 10 November 2020 (26–35 years-old)

> Black people are washed up over here. As we are considered the minority, the few black voices are either tokenised once a year during black history month or rarely celebrated at all. It almost feels like our experience does not matter as much and that we should just feel grateful.
>
> 27 October 2020 (26–25 years-old)

> This [representation of Black people in Scotland in the media] is limited. Particularly in terms of representing those born here. I especially think people outside of Scotland have no idea of the prevalence or experience of Black people in Scotland.
>
> 17 October 2020 (26–35 years-old)

The words of someone else who responded to our survey and who wrote about their experience in the Highlands is a reminder of the fact that discourse, collective action, and structural change concerning the lives of Black people in Scotland is moulded by the particularities of regional and rural contexts, as well as national and urban ones. When asked 'If you could implement a new policy in Scotland to address issues faced by Black people there, what would the policy be and why?' the person wrote the following regarding the need for Black people's experiences in public life to no longer be side-lined:

> To ensure councils such as Highland Council (HC) facility [sic] the formation of representative community groups to amplify local voices because according to HC in their 2017–2019 'Mainstream Equality and Equality outcomes Progress Report', 'there are no umbrella networks to provide a single representative voice for any of the individual equality strands. . . . (but) . . . there is continual engagement with the groups on the equality contacts database.' This means groups without the resources or know how are left out. This means that because there has not been any BAME group which they can consult, they are excluded from everything HC organises and communicates. Further alienating this community.
>
> 19 March 2021 (56–65 years-old)

Accounting for such comments and experiences, our discussion of representation in public life in Scotland focuses on political and public sector arenas, as well as marketplace contexts, alongside our analysis of media activity and issues. Our writing in this chapter is partly inspired by prior analysis of images of Black people in media and marketing in Britain in previous decades, such as the 'Black Markets: Images of Black people in Advertising & Packaging in Britain (1880–1990)' publication which accompanied the exhibition Black Markets which was showcased in Manchester in 1990, and in Wolverhampton, London, and Coventry in 1991.

The publication opens with the following words: 'Images of Black people have been employed by every type of advertiser to increase the appeal of their products. These advertisements directed primarily at the white consumer have been born out of a definite history of enslavement and colonisation' (1). The exhibition that the publication is based on is referred to as being 'an attempt to bring together both historical and contemporary advertisements in order to trace the roots of some of the images we see today. Developing at a time of massive industrialization, advertising became essential to shift the mass of goods produced by Britain's industry'.

In this chapter we continue to consider components of 'the complex interrelationship between marketing, commercial representation, and discourses of identity, inequality, and structural change' (Rosa-Salas and Sobande 2022). So, we think about how consumer culture and societal changes have resulted in more commercial organizations attempting to appeal to Black people in Britain and elsewhere, including in ways that are presented as 'empowering' and 'representing' Black people, but which ultimately serve profit-making brands who do not have Black people's interests at heart. In other words, we approach this topic with an awareness of 'how and why ideas regarding "intersectional" approaches to feminism and Black activism are drawn on in marketing content related to the concept of being "woke" (invested in addressing social injustices)' (Sobande 2020b: 2723).

Our words on such matters reflect our critical perspective concerning the rise of marketing and consumer culture studies that explicitly position brands as being activists. Such positioning even occurs within some recent literature which, on the surface, appears to be critical of brands co-opting activism, but which upholds the commerce-orientated belief that brands can be activists, and even offers ways for them to position themselves as such (Sobande 2021). Our discussion of related issues in this chapter also attends to how the decline of the more traditional 'one to many' (wan tae mony) media broadcast model and the rise of the 'many to many' (mony tae mony) dialogue that social media facilitates has contributed to contemporary media and digital discussions and depictions of the lives of Black people in Scotland.

Observing Scotland's media in the summer of 2020 and the months that followed, demonstrated a recognition that, Black people in Scotland do, in fact, exist. From the mainstream to independent media, public, private to voluntary and third-sector organizations, across print, television, radio, podcasts, blogs and social media, interest was shown in the lives of Black people in Scotland. Within the mainstream media, many of the stories and debates featured Black people, sought out by journalists to speak about racism and their experience of 'dealing with being different'. Many chose to address calls to acknowledge Scotland's 'dark and shameful past' – its role in the transatlantic slave trade and the wealth generated from it. Histories and lives which were of little societal significance previously, were now a source of 'new' news.

Indeed, some chose to focus on the backlash against the renaming of street names and removal of statues – which has been credited to Celtic Football Club fan group, the Green Brigade – as supporters of British unionism and loyalism in Scotland – often Glasgow-centric –aligning their beliefs towards the global far right (Leask 2020). Sectarianism was also, arguably, echoed in an article by one of Scotland's leading political journalists, in which he wrote that 'No society is free from racism but Scotland's record isn't bad' (Macwhirter 2020). The journalist attributed the small numbers of African-Caribbean people as the reason why there is no real racism in Scotland and suggested that the plight of working-class Scots – while equating the working-class with whiteness – is a matter which should be of greater concern to the Scottish government than their diversity and anti-racism agenda.

Shortly after that article, the National Defence League (NDL) called on followers to attend a rally in George Square in Glasgow, at the same time as a demonstration by campaign and activist group Glasgow No Evictions was being staged, to raise awareness of the treatment of asylum seekers sent to live in hotels during the pandemic. In response to the 'latest protests and disorder in George Square', the Scottish Police Federation (SPF), which represents 98% of all police officers in Scotland, put out a news release titled, 'Coronavirus – What Coronavirus?'. Despite the NDL's links to neo-Nazis and fascists, the SPF did not acknowledge the role of racism which directed many of these actions, merely reducing them to opposing factions and sectarianism. Reflecting on such matters is important when considering how Black people's lives are not only shaped by media coverage of their experiences and depictions of them, but are also impacted by broader media, public, and police discourse and (in)action concerning racism.

Although the perspectives of Black people in Scotland often continue to be side-lined in much of Scottish media and public life, it is crucial to note that Black-led media has a long history within the UK (Benjamin 1995), often highly political and international in its outlook, owing to their beginnings as an effective campaigning tool against racism and imperialism. Activist journalism has allowed a rapid transportation of ideas throughout Black communities in Britain and abroad (Boyce Davies 2008: 74). Publications such as the *West Indian Gazette* and the *Race Today* are examples of Black self-expression, radical Black journalism in the UK, and contribute to the rich Black radical tradition.

Trinidadian journalist and political activist Claudia Jones was 'central to the Caribbean diaspora community organizing abroad, the founder of the London Carnival and of one of the first black newspapers in London, the *West Indian Gazette and Afro-Asian-Caribbean News*' (Boyce Davies 2008: 1). Jones, who founded the *West Indian Gazette* in 1958, had been deported from the United States for being a communist and a Black woman and saw her '"activism through writing" as always linked to struggles for social change and for the creation of equitable societies' (Boyce Davies 2008: xiii). The *Race Today* journal, which operated from 1974–1988 and which 'placed race, sex and social class at the core of its analysis of events in Britain, and across the world' (Field et al. 2019: 1), had Jean Ambrose, Patricia Dick, and Leila Hassan as members of the *Race Today* Collective and featured contributions from C.L.R James and Darcus Howe, among many leading activists of the time.

Perhaps, with the perceivable rise in Black consciousness since the impact of BLM organizing in 2020, a radical Black media such as those developed by Claudia Jones and the *Race Today* Collective could begin to flourish in Scotland. This could do much for Black Scottish self-expression and enable various political ideas and theoretical positions to reach Black people and communities. Furthermore, analysis or opinion by a Black radical media on press releases by organizations such as the Scottish Police Federation – or indeed the many media releases and public statements made by government, organizations – could do much to hold such organizations to account and provide a more accurate reflection of Scotland.

We recognize that media organizations (and individuals) who draw attention to the failings of those in power, quickly become the focus of threats and intimidation, and historically this has been true of African and Black media and writers across the world up to the present day. As questions of economic and climate justice intersect with conflicts over national identity, race and class, the openings for new media narratives exist and perhaps pre-existing media channels – particularly those who claim to hold power to account – could work towards creating a reflective media which is collaborative and representative of our society, exchanging ideas and information in ways which are healing and helpful, instead of harmful. However, alongside changes to existing media spheres, attempts at a Black radical media, which exists outside of current institutions, could - and should – find a place within Scotland.

Wanting tae see yersel, that's aw':
Feeling seen and supported?

When asked about their 'thoughts on the media representation of Black people in Scotland and/or their experiences in the media industry', people who responded to our survey had many comments to share:

> I am not aware of much media representation in Scotland regarding black people or people of colour. The national media agenda of black representation is more evident. Perhaps that is due to the press that I read.
>
> 5 April 2021 (56–65 years-old)

> The representation is episodic rather than comprehensive or inclusive. To my knowledge, there are very few Black people working in Scotland's media sector.
>
> 6 February 2021 (77+ years-old)

> I think it's good considering the percentage of black people in the population. It's more than in Brazil where black people are 54% of the population. It was here that I saw for the first time a black woman in a car ad. My daughter used to watch 3 tv shows with black protagonists, something unthinkable in Brazil.
>
> 12 January 2021 (46–55 years-old)

> It's not great. Still stuck on, 'Is it racist to ask someone where they're from?' I think the 'awakening' (I hope) of 2020 has moved things on slightly. But I want to see Black Scottish people/Black people living in Scotland on TV and on Radio talking about things that aren't always about racism, or even race. While also beginning to analyse the complexity of structural racism and colonial legacies.
>
> 5 February 2021 (26–35 years-old)

> Poor, suffering and destitute. The world and Scotland has failed to see the good in black people. Everything good about us has been relegated to the background and most people have assumed the place assigned to them especially when they are not given the opportunity to express themselves.
>
> 29 January 2021 (36–45 years-old),

I feel that black people are missing from the cultural landscape of Scotland.

23 January 2021 (26–35 years-old)

Black Scottish lives are still largely invisible on screen. We're missing from popular narratives about Scottish identity. It's always jarring when shows like Still Game or Two Doors Down, seen to encapsulate so much of our culture, are ultimately presenting a vision of an imagined Glasgow where Black people don't exist.

13 January 2021 (26–35 years-old)

Another notably detailed survey comment that connects to the media depiction of Black people in Scotland is the following:

We were the only black family that I ever saw as a child. There were no Asians nearby either. We lived on the outskirts of the city. During holidays relatives used to come and stay and that was my only experience of being with a larger group of black people who were like my parents. My parents did not particularly discuss any racism that they experienced neither did we as children involve them in our daily experiences. We grew up in the 70's where British television ridiculed black people and that had a big impact on my confidence. We watched a lot of American cinema also and despite seeing plantations in film, I was traumatised by seeing the TV series 'Roots' when I was 12 years old. We watched as a family and strangely never talked about it afterwards. The annual arts festival was a real eye opener to various cultures and cultural backgrounds. With hindsight, I was really naive about other black experiences and when I moved into the city the urban experience was very different. Now there are many different races in Scotland, and shops selling foods from around the world. There are many more mixed race children too. There are still whole communities that do not have any black residents, mostly as one moves further from cities . . . I remember when I realised I was different. At primary school around the age of 7. I understood then that my colour would always be mentioned. I have experienced much racism by assumption. Eg people speaking about and to me as a stereotype. Believing everything they see or read in the media. If I fall out with someone or someone is unpleasant to me, I always consider that race may play a part in what has happened. I am less likely to discuss my feelings, my hair or hot topics, (eg Meghan Markle) as a black in a mainly white environment.

5 April (56–65 years-old)

Comments made during research interviews also emphasized the limited nature of the media representation of Black people in Scotland, as well as various experiences of being societally tokenized, exoticized, and hypersexualized that are part of some Black people's lives:

... to me there's nothing that really gets shared about being Black in Scotland, apart from the one character in *Porridge*... You don't see any discussion. I think one of the things that I hadn't fully taken into account, and I think some of that is because of my naivety and being young, is you kind of get used, and I would even say abused at times, that you are the token Black friend, or the token boyfriend, or something. This exotic peculiar creature. It sounds daft that I never thought about it. But I was acutely aware of my identity and I knew that peoples' heads would turn, I'm black, when I walk into a room, but it never dawned on me that once people knew me, listened to what I had to say and got to know me, that those stereotypes would be maintained and remain ...

The notion of 'predatory inclusion' (McMillan Cottom 2020: 443) is highly relevant to such matters and refers to 'the logic, organization, and technique of including marginalized consumer-citizens into ostensibly democratizing mobility schemes on extractive terms' (ibid.). When reflecting on survey responses such as the following, arguably, some Black people in, from, and connected to Scotland regard practices that may be referred to as forms of 'predatory inclusion' as being part of the media and creative and cultural industries. In the words of one person who responded to our survey:

Black people only appear/mentioned or even shown during Black history month and refugee week. Rarely on the 6pm news. We had a young weather girl that was never promoted any further by Scotland news agency/broadcasters. There is also a Black newsreader that appears on the 6am news but she is never really seen elsewhere. I don't think people really know that she's on the news. Singers, models and actors etc. are only seen/shown during moments of special inclusive programming that cover Black history or racial issues. Black media has no real open presence in Scotland.

11 October 2020 (26–35 years-old)

Nikko Dingani also shared his thoughts on media representations of Black people in Scotland:

The media is horrible. Every time something bad happens and it is not Black people, you just think thank god we survived. The media is terrible when it comes to Black people, it is horrible. How my country, for example is represented by the BBC. When there is something going on there, they will show the worst part. But there are good parts of the country and there are some beautiful things happening. But it will always be labelled as bad.

When it comes to Scotland for media, I always wanted opportunities in Scotland on the BBC, as an entertainer, to do some sketches but it's very very rare to see that given to Black people here. They will give you, BBC The Social, but it has no value. It's not going to take me anywhere.

There is a very small chance as a Black person to be on the media in the good terms. If I do something like crime, oh my God, I'll be famous tomorrow. The media is not doing well at all for Black people in Scotland. It's one of the most dangerous things dividing people in the world. I try to stay away from the media. The only way to give awareness of this is, if I got a question like this from the BBC, I'd be saying the same thing, but they would delete it. They would never put it out there because they know it's true.

The media is always twisting things. They are always going to make us fight. It's up to us as well, just to ignore those kind of things cause, otherwise it's just going to fill us with fear and negativity.

Evans' (1995) *African/Caribbeans in Scotland: A socio-geographical study* thesis includes a comprehensive analysis of the representation of Black people within Scottish media, including an examination of some Scottish newspapers such as *The Scotsman* and the *Glasgow Herald*. From this analysis, Evans (1995: 113, 115, 117) draws the following conclusions:

A scrutiny of The Scotsman and the Edinburgh Evening News a year before the murder of the African student Ahmed Shek [sic] in Edinburgh in January 1989 for reference to African/Caribbean people in Scotland indicated that although people of African origin or descent were written about, often accompanied by the inescapable large photographs which dominate the page on which they are on, most of those featured have no permanent residential connection with Scotland. There are photographs of musicians, singers, actors, actresses and sportsmen/women, but very few of them live in Scotland.

For the purpose of balance the Glasgow Herald was also examined for the month of January 1989 to see if the larger number of ethnic minorities living in Strathclyde might have some impact on what is reported on African/Caribbeans in Scotland. However, the same pattern of invisibility of the African/Caribbean presence in Scotland was observed. While it can be argued that people of African origin or descent are featured, of the six articles/ photographs, none was of African/Caribbeans in Scotland. The murder of the African man in Scotland seems not to have been featured in the Glasgow press.

Although people of African origin or descent are seen or read about in Scotland they are viewed through images which have no connection with Scotland. The invisibility of African/Caribbeans living in Scotland is enhanced by the visibility of those who do not. While people of African origin or descent from elsewhere are recognised and celebrated those in Scotland are marginalised with little or no notice taken of their presence.

...While it is pleasing to see Africans and diasporan Africans on television and to read about them in Scottish newspapers it is disconcerting not to be seeing, or reading about, those for whom Scotland is home. Since these articles/photographs are rarely balanced by reports of the African/Caribbean presence in Scotland the impression created and perpetuated is that African/Caribbean are transients and do not belong to Scotland.

What is evident from an African/Caribbean perspective is that Scottish newspapers are more about giving visibility and voice to people of African origin or descent who live outwith Scotland than it is about recognising those who live in Scotland.

Despite Evans' vital research having been undertaken between 1989–1993, the similarities to today's media representation seem indisputable.

Responses to questions in our survey such as 'Have there been any events which have happened in Scotland which have affected you as a Black person living in Scotland? Please describe/explain', included the following which relate to the media experiences of Black people:

When Lee Rigby was murdered it was as if every single black person conspired and was part of that evil act. I recall crying when I saw the terrible news that an innocent man was beheaded in public. There was a huge outcry and public protests in Glasgow and Edinburgh. I was completely devastated at the loss of human life. But I became devastated at the hate towards black people that followed. Facebook was no longer a space to connect with Friends. There was a lot of covert and overt acts of racism and violence towards many Black people. Being outside was not safe. It was even more shocking that this was experienced in Scotland even though the crime never took place in Glasgow or Edinburgh. I recall being openly accused of being affiliated with his death. I recall many young and old white people advising that Scotland and Britain in general should not accept Black folks because 'this is what they do!'. It's difficult to comprehend why the murder of a white man by a black man in 2013 can hold such power. White supremacy I guess. The irony is that Glasgow had a long standing record for being the murder capital in Europe. The main perpetrators being white - not too many outcrys regarding many murders.

11 October 2020 (26–35 years-old)

Another person who responded to our survey highlighted that their life had been impacted by 'BLM, racism in the workplace, lack of diversity in the media, creative, cultural, and business community'. Additionally, survey responses on the media representation of Black people in Scotland included remarks such as the following which make clear the challenges that Black people encounter when working in the media industry in Scotland:

I work in the media industry in Scotland and my experience has been a VERY bitter sweet one. In London, I never felt as though my race was an issue for people. But in Scotland everywhere I turn I am confronted with direct and indirect discrimination, and it has got no easier now that I run my own media company.

17 March 2021 (26–35 years-old)

Other comments indicated some positive perceptions of certain creative and cultural industry organizations:

I know there are many groups that have funding and support from Creative Scotland. There are artistic and creative forums for theatre, art, music and dance. There are support groups for non-English speaking females with children in mainstream schools. There is a multicultural festival raising awareness of cultural identities. There is a support group for children from ethnic backgrounds.

5 April 2021 (56–65 years-old)

Oftentimes, if traditional sources of funding cannot be accessed, online crowd funders and other digital forms of fundraising can be used to raise money to enable the work of Black individuals and projects to be undertaken. However, the success of these avenues for fundraising are often dependent on who or what the project is, the networks and reach of the person(s) and can often feed into the white saviour complex, which 'while seemingly harmless, is in fact, an extension of privilege and white supremacy' (HipLatina 2021). As Charmaine Blaize reflects:

That notion of the individualistic mindset as opposed to that community and that sense of collectiveness that other cultures – Caribbean cultures have to an extent – that is different here. I think the community might be reflected in charities and raising funds for a good cause. We don't have that back home as much, because the communities help who is in the communities. I think that kinda transfers into, 'I am running to raise funds for this one', 'I'm bungee jumping to raise funds for this'. You really wouldn't get many people from my country doing that naturally.

Though the act of giving can demonstrate solidarity with the cause, as Charmaine describes, this can sometimes be individualistic, with no desire to engage with the person or purpose beyond donation. Or indeed the cause or project which funds are being requested for, might be an individualistic pursuit, with no connection or contribution to the collective. In recent times, there appears to have been an increase in the visibility of some Black people – rightly – asking to be paid for work and these asks have sometimes included payment for emotional labour, or contributions to help make lives easier under capitalism. However, prevailing discourses around 'white privilege' can lead to the transference of money serving as a means to appease 'white guilt', which can lead to a lack of accountability as to where and to whom the money is going and may bypass those who are truly in need of financial support.

In 2020, in response to the COVID-19 pandemic, '[f]rom theatres and galleries, to museums and archives – arts and cultural organizations have made the difficult but necessary decision to close their doors for the foreseeable future. Amid the anxiety of adjusting to life in this current climate, creative workers are having to quickly figure out how to continue their work in a way that is financially sustainable and not as dependent on certain physical spaces, audience footfall, and in-person events than it usually is. Even individuals whose work is closely tied to digital sites, social media, and online outlets, are likely to be impacted by current circumstances to such an extent that they are required to re-evaluate their plans for the rest of the year' (Sobande 2020c)

Relatively recent groups and organizations with a clear commitment to supporting the creative work of Black people include We Are Here Scotland which 'exists to support and amplify the voices of BIPOC artists across Scotland' (Qureshi 2020) and was officially launched in November 2020, due to the work of Aberdeen-based creative practitioner Ica Headlam who 'is the driving force' (Qureshi 2020) behind this new creative platform. As Ica Headlam outlined, during an interview with writer Arusa Qureshi for Scottish online publication *Bella Caledonia:*

> We Are Here Scotland came about through my sheer frustration of seeing the constant lack of consistent BIPOC representation within Scotland's creative industries whilst also recognising that there needs to be a platform in which we are given the chance to showcase ourselves, connect and seek funding and grant opportunities. I've had a lot of conversations with BIPOC artists and creatives and we have all noted that we face constant barriers in terms of funding and employment opportunities within Scotland. There are also hurdles when it comes to the recognition of our work and people not valuing our time.

Another example of activity in Scotland which includes a focus on the creative work of Black people and people of colour is Fringe of Colour, founded/directed by writer, producer, and psycholinguistics PhD student Jess Brough. Since 2018, the Fringe of Colour initiative has been 'dedicated to supporting Black people and People of Colour at arts festivals in Scotland and beyond' and, since 2020, such work has included an online arts festival, Fringe of Colour Films, which 'celebrates the creative work of Black, Asian, Indigenous and Latine people in

Scotland and around the world, through an online streaming service, publishing platform and podcast series'.

Other indications of changes amid Scotland's creative and cultural landscape include what appear to be the intentional efforts of some arts organizations to more substantially, and, sustainably, support the work of Black artists. Are we witnessing a crucial turning point in terms of how the realities of racism, colonialism, and the legacy of slavery and empire is being reckoned with across Scotland? Only time will tell. However, we are buoyed by the efforts of individuals who, often without the backing of high-profile organizations and without access to networks or large amounts of funding, continue to do invaluable grassroots and community-orientated work that supports Black people in nuanced ways, without appeasing institutions that search for Black people to individualistically tokenize.

Despite the fact that 'Urban ethnicities were increasingly penetrating media culture' (Hesse 2000a: 10) in the 1990s in Britain, well-developed depictions of Black people in, from, or connected to Scotland were, and continue to be, relatively scarce. Also, even though the annual Edinburgh International Festival is international in nature, as Gary Younge said when interviewed by us, 'I remember the festival just feeling like the whitest show on earth'. That said, as Hesse (2000a: 10) states when writing about media and marketplace activity at the turn of the second century, 'the undoubted commodification of "non-western", "non-white" cultural differences and their dissemination as signs of style, exoticism, pleasure and connoisseurship, was more populist than liberal, more capitalist than constitutional, more ethnographic than historiographic ...' (ibid.). Hence, the mere inclusion of Black people in media and creative and cultural industry contexts does not magically result in structural changes related to racism, white supremacy, and capitalism.

Arusa Qureshi's (2021b) report on 'People of Colour and the Creative Industries in Scotland: A Post-2020 Reflection' pushes against the tokenizing gestures of institutions and considers 'the prospects for post-Covid recovery in the arts, and the challenges for representation, "diversity" and power relations in Scottish cultural institutions and forums'. When reading Qureshi's in-depth report, we were reminded of the groundbreaking creative work of people such as Kubara Zamani who, in Kubara's words, was in 'one of the first reggae bands in Scotland to go digital. We used that old way of playing reggae and then went digital ... we were one of the first bands to go digital in Scotland using digital reggae which is now what you would look on as 'club music' or 'dance music' ... we were one of the first ones to use digital drumkits live on stage ... supported Dennis Brown when he came up'.

Kubara spoke in detail about activism and Black creative work in Scotland. When asked if Black activism in Scotland has changed, Kubara said the following, which also relates to the history of Black creative, artistic, and cultural work and experiences (t)here:

> Black activism in Scotland ... has changed because more people have gone there. I left in 88 and at that time ... we would know ... between my family and friends ... we would kind of know most Black people who came into Edinburgh if they stayed for any length of time ... it's one city centre and also the university is open campus ... I lived all over the Southside ... after I moved out of my parents' I lived in many flats over the Southside ... we would kind of ... even though I wasn't at the university you could go in the university and we would have meetings in there and we knew people studying in there ... so most of the Black people between us we would know ... because it was literally that few ... people would come up for the festival then there would be ya know things like market theatre of Johannesburg ... mystic revelation of Rastafri, Benjamin Zephaniah, Black theatre cooperative, Linton Kwesi Johnson, Last Messenger, I saw all of them in Edinburgh ... Curtis Mayfield ... saw all those people in Edinburgh ... Dennis Brown as well ... that was different from supporting Dennis Brown ... we saw him there as well, so I would say at that time we knew most of what was going on ...

While navigating landscapes which both erase and promote Black people when it suits, Black creative practitioners should speak, and talk back, because as Black feminist writer, scholar, and activist bell hooks (1989: 8) states, 'for us, true speaking, is not solely an expression of creative power; it is an act of resistance, a political gesture which challenges politics of domination that would render us nameless and voiceless. As such, it is a courageous act – as such it represents a threat'. In addition, it is equally necessary for Black creatives to be amenable to self-critique. As hooks wrote in 1989 and which remains relevant today:

> if much of the recent work on race grows out of a sincere commitment to cultural transformation, then there is serious need for immediate and persistent self-critique. Committed cultural critics—whether white or black, whether scholars, artists, or both—can produce work that opposes structures of domination, that presents possibilities for a transformed future by willingly interrogating their own work on aesthetic and political grounds. This interrogation itself becomes an act of critical intervention, fundamentally fostering an attitude of vigilance rather than denial.

The lives of Black people in Scotland can never wholly be understood or (re)told whilst substantial and sustained avenues for Black self-expression fail to exist. As

Scotland moves towards a 'post-Covid' recovery, we hope that new (and old) Black-led creative, intellectual and media pursuits can thrive and produce generative critiques. However, large-scale events such as the 26th UN Climate Change Conference of the Parties (COP26), held in Glasgow in November 2021 and the 2014 Commonwealth Games, which place Scotland on the international stage and allow soft powers to be cultivated and deployed, are often at the expense of those who live there. Funding opportunities become quickly available to help shape a narrative which projects Scotland as an attractive and progressive place to live, visit, work and, crucially, invest in.

As Wilson (2017: 123–124) describes:

> Marginality, more deeply than before, is ascribed to the visual, what people are seen to represent. Appear poor, and the proper place for you in the city is in the caverns of the urban's forgotten spaces. Appear creative, and your proper place is neighborhoods and zones that are boldly illuminated and heralded. The new marginality, ignoring plight and circumstance, identifies beings that are supposed contaminants of pristine, sellable entrepreneurial space.

Though this speaks to, and will be more keenly felt within urban settings, gentrification packaged as redevelopment, happens in rural areas too and will possibly increase in post-Covid landscapes. We are encouraged by emerging new creative and media endeavors from individuals, groups, and organizations such as the Black and asylum-seeker-led, Siyakhuluma WeTalk Podcast, able to provide a counter-narrative and much-needed avenue for Black self-expression, whilst also resisting the commodification of their identities.

But thurs broon faces in white places: (No) Black people in Scottish politics

We also need to see more Black politicians in Scotland.

17 March 2021 (26–35 years-old)

I think that Scotland will get closer to embracing any kind of Black Scottish activity ... even if there are less people there than certain parts of England ... certain parts of England they see everything as if you get something you're taking it from me ... anything you get its cause you're taking it from me ... what they've got in the first place they were given or they were false beneficiaries of all the slaughter and genocide ... I'm not a supporter of any political party but I think that the SNP make it easier to have certain discussions just because they have to have difficult discussions about independence, so if we're having that difficult discussion … let's have that other difficult discussion as well.

30 April 2021 (Kubara)

In the immediate aftermath of the 6 May 2021 Scottish Parliament election, much was made of Scotland's 'newly diverse parliament', 'with MSPs that more accurately reflect the country's multiculturalism' (Garavelli 2021).

Framed by many commentors as a rejection of the controversial Alba Party (founded by former First Minister Alex Salmond several weeks before the election) and the All For Unity party (led by George Galloway), the election of more women (45%), more representatives from ethnic minority backgrounds and more MSPs with visible disabilities, would all certainly indicate that 'Scotland is no country for old men with outdated attitudes, but a progressive, multicultural nation with its eyes firmly fixed on the future' (Guardian 2021). Indeed, the variety of languages used for the swearing in ceremony on Thursday 13 May, helped to further reinforce a narrative of diversity and multiculturalism. However, this progressive and multicultural nation has still failed to return any Black MSPs to the Scottish Parliament and the oath in Zimbabwean Shona, was taken by Scottish Greens MSP Maggie Chapman, a white woman who was born and spent most of her life in Zimbabwe, before moving to Scotland.

Prior to the 2021 elections, the Scottish Parliament had two BAME MSPs – Humza Yousaf of the Scottish National Party (SNP) and Anas Sarwar of the Scottish Labour Party, elected in the 2017 election. This was in stark contrast to Westminster which returned 20 Black MPs – 13 of whom are Black women – in the 2019 General Election. Since the formation of the Scottish Parliament in 1999 and prior to 2021, a total of four BAME people have been elected as MSPs – each of them men of Scottish and Pakistani heritage, representing the city of Glasgow.

The Pakistani population is the largest BAME ethnic group in Scotland, thus it could be argued that this is why BAME representation within institutional – and inherently male-dominated – politics is weighted towards men of Pakistani heritage. However, the Chinese population is the second largest BAME ethnic group in Scotland (Scotland's Census 2011) and has yet to be represented at Holyrood. Yen Hongmei Jin, who briefly represented the SNP in Dumfries and Galloway was 'Scotland's first Chinese councillor' but became an Independent representative after experiencing racism and a lack of support from the party in addressing this. Yen Hongmei Jin later attempted to stand as a Parliamentary candidate and after failing to be selected, took the SNP to court for racial discrimination, but lost her claim (Donnelly 2016).

The newly diverse Scottish Parliament returned six BAME MSPs, Foysol Choudhury (Labour), Pam Gosal (Conservatives), Sandesh Gulhane (Conservatives), Anas Sarwar (Labour) Kaukab Stewart (SNP) and Humza Yousaf (SNP). In the weeks, prior to the Scottish Parliament 2021 elections, Anas Sarwar became the first Muslim and person of colour to lead a major political party in Scotland, and in the UK. Pam Gosal became the first woman MSP elected to the Scottish Parliament from an Indian Sikh background. Having unsuccessfully stood as the first BAME candidate in the 1999 elections, Kaukab Stewart's constituency was one of the first to be announced, making her the first woman of colour and Muslim woman to become an MSP. As part of her acceptance speech Kaukab Stewart (BBC 2021) said:

> It is without doubt an honour, to be elected as the first woman of colour, to the Scottish Parliament. It has taken too long. But to all the women, and girls, of colour out there, the Scottish Parliament belongs to you too. So, whilst I may be the first, I will not be the last.

Nicola Sturgeon's words followed a similar framing:

> While I'm delighted about all the SNP MSPs elected. I am thrilled beyond words to see Kaukab Stewart elected. It has taken us far too long, more than twenty years, but today she becomes the first woman of colour to be elected to our national parliament. So, party politics aside, this is a really special and a very significant moment for Scotland, and I could not be prouder right now.

The lack of Black people within institutional politics could be easily dismissed as Black people having a lack of interest in it or, as we have highlighted in earlier chapters, Black people being perceived as 'too difficult' to engage with. However, Black people have been interested and have engaged with Scottish politics, since at least the formation of the Scottish Parliament, as trade unionist, educator, and activist Anita Shelton (2001:51) describes:

> In the new political environment, where issues of social inclusion were foremost on party agendas, it was a bitter disappointment that no black ethnic minority members – male or female – became members of the Scottish Parliament. Overall, networking among black women around the establishment of the Scottish Parliament took the form of participation in civic and party-sponsored campaign activities. The candidate selection process, viewed by many blacks [sic] as flawed, and inadequate support to black candidates by their respective parties, removed any realistic chance of success for black candidates. Black women's efforts, therefore, were in area of wider concern and interest, including the increase in women's representation in Scottish political and public life.

Several initiatives such as Women 50:50 and the Coalition for Racial Equality and Rights (CRER) Political Shadowing Scheme (2020c) exist to encourage BAME people into politics and public life. CRER's Political Shadowing Scheme has been running for over 10 years and 'gives those involved an opportunity to gain first-hand experience of the work of an MSP or Councillor, which can often provide a stepping stone into Scottish politics' and seeks to 'address the severe under representation of Black and minority ethnic (BME) individuals in the Scottish political arena'. Despite the popularity and support of these initiatives – including by MSPs – given the lack of Black people in mainstream politics, there appears to be much work still to do.

The Scottish Government's own response to research which highlighted the dearth of BAME people within the civil service, has been to launch a similar initiative, the Minority Ethnic Emerging Leaders Programme. The £470k Scottish-Government-funded programme will be delivered by the John Smith Centre at the University of Glasgow and 'up to 50 minority ethnic people between the ages of 18–29 across Scotland' will be provided with 'a part-time internship for 9 months with a host organization working within the public, third/voluntary sector or a politician'.

When asked, 'If you could implement a new policy in Scotland to address issues faced by Black people there, what would the policy be and why?', people who responded to our survey shared some of the following recommendations:

Mental health support for Black people. I think racism can't be changed by a single policy and systematic change takes time. Something that would help us know is mental health support to help Black people with day to day challenges to their/our mental health. Be it group therapy in Black safe spaces, 1to1 sessions with Black therapists, sessions for children, families to talk about racism.

9 October 2020 (26–35 years-old)

Education, Housing and Welfare because of racial disparities that exists in these departments.

4 February 2021 (56–65 years-old)

The race equality act needs to be reviewed and be an active document. At the moment the document is dormant.

7 February 2021 (46–55 years-old.

My policy would be inclusion of black history in Scotland and how we shaped the country. I'd love inclusion of our culture and music into schools. All policies should be in education as that's where we need it to filter from.

29 January 2021 (36–45 years-old)

I would focus on promoting education and cultural expression linked to addressing Scotland's visible and invisible role in colonialism. As in all of Britain there needs to be serious reform of the police and criminal justice system as one small interaction with them can destroy people's lives.

4 April 2021 (56–65 years-old)

We have never had a Black MSP since Holyrood was founded. I'd suggest all Black shortlists to push for a cultural shift; when Blair did this for women at Westminster, it dramatically changed representation for women.

13 January 2021 (26–35 years-old)

Anti-racism training being mandatory for every workplace. Holding work positions for black applicants. Work places following their own anti-racism policies.

24 January 2021 (36–45 years old)

Multiracial, progressive schools curricula promoting awareness and empathy from P1 forward.

2 May 2021 (56–65 years-old)

In 2017, after nearly four decades in power, the Scottish Labour party lost control of Glasgow City Council and candidates Graham Campbell of the Scottish National Party (SNP) and Ade Aibinu of Scottish Conservative and Unionist Party were elected as the 'first' Black councillors of the council. Though Campbell and Aibinu's status as such, received considerable press coverage, Black mixed-race SNP candidate, Michelle Campbell, who was elected to Erskine and Inchinnan Council in the same election, received little attention. Speaking in 2019 about her experiences as a Black woman in public life in Renfrewshire and on the campaign trail, Michelle reflected in *The Gazette* (Haugh 2019):

> When I walk into a room, it's the first thing people see. People don't hear an accent when I walk past them. Some make an assumption and don't realise I was born in this country. I've had people when you knock on their door they just look you up and down and say, 'You've got to be kidding me'. They then go on a rant about how 'people like me' are the problem. I can't do anything when that happens.

Mere months before the 2021 Scottish Parliament election, the SNP National Executive Committee (NEC) put forward a proposal which would put disabled or BAME candidates at the top of regional lists (The National 2021). It is worth noting the context of these changes; the SNP was going through a shaky period, not limited to; internal shifts, fragmentation, questions raised over the management of the pandemic, and the First Minister herself being subjected to two separate investigations to establish if she had broken the Ministerial Code. As the impact of these events on the general public's perception of the party, government, and how they vote can never be certain until election day, these actions could be seen as tactical.

Furthermore, the policy applied only to regional lists and not constituency seats, meaning that if the SNP did well in constituency votes, a BAME or disabled candidate gaining a regional list seat would be unlikely. This is due to the additional member system (AMS), which means the number of seats a party gets in total is about the same as the percentage of votes it receives. Unsuccessful candidates for the 2021 Scottish Parliament election, included Roza Salih (SNP), one of the 'Glasgow Girls' who fought against the practice of dawn raids and mistreatment of asylum seekers, and Nadia Kanyange (Scottish Greens), also a former asylum seeker from Burundi. Had they been elected, the Scottish Parliament would have been more reflective of a progressive and diverse parliament. Roza Salih has since been elected as the 'first' refugee to be elected as a councillor in Scotland, representing the SNP in the Greater Pollok ward at Glasgow City Council.

As seen in the US and England, the Black vote plays an important part in politics and, as Scotland's demographics continue to change, it could be that politicians are recognizing the value of the Black vote here too. Whilst undertaking research for this section of the book, we discovered two Freedom of Information (FOI) requests of note, submitted to the Scottish Parliament and Scottish Government in July 2020 (Scottish Government 2020d). Of the request made to the Scottish Parliament on 20 July 2020, the Parliament was asked to:

> provide the information which confirms which members of the Scottish Parliament are also members of the Black Lives Matter protest group. Provide the information which confirms which members of Scottish Parliament hold positions of power and influence within this organisation.

The relatively global nature of the 2020 BLM protests has taken many by surprise and, unsurprisingly, has led to speculation around the origins, financial backing, and agenda(s) of the movement, ranging from being perceived as an alleged 'terrorist organisation' (The Root 2020) – akin to the threat the Black Panthers posed in the 1960-1970s – to being aligned with Wall Street interests, supported by the ruling class.

Of the request made to the Scottish Government on 27 July 2020, the government was asked to provide information related to racist incidents 'committed against any black employee by any white employee or any white employee against any black member of the public' and curiously, 'for information about when a black person will become First Minister' (Scottish Government 2020). We don't know who submitted these FOIs and, indeed, if they were submitted by the same person, but it made us think about the way BLM has – at the very least – resulted in more people asking more questions about Black people in Scotland and their experience of politics.

While being far from tokenistic in nature, we imagine that the election of two women of colour to the new Scottish Parliament may have brought a sense of relief not just to the SNP, but to all Scottish political parties. Finally, Scotland's devolved seat of power has the diversity it claims to endorse and embrace but has been lacking, potentially sidestepping some critiques of it being anything other than progressive. Raising the absence of Black women in the political sphere may become even more difficult, now that some racial diversity can be 'seen' in the Parliament.

Furthermore, over the SNP's time in government, at certain points, sex workers and trans people have been offered the party's support, but when narratives have become toxic and discriminatory, that support is nowhere to be found. We hope that the new Scottish Parliament – and those which follow – takes heed of some of the policy recommendations highlighted by our survey responses. In addition, we hope the women of colour who have been elected, are not subjected to similar experiences as those expressed by Michelle Campbell and Yen Hongmei Jin and are able to interrogate the omission of Black people from Scottish politics and beyond.

Fae nane/yin tae plenty: Digital media and a global gaze on Black Scottishness

Since the rise of online content-sharing and social media platforms such as Twitter, Instagram, Facebook, YouTube, and TikTok, it has become easier for some Black people to create and share online content with a potentially global reach. The move away from the 'one to many' broadcast model that was once strongly associated with media such as newspapers and televised news has made way for 'many to many' communication approaches that are more dialogic in nature and can involve people '[d]eploying the Internet as a creative material . . .' (Russell 2020: 9). Black digital studies scholarship highlights the creative and community-orientated ways that Black people have made use of digital tools to communicate and connect with other Black people in different parts of the world.

When writing about *Distributed Blackness: African American Cybercultures*, scholar André Brock Jr. (2020: 1) states that '[o]ver the last decade' there is evidence that 'Black digital practice has become very much a mainstream phenomenon, even if its expert practitioners rarely receive economic compensation for their brilliance or political compensation for their activism'. Elaborating on this point, Brock (2020: 1) asserts that '[t]he visibility of online Blackness can be partly attributed to the concentration of Black folk online in ways that the mainstream is unable to disavow'. Further still, the work of writer and curator Legacy Russell (2020: 6) captures some of the generative experimental dimensions of digital culture when stating '[f]or my body, then, subversion came via digital remix, searching for those sites of experimentation where I could explore my true self, open and ready to be read by those who spoke my language'.

When reflecting on the work of scholars such as Brock (2020), and considering the particularities of the context of Scotland, we have thought about the gradually increasing and digitally mediated global visibility of the experiences and perspectives of Black people in Scotland. Examples of this include the expanding number of podcasts that are created by Black people in Scotland, as well as impactful journalistic writing and dynamic Black Scottish multimedia content.

Since our childhoods in Scotland in the 1990s, certainly, there have been changes concerning both the media depictions and experiences of Black people in, from, and connected to Scotland. Among the most significant of these changes is the impact of social media and online content-sharing sites that are sometimes used in ways that contribute to Black digital diasporic discussions, collaborations, and solidarity formations. Some of our own experiences are included in this, such as when meeting Black people elsewhere 'in real life' (IRL) and continuing to find ways to support one another and learn about what is happening where everyone lives, via digital spaces. In the words of Russell (2020: 4), 'I was a digital native pushing through those cybernated landscapes with a dawning awareness, a shyly exercised power. I was not yet privileged enough to be fully formed as cyborg, but in reaching, surely on my way'.

While we undeniably acknowledge the potential for Black people in, from, and connected to Scotland to form and/or continue meaningful relationships and collective work with Black people from/based in other parts of the world, we also note how the somewhat increasing digital visibility of a 'Black Scottish experience' can result in interest expressed by organizations that identify new potential audiences and target markets. We also take note of Essed's (2009: xiv) cautionary words, '[i]n the age of the virtual, illusions sometimes count as real'.

Slowly, but surely, there has been indication of brands and organizations, including in the media and tech sectors, attempting to distinguish between the experiences of Black people in different parts of Britain. Perhaps, at times, such acknowledgement is linked to an awareness that for some Black people in Britain there is 'little meaningful identification with Britain' (Hesse 2000: 96). On the surface, this may appear to be helpful and reflect that the experiences of Black people in, from, and connected to Scotland are being treated and understood with more nuance than ever before. However, when accounting for the existence of 'predatory inclusion' practices (McMillan Cottom 2020) and Hesse's (2000b) work on 'Diasporicity: Black Britain's Post-Colonial Formations', the increase in brands and organizations attempting to depict and connect to a 'Black Scottish experience' may be interpreted as an example of how institutions seek to commercialize or capitalize on the nationally and regionally distinct identities and lives of Black people.

Perhaps, Black digital diaspora (Everett, 2019), or alluding to it, is sometimes treated as a branding strategy by corporations. Furthermore, Black Scottish influencers have already spoken out about being paid less by big brands (Ong 2020), though when compared to white influencers, factors such as age, gender, and region – which also affect pay – are not considered. On that note, in 2000 Hesse wrote the following:

> Although since the late 1970s and the early 1980s the relationship of Black people to the British landscape has become more visible in its coherence and complexity, the idea of Black Britishness still retains the resonance of an oxymoron . . .

In the present day, tensions surrounding the idea of Black Scottishness persist, including due to the exclusionary associations of nationalism that Hesse (2000b) reflects on when writing about Black Britishness. Just as Hesse (2000: 97) argued that 'Black Britishness is a discourse whose increasing currency has yet to be conceptualized seriously', we affirm the need for more work that attends to the conceptualization of Black Scottishness and being Black in Scotland.

Still, while we call for and contribute to such work, we also observe how the digital creativity, content, commentaries, archives, and articulations of Black people in, from, and connected to Scotland are crucial forms of knowledge production and knowledge sharing that include conceptualizations, and experiences, of Black Scottishness. To be more direct, the relative dearth of institutionally affiliated written scholarship on the details of Black Scottishness (not just Blackness and Black people in Scotland), does not mean that conceptualizing, theorizing, and research on this is absent elsewhere.

Just as Hesse (2000: 97) posed the question 'What is signified by Black Britishness?', we are interested in what is and is not signified by Black Scottishness, including in ways that both relate to and depart from understandings of Black Britishness. How might the future of digital media and culture shape ideas about and representations of Black Scottishness, and the lives of Black people in Scotland? What risks are involved in the digital visibility of Black people in, from, and connected to Scotland? How and why might brands and organizations attempt to engage such Black people? Future research related to the lives and media experiences of Black people in, from, and connected to Scotland may benefit from considering these questions, and more.

When reflecting on 'a possible analytics of Black Britishness, defining its theoretical specificity by way of its intra-national and transnational relations with the African diaspora' (Hesse 2000: 97), future work on the lives of Black people in Scotland may be helped by an attentiveness to how the mechanics of different regional experiences shape notions and embodied experiences of Black Scottishness. While writing about digital media, culture, and Black people in, from, and connected to Scotland, we always do so with an understanding of the fact that *not all* such people have access to the internet, digital technology, and the time and financial resources that are required to participate in digital spaces and dialogue. Therefore, we hope that continued work in this area, and related future policymaking, will be sensitive to the wide range of material conditions that Black people in, from, and connected to Scotland deal with, particularly those who are most marginalized.

5

Tis nae th' end: Some not so final thoughts

I appreciate how black Scots support each other. From the little nod we do
when we see each other in the street or in a bar (even when we don't know
each other), to supporting each others' businesses/projects, sharing hair tips or
complimenting each other when passing in a shop. This is an absolute gem of
black Scottish culture.

3 February 2021 (26–35 years-old)

The lives and history of Black people in, from, and connected to Scotland are so much more than the sum of this book, or any other publication for that matter. While working on this project we have always been acutely aware of the impossibility of understanding and accounting for the exact experiences of *all* Black people. We also spent a lot of time questioning who and what this book could and would focus on, and why.

Often Black and marginalized people are assumed to seek forms of public visibility and inclusion, whether in the form of on-screen depictions or representation within the chapters of a book. However, public visibility and representation are far from being desired by every Black person, and can result in increased risks and dangers, particularly for Black people who are not regarded as the palatable, politically malleable, and middle-class face of Blackness that institutions may seek to platform and see as 'non-threatening'. For those reasons, when writing this book, we attempted to avoid fetishizing and glamourizing forms of public representation and recognition of Black people, including by being attentive to both the perspectives of Black people who are public figures, and those who are not regarded as such.

We've stayed critical and cognizant of the limitations of representational politics which often predominantly propels the public image of institutions and a select few marketable individuals, rather than substantially tackling intersecting oppressions that impact Black people's lives. However, that does not mean that Black people's pursuit of various forms of representation in Scotland should be completely dismissed, especially if such forms of representation are connected to the possibility of enacting change. In other words, critiquing the lack of radical and transformative potential of certain, particularly commercial, representations of Black people and public platforms that they are afforded should not be confused for denying that forms of representation can play a generative, meaningful, and even joyful role in the lives of some Black people.

The terrain of representational politics is fraught with friction and is as uneven as the landscape of Scotland itself. Do all representations of Black people need to involve explicit declarations of an activist intent to address anti-Black racism and interconnected oppressions to be understood as valuable to Black people? How is the political potential of representations of Black people determined, and who by? Beyond the language and idea of representation, what are some of the many ways that Black people in, from, and connected to Scotland are expressing themselves, creating, and reimagining the future? These are a few of a series of ever-expanding questions that we continue to wrestle with and think about when engaging with, being part of, and commenting on the representation of Black people in, from, and connected to Scotland.

Of course, there is, and always will be, much more to say and write about the lives and history of Black people in, from, and connected to Scotland. We view *Black Oot Here* as neither a starting point nor summary of considerations and conversations concerning Black people's lives (t)here. To return to the powerful words of interdisciplinary scholar and artist Derrais Carter (2018: 40) on 'Black Study': 'Blackness somehow remains both in and out of time, pushing against the attempts to be ordered in the present, revisiting and reimagining the past, and producing future possibilities.' Thus, although *Black Oot Here: Black Lives in Scotland* mainly focuses on the contemporary experiences of Black people in Scotland, we also feel and hope that this book does the work of oscillating between the then, here, and now, and the yet to be.

The lives of Black people in Scotland are both old and new. They are seen and disappeared. They are documented and datafied. The lives of Black people in Scotland are significantly impacted but not defined by antiblackness. Such lives have been discussed and described in Scotland with the use of many different words which rarely, if ever, get close to articulating *all* that it means to be a Black person (t)here. The lives of Black people in Scotland are both fleeting and forever. They are rural and urban. Such lives are known and unknowable. *Black Oot Here: Black Lives in Scotland* is best understood as an unfinished and always expanding collection of thoughts, experiences, perspectives, and memories.

Just as 'Black Europe' is a descriptive category, an identity category, an unsatisfactory identity, no doubt to be contested by readers now and into the next generation' (Essed 2009: xii), 'Black Scotland', 'Black Scot', 'Black Scottish', and 'Afro Scot' continue to be unsettled terms that despite having the potential to represent elements of the experiences, lives, and geographies of Black people in, from, and connected to Scotland, can never fully encompass the nuances of all of what it means to be such a person.

As historian Olivette Otele (2020) observes in the introduction to the landmark book, *African Europeans: An Untold History*, '[p]ublished work often pairs the term "black presence" with a specific geographical area. From "black presence in Europe" to "black presence in Wales", these volumes map out the lives of black people of African descent in the named places' (1). While we view our work as being part of this broader body of research and writing, in co-authoring *Black Oot Here: Black Lives in Scotland* we also sought to speak to how the experiences of Black people (t)here are connected to those of Black people elsewhere, and are linked to regional, national, and transnational dynamics that are part of the geo-cultural contexts where Black people live.

Furthermore, as Otele (2020) outlines, many books about the lives of Black people in particular places are 'often about known men and women' (1). Although *Black Oot Here: Black Lives in Scotland* includes a discussion of some of the experiences of people who are public figures and representatives of various kinds, the voices included in our book are many, and mainly those of individuals whose lives have rarely, if ever, been the source of much public interest. Furthermore, *Black Oot Here: Black Lives in Scotland* may be understood as contributing to a history of 'grounding "black" experiences and definitions of reality in national stories—past and present' (Essed 2009: xii).

While writing this book we reflected on the words of many Black writers and scholars, including Katherine McKittrick (2021) who has asked 'questions about how black worlds are not always wholly defined by scientific racism and biological determinism' (1), and has written about 'black livingness and ways of knowing' (3). We were inspired by McKittrick's (2021) work *Dear Science and Other Stories* which 'argues that black people have always used interdisciplinary methodologies to explain, explore, and story the world, because thinking and writing and imagining across a range of texts, disciplines, histories, and genres unsettles suffocating and dismal and insular racial logics. By employing interdisciplinary methodologies and having interdisciplinary words, Black people bring together various sources and texts and narratives to challenge racism. Or, Black people bring together various sources and texts and narratives not to capture something or someone, but to question the analytical work of capturing, and the desire to capture, something or someone'.

The relative dearth of disaggregated data on life at the intersections of race, ethnicity, gender, and class in Scotland means that the specific experiences of Black people are seldom meaningfully societally acknowledged, including the nuances of what it means to be a Black woman, man, or nonbinary person (t) here. Then again, Black people *are not*, and should not be treated as, data. We contend that their/our lives can never be comprehend by datafication processes that reduce realities to little more than percentages and bullet-pointed statements, so we hope that future work will include writing which pays attention to expansive Black expressivity, ephemera, and oral histories that will be of importance and interest to generations to come.

When working on our book we also consistently thought about June Evans' (1995: 271) concluding words:

> Many African/Caribbeans enjoy living in Scotland which they regard as home in spite of racism, the inability to obtain jobs suited to educational level of qualification and the uncertainty about the future of their offspring, AfroScots. Though the historical presence of African/Caribbean people in Scotland is eroded and contemporary presence denied they look forward to a future in Scotland in which their talents and contribution would be recognized. This thesis challenges academics, policy makers and service providers to make this possible.

While thinking about our own concluding words that we wanted to share in this final chapter, we spent a lot of time revisiting the comments of everyone who kindly agreed to speak to us and shared their thoughts and experiences as part of the research that informed our book. We sat with the fears that people shared, including when they spoke of the 'heart-wrenching and terrifying' impact of COVID-19 and being 'worried that this could be used as a reason to "discriminate" under the guise of caring'. We also reread the words of people who reflected on how, since 2020, '[o]n one side people [in Scotland] are talking and listening more to the experiences of Black people in Scotland. But a lot of other people feel threatened and double down on their prejudices to avoid taking personal responsibility for the work they have to do'.

When we started this project, truth be told, we did not know the direction and details of what would become this book – *our* book, as well as the many 'disruptions' we would encounter, including in the form of personal health circumstances and a global pandemic that is still very much present. Researchers often face an impulse to present everything as methodical, systematic, linear, and structured, but this book took shape somewhere between meaningful meanderings, musings, remembering, revisiting and many, many voice notes to each other. This project involved more wondering and wandering than it did following a planned and paved path. Always mindful of our aim to 'finish' this book but without forcing it, we tried to allow the research and writing process to ebb and flow, while being buoyed by the prospect of our words connecting with someone else.

There is often an expectation that concluding chapters include some pithy closing words that leave the reader(s) with a neat soundbite that summarizes the core sentiments of the book. We would be lying if we suggested that we did not feel the pressure to do just that, but the lives of Black people in Scotland cannot and should not be reduced to any single statement or commodifiable caption. Instead of simply 'closing' this book by reiterating the reflections and ruminations that are woven throughout it, we decided to share six more images. What the images mean to you may differ to what they mean to us. How the images relate to all that is discussed in this book may be ambiguous or palpable, depending on your personal perspective and the ways that you have felt and interpreted the words on these pages.

The conflicted feeling of being 'oot here' that courses throughout the chapters of our work is one that may be comfortingly or painfully familiar to you, or someone that you know. With this in mind, we hope that our book does the work of acknowledging the collective nature of such feelings which are part of the lives of many Black people in Scotland. Finally, regardless of whether you read our work from the first page to the last or have found yourself reading these words out of curiosity without having explored the other parts of our book, we thank you for taking and making the time to engage with *Black Oot Here: Black Lives in Scotland*. Our book is the outcome of the work, words, and shared world(s) of many people, whose lives and living archives are part of Black pasts, present day experiences, and futures in Scotland, where Black people continue to find, forge, fight for, and feel, a sense of history, here and now, and 'home'.

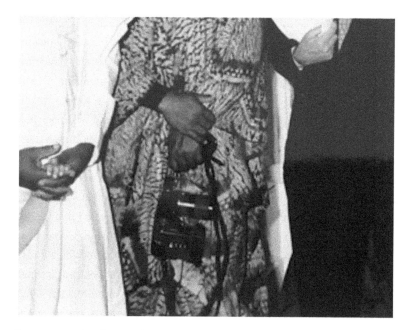

37 From personal collection featuring family and friends. Courtesy of Francesca Sobande

38 Silhouette of myself taking a photograph in the meadows in Edinburgh. Photograph by Francesca Sobande

39 Seal resting on a sea buoy near South Queensferry. Photograph by layla-roxanne hill

40 Tree in bloom in April 2021. Photograph by Francesca Sobande

41 Bird amongst bins in April 2021. Photograph by layla-roxanne hill

42 From personal collection featuring family celebrating an occasion in Kano, Nigeria. Courtesy of layla-roxanne hill

Notes

Chapter 1

1 *Post-racial* is a term that is typically used to encompass a point in time and/or part of society that is thought to exist in a way that is not impacted by, or transcends, issues concerning race and racism. Our position aligns with what is outlined in the vital work of communication scholar Ralina L. Joseph, who uses the term 'postrace' as a way 'to name the ideology – sceptically – and to point out the continued centrality of race in this ideology where race is ostensibly immaterial' (Joseph 2018: 8).

2 We use the term *(t)here* to allude to the fact that, at present, only one of us (layla-roxanne hill) lives in Scotland. We also use this term to allude to the sense of 'in-betweenness' that can be part of the experiences of diasporic people who, as Henry (2015: 239) notes in relation to what the work of Stuart Hall highlights, 'carry loss, grief, nostalgia and displacement'.

3 When we refer to class, we are referring to the socio-economic material conditions that different people deal with and which impact their proximity to, distance from, or experience of poverty, precarious work and employment situations, poor health, and forms of societal oppression, exclusion, and harm that can be fatal.

4 We use the term *racialized people* to collectively refer to Black, Asian and other racialized individuals, including, but not limited, to those who may identify as Arab and/or People of Colour (POC).

5 For more information about *Black Feminism, Womanism and the Politics of Women of Colour in Europe*: see https://woceuropeconference.wordpress.com/2016-conference/.

6 'The term "mixed-race" is commonly used in Britain to refer to a person who is biologically related to parents from different racial backgrounds – broadly defined – including a person with one Black parent of African descent. "Mixed-race" is one of many terms that has been used as part of essentialising, homogenising, racist and purist white supremacist pseudoscience discourse regarding race and eugenics. The term "mixed-race" has also been used as part of some people's self-identifying efforts to distance themselves from their Blackness, in ways that may ultimately be rooted in anti-Black positions and a rejection of Black identity' (Sobande 2020: 19). We use the words 'mixed-race' with caution and 'an unwaveringly critical perspective of this term, including due to how it can obscure particularities of the experiences of

racialized people and can function as part of rhetoric and research which upholds oppressive and racist notions of racial purity' (ibid.). However, we use the words 'mixed-race' in our book when referring to the exact words of others, and to acknowledge how our own Black identities are often perceived, described, and categorized by others in the context of Britain's history and contemporary notions of racial identity and Blackness.

7 For more information about *Black Oot Here: Black Lives in Scotland*, visit the project website: www.blackinscotland.com/.

Chapter 2

1 For more information about the extensive work of Palmer, who is leading a review of Edinburgh's slavery's legacy, see www.scottishlegal.com/article/sir-geoff-palmer-to-lead-review-of-edinburgh-s-slavery-legacy.

2 We use the term *skilled* critically and with ambivalence, but we use the term to reflect how certain jobs and experiences of work and labour are typically discussed within Scottish public and political discourse. However, we remain critical of how the notion of being skilled is defined and interpreted in ways that uphold inherently capitalist, hierarchical, and classist distinctions between different types of work (e.g. what is often referred to as 'manual labour' and 'office work'). Moreover, we note how the notion of being skilled is a slippery one that is used by institutions to oppressively suggest that the perceived societal contributions of individuals should be measured in relation to their socio-economic productivity (Cowan 2021). Put briefly, when using the term *skilled* we do so from a critical vantage point, and we aim to avoid upholding oppressive and classist socially constructed distinctions between forms of work and labour.

Chapter 4

1 *Black Women and the Media – National Union of Journalists* which took place on 6 October in 2016 involved public discussions between Samantha Asumadu, layla-roxanne hill, Briana Pegado, and Francesca Sobande. While the event focused on the media experiences and depictions of Black women in Britain, there was a strong focus on the Scottish context. Since then, public discourse on these specific matters has significantly expanded and resulted in events such as *Telling Our Own Stories: People of Colour in Scotland's Media* (Kinning Park, Glasgow, 27 September, 2019) organized by layla-roxanne hill and others involved in the National Union of

Journalists (NUJ) Glasgow Branch and Race Beat, *In Our Own Voices: Women of Colour in Scottish Media* (University of Strathclyde, Glasgow, 23 October, 2019) organized by Gender Equal Media Scotland, and the *Pass the Mic* project founded in October 2019 and delivered by Talat Yaqoob who is a campaigner, consultant and co-founder of Women 50:50.

References

African & Caribbean Women's Association – ACWA (2020), *New Shoots Old Roots: Volume II*, Glasgow: Street Level Photoworks.

African Women Group Scotland (date unknown), 'Our Invisibility in Scotland: Aberdeen 1998,' *African Women Group Scotland*. Available online: https://africanwomenscotland.org.uk/conference-1998/.

Agbemetsi, M. (1990), 'Our Day of Awakening. The African & Caribbean Women's Association, Glasgow', in S. Henderson and A. Mackay (eds), *Grit and Diamonds: Women in Scotland Making History 1980–1990*, pp. 121–122, Edinburgh: Stramullion.

Andrews, K. (2016), 'The problem of political blackness: lessons from the Black Supplementary School Movement', *Ethnic and Racial Studies*, 39 (11): 2060–2078.

Anon (date unknown but appears to be 1990 or 1991), *Black Markets: Images of Black people in Advertising & Packaging in Britain (1880–1990)*, Cornerhouse/Arts Council Funded.

Arshad, R. and M. McCrum (1989), 'Black Women, White Scotland', in A. Brown and D. McCrone (eds), *The Scottish Government Yearbook 1989*, pp. 207–227, Edinburgh: Edinburgh University Press.

Arshad, R. (1990), 'The Scottish Black Women's Group', in S. Henderson and A. Mackay (eds), *Grit and Diamonds: Women in Scotland Making History 1980–1990*, pp. 118–120, Edinburgh: Stramullion.

Asani, F. (2020), 'When the world crumbles, migrant lives are shattered – after being threatened with deportation, I know', *The Independent*, 15 May. Available online: www.independent.co.uk/voices/coronavirus-lockdown-migrants-hostile-environment-home-office-furaha-asani-a9512826.html.

Association of African Communities in Renfrewshire (date unknown). Available online: www.facebook.com/Association-of-African-Communities-in-Renfrewshire-368035099935299/.

Bailey, M. (2021), *Misogynoir Transformed: Black Women's Digital Resistance*, New York: New York University Press.

Barber, A. (2021), *Consumed: The Need for Collective Change: Colonialism, Climate Change & Consumerism*, London: Brazen.

Bassel, L. and A. Emejulu (2017), *Minority Women and Austerity: Survival and Resistance in France and Britain*, Bristol: Policy Press.

BBC (2019a), 'Black and Scottish' [documentary], *BBC*. Available online: www.bbc.co.uk/programmes/m00098n0.

BBC (2019b), 'Black and Scottish: "Are you a Protestant Rasta or a Catholic Rasta?"', *BBC*, 7 October. Available online: www.bbc.co.uk/news/uk-scotland-49894363.

BBC (2019c), 'Slavery: Scotland's Hidden Shame – Episode 1' [documentary], *BBC*. Available online: www.bbc.co.uk/programmes/b0bqvv10.

BBC (2019d), 'Slavery: Scotland's Hidden Shame – Episode 2' [documentary], *BBC*. Available online: www.bbc.co.uk/programmes/b0bqvv10.

BBC (2020a), 'Scotland, Slavery and Statues' [documentary], *BBC*. Available online: www.bbc.co.uk/programmes/m000nrpb.

BBC (2020b), 'Edinburgh University renames David Hume Tower over "racist" views', *BBC*, 13 September. Available online: www.bbc.co.uk/news/uk-scotland-edinburgh-east-fife-54138247.

BBC (2021a), 'Scottish election 2021: First women of colour elected to Holyrood', *BBC*, 8 May. Available online: www.bbc.co.uk/news/uk-scotland-scotland-politics-57038919.

BBC (2021b), 'Scotland's papers: People power and teen jabs to tackle variant', *BBC*, 14 May. Available online: www.bbc.co.uk/news/uk-scotland-57111375 www.bbc.co.uk/programmes/b0bqvv10.

Benjamin, I. (1995), *The Black Press in Britain*, London: Trentham Books.

Bento, K. and A. Johnson (2021), 'Spoken Gems: When Academia Meets Self-Care – A Conversational Piece', *Retrospect Journal: Race in Retrospective*, 29: 14–18.

Bilge, S. (2013), 'Intersectionality Undone: Saving Intersectionality from Feminist Intersectionality Studies', *Du Bois Review: Social Science Research on Race*, 10 (2): 405–424.

Boyce Davies, C. (2008), *Left of Karl Marx: The Political Life of Black Communist Claudia Jones*, Durham, NC: Duke University Press.

Brock Jr, A. (2020), *Distributed Blackness: African American Cybercultures*. New York: New York University Press.

Brown, J. N. (2009) 'Black Europe and the African Diaspora: A Discourse on Location', in D. Clarke Hine, T. Danielle Keaton, and S. Small (eds), *Black Europe and the African Diaspora*, pp. 201–211, Urbana and Chicago: University of Illinois Press.

Bryan, B., Dadzie, S. and Scafe, S. (1985), *The Heart of the Race: Black Women's Lives in Britain*, London: Virago Press.

Campaign Against Racism & Fascism (CARF) (2001), 'Summer of rebellion: the CARF report', *CARF* 63: 11. Available online: https://irr.org.uk/resources/carf-magazine-archive-1991-2003/.

Campt, T. M. (2017), *Listening to Images*, Durham, NC: Duke University Press.

Carby, H. V. (2019), *Imperial Intimacies: A Tale of Two Islands*, London: Verso.

Carter, D. (2018), 'Black Study', in A. Johnson, R. Joseph-Salisbury, and B. Kamunge (eds), *Fire Now: Anti-Racist Scholarship in Times of Explicit Racial Violence*, pp. 38–43, London: Zed Books.

Centre for the Study of the Legacies of British Slavery (date unknown), 'Trinidad 1754 (Palmira Estate)', University of London College. Available online: www.ucl.ac.uk/lbs/claim/view/28718.

Christoffersen, A. (2020), 'The politics of intersectional practice: Towards an intersectional gender equality architecture', *One Scotland*. Available online: https://onescotland.org/wp-content/uploads/2020/08/NACWG-Webinar-2-Ashlee-Christofferson-Webinar-Slides-20200824.pdf.

Clements, L. and R. Flint (2021), 'Black history lessons to be made mandatory in Welsh Schools', *BBC News*, 19 March. Available online: www.bbc.co.uk/news/uk-wales-56447682.

Coalition for Racial and Equality Rights (CRER), Cllr. Graham Campbell, and Hoskins Architects & Stuco Design (2020a), 'Black History Month Scotland 2020', *CRER*. Available online: www.blackhistorymonthscotland.org/resources.

Coalition for Racial Equality and Rights (CRER) (2020b), 'New research from CRER: Ethnicity and Poverty in Scotland 2020', *CRER*, 18 December. Available online: www. crer.scot/post/new-research-from-crerethnicity-and-poverty-in-scotland-2020.

Coalition for Race Equality (CRER) (2020c), 'CRER's Political Shadowing Scheme', *CRER*. Available online: www.crer.scot/political-shadowing-scheme.

Collins, P. H. and S. Bilge (2016), *Intersectionality*. Cambridge, Malden, MA: Polity Press.

Collins, P. H. (2000), *Black Feminist Thought: Knowledge, Consciousness, and the Politics of Empowerment*, New York: Routledge.

Combahee River Collective (1978), '*Combahee River Collective* Statement', in Z. R. Eisenstein (ed), *Capitalist Patriarchy and the Case for Socialist Feminism*, pp. 210–218, New York: Monthly Review Press.

Cowan, L. (2021), *Border Nation: A Story of Migration*. London: Pluto Press.

Crenshaw, K. (1989), 'Demarginalizing the Intersection of Race and Sex: A Black Feminist Critique of Antidiscrimination Doctrine, Feminist Theory and Antiracist Politics', *University of Chicago Legal Forum*: Vol. 1989(1), Article 8.

Crenshaw, K. (1991), 'Mapping the Margins: Intersectionality, Identity Politics, and Violence against Women of Color', *Stanford Law Review*, 43(6): 1241–1299.

Curry, G. (2020), 'Covid pandemic: Impact of racism and discrimination on death rate cannot be ignored – Dr Gwenetta Curry', *The Scotsman*, 3 June. Available online: www.scotsman.com/news/opinion/columnists/covid-pandemic-impact-of-racism-and-discrimination-on-death-rate-cannot-be-ignored-dr-gwenetta-curry-3258586.

Curry, G. (2021), 'But they said we wouldn't find it here: Racism, discrimination and Covid-19', *Scope*. Available online: https://blogs.ed.ac.uk/scope/2020/09/17/but-they-said-we-wouldnt-find-it-here-racism-discrimination-and-covid-19/.

Dadzie, S. (2020), *A Kick in the Belly: Women, Slavery & Resistance,* London: Verso.

Davidson, N. and S. Virdee (2018), 'Introduction: Understanding Racism in Scotland' in N. Davidson, M. Liinpää, M. M. McBride, and S. Virdee (eds), *No Problem Here: Understanding Racism in Scotland*, pp. 9–12, Edinburgh: Luath Press.

DAWSUN (2021), 'Voices Within: The Social Economic Status Of Africans In Scotland: What Can We Learn?', Available at: https://www.dawsun.org/research-publications/voices-within-research-project

de Lima, P. (2012), 'Migration, "race" equality and discrimination: a question of social justice, in G. Mooney and J. Scott (eds) *Social Justice and Social Policy in Scotland*, 97–112. Bristol: Policy Press.

Donnelly, B. (2016), 'Judge rejects councillor's racism claim against SNP', *The Herald*, 2 April. Available online: www.heraldscotland.com/news/14397545.judge-rejects-councillors-racism-claim-against-snp/.

Dosekun, S. (2020), *Fashioning Postfeminism: Spectacular Femininity and Transnational Culture*. Urbana: University of Illinois Press.

Dundee Courier and Argus (1875), 'On Tuesday a man named James Crow, inmate of the Convalescent Home, was drowned while bathing at West Bay, Dunoon', *Dundee Courier and Argus*. Available online: www.britishnewspaperarchive.co.uk/viewer/bl/0000162/18750918/035/0003?browse%20=%20false.

Elliot–Cooper, A. (2021), *Black Resistance to British Policing*, Manchester: Manchester University Press.

Emejulu, A. and L. Bassel (2015), 'Minority women, austerity and activism', *Race & Class*, 57 (2): 86–95.

Essed, P. (2009), 'Foreword', in D. Clark Hine, T. Danielle Keaton, and S. Small (eds), *Black Europe and the African Diaspora*, pp. ix–xv, Urbana and Chicago: University of Illinois Press.

Evans, J. (1995), 'African/Caribbeans in Scotland: A socio-geographical study', *University of Edinburgh*. Available online: https://era.ed.ac.uk/handle/1842/7187.

Field, P., R. Bunce, L. Hassan, and M. Peacock (eds) (2019), *Here to Stay, Here to Fight: A Race Today Anthology*. London: Pluto Press.

Folorunso, T. (2020), 'Police brutality against black people isn't shocking or surprising', *The National*, 7 June. Available online: www.thenational.scot/news/18501323.police-brutality-black-people-isnt shocking-surprising.

Foloruso, T. (2020), 'The Black Women Shaking Up the Scottish Arts Scene' *Black Ballad*, 24 January. Available online: https://blackballad.co.uk/arts-culture/the-black-women-shaking-up-the-scottish-arts-scene?listIds=5bb46fe7526cbf2b64fa9180.

Ford, A. (1985), *Telling the Truth: British Honduran Forestry Unit in Scotland, 1941–44*, Kent: Karia Press. Available online: https://ambergriscaye.com/art8/Ford-TellingtheTruth.pdf.

Foy, S. L., V. Ray, and A. Hummel (2017), 'The Shade of a Criminal Record: Colorism, Incarceration, and External Racial Classification', *Socius: Sociological Research for a Dynamic World* 3: 1–14.

France, M. (1992), 'The lady vanishes', *The List*, 6 November. Available online: https://archive.list.co.uk/the-list/1992-11-06/56/.

Garavelli, D. (2021), 'Scotland will benefit from its newly diverse parliament', *The Guardian*, 12 May. Available online: www.theguardian.com/commentisfree/2021/may/12/scotland-benefit-diverse-parliament-holyrood-msps.

Gemmell, J. (2021), 'From the Editor', *Retrospect Journal: Race in Retrospective*, 29: pp. 4–5.

Gill, R. (2007), 'Postfeminist media culture: Elements of a sensibility', *European Journal of Cultural Studies*, 10(2): 147–166.

Gill, R. (2016), 'Post-postfeminism?: New feminist visibilities in postfeminist times', *Feminist Media Studies* 16(4): 610–630.

Gilmore, R. W. (2020), 'Geographies of racial capitalism with Ruth Wilson Gilmore – An Antipode Foundation Film', *Antipode*, 1 June. Available online: www.youtube.com/watch?v=2CS627aKrJI.

Gilmore, R. W. (2021), *Change Everything: Racial Capitalism and the Case for Abolition,* Chicago: Haymarket Books.

Glasgow School of Art (GSA) People of Colour Collective (2021). Available online: www.facebook.com/gsapoccollective.

Glencorse, M. (2016), '10 reasons why Scottish girlfriends are the best', *The Daily Record,* 1 June. Available online: www.dailyrecord.co.uk/scotland-now/10-reasons-scottish-girlfriends-best-8540811.

Hall, S. (2019), 'The Multicultural Question', in D. Morley (ed), *Essential Essays Vol.2: Identity and Diaspora,* 95–133. Durham, NC: Duke University Press.

Hamad, H. (2018), 'The One with the Feminist Critique: Revisiting Millennial Postfeminism with *Friends*', *Television & New Media* 19 (8): 692–707.

Hargreaves, J. D. (1994), 'African students in Britain: The case of Aberdeen university', in D. Killingray (ed), *Africans in Britain,* 129–144. Essex: Frank Cass.

Harnois, C. E. (2013), *Feminist Measures in Survey Research,* London: SAGE.

Hassan, L., R. Bunce, and P. Field (2019), 'Introduction', in P. Field, R. Bunce, L. Hassan and M. Peacock (eds), *Here to Stay, Here to Fight. A 'Race Today' Anthology,* pp. 1–7. London: Pluto Press.

Haugh, J. (2019), 'Councillor opens up about modern day racism in Renfrewshire', *The Gazette,* 19 February. Available online: www.thegazette.co.uk/news/17583948.councillor-opens-modern-day-racism-renfrewshire/.

Henderson, S. and A. Mackay (1990), *Grit and Diamonds: Women in Scotland Making History: 1980–1990.* Edinburgh: Stramullion.

Henry, A. (2015), '"Nostalgia for what cannot be": an interpretive and social biography of Stuart Hall's early years in Jamaica and England, 1932–1959,' *Discourse: Studies in the Cultural Politics of Education,* 36(2): 227–242.

Hepburn, E., M. Keating, and N. McEwen (eds) (2021), *Scotland's New Choice Independence after Brexit,* Edinburgh: Centre on Constitutional Change.

Hesse, B. (eds) (2000a), *Un/settled Multiculturalisms: Diasporas, Entanglements, Transruptions,* London: Zed Books.

Hesse, B. (eds) (2000b), 'Diasporicity: Black Britain's Post-Colonial Formations,' in B. Hesse (ed), *Un/settled Multiculturalisms: Diasporas, Entanglements,* pp. 96–120. *Transruptions.* London: Zed Books.

Hine, D. C., Keaton, T. D. and S. Small (eds) (2009), *Black Europe and the African Diaspora.* Urbana, IL: University of Illinois Press.

hill, l.r. and Sobande, F. (2018), 'In our own words: Organising and experiencing exhibitions as Black women and women of colour in Scotland', in R. Finkel, B. Sharp, M. Sweeney (eds), *Accessibility, Inclusion, and Diversity in Critical Event Studies,* 107–121. London: Routledge.

hill, l.r. (2018), 'An Other World,' *Bella Caledonia,* 8 May. Available online: https://bellacaledonia.org.uk/2018/05/08/an-other-world/.

hill, l.r. (2019), 'Let's Talk about Sex (and Race and Colonialism)', *Bella Caledonia,* 9 June. Available online: https://bellacaledonia.org.uk/2019/06/09/lets-talk-about-sex-and-race-and-colonialism/.

hill, l.r. and Sobande, F. (2020), '(Re)viewing race, the marketplace, and public space through the lens of photography', *Journal of Marketing Management*, 36 (13–14): 1169–1177.

hill, l.r. (2021), 'On cosplaying community' [WhatsApp voice message], 5 January 2021.

Hillhouse, R. (1909), 'Reminiscences. Byegone years of the West of Scotland Convalescent Seaside Homes, Dunoon', *University of Glasgow*. Available online: https://wellcomecollection.org/works/rfzt7b4q/items?canvas=6.

HipLatina (2020), '5 Ways to Tell if you have White Savior Complex', *HipLatina*, 25 June. Available online: https://hiplatina.com/white-savior-complex-is-real.

Hirsch, L. and N. Jones (2021), 'Incontestable: Imagining possibilities through intimate black geographies', *Transactions of the Institute of British Geographers*, 46(4): 796–800.

HMSO (1994), *Challenging Racism in The Early Years: The Role of Childcare Services in Scotland and Europe*, Edinburgh: HMSO.

hooks, b (1989), *Talking Back. Think Feminist, Thinking Black*, Boston: South End Press.

Horne, J. (1995), 'Racism, sectarianism and football in Scotland', *Scottish Affairs* 12: 27–51.

House of Commons Library (2021), 'UK Prison Population Statistics', *UK Parliament*, October 2021. Available online: https://commonslibrary.parliament.uk/research-briefings/sn04334/.

Howard, S., K. Kennedy, and F. Tejeda (2020), 'Social Media Posts About Racism Leads to Evaluative Backlash for Black Job Applicants', *Social Media + Society*, October-December 2020: 1–7.

Huskisson, S. (2020), 'Welsh government told to include Black history in new curriculum bill', *The Voice*, 21 December. Available online: www.voice online.co.uk/news/uk-news/2020/12/21/welsh-government-told-to-include-black-history-in-new-curriculum-bill/.

Iredia, P. (2020), 'New Shoots Old Roots', in African & Caribbean Women's Association (ed), *New Shoots Old Roots: Volume II*, 5, Glasgow: Street Level Photoworks.

Isoke, Z. (2013), *Urban Black Women and the Politics of Resistance*, New York: Palgrave Macmillan.

Jackson, J. A. (2020), *Writing Black Scotland: Race, Nation and the Devolution of Black Britain*, Edinburgh: Edinburgh University Press.

Jackson, L.M. (2021), 'Dave Chappelle, Netflix, and the Illusions of Corporate Identity Politics', *The New Yorker*, 25 October. Available online: www.newyorker.com/culture/cultural-comment/dave-chappelle-netflix-and-the-illusions-of-corporate-identity-politics.

Jameela, M. (2021), 'Violence, Above All, is What Maintains the Breach: Racial Categorisation and the Flattening of Difference', in C. Nwonka and A. Saha (eds), *Black Film British Cinema II*, 55–68, London: Goldsmiths Press.

Johnson, A, R. Joseph-Salisbury, and B. Kamunge (eds), *Fire Now: Anti-Racist Scholarship in Times of Explicit Racial Violence*, London: Zed Books.

Johnson, A. (2019), 'Throwing our bodies against the white background of academia', *Ethics In/Of Geographic Research.* https://doi.org/10.1111/area.12568

Johnson, A. (2020), 'Refuting "how the other half lives": I am a woman's rights', *Area* 2020; 52: 801–805.

Jones, O. (2021), '"You're a fascist and a racist." Massive kudos to @NicolaSturgeon for facing down these far right thugs', *Twitter*, 6 May. Available online: https://twitter.com/OwenJones84/status/1390336734697828362.

Joseph, R. L. (2018), *Postracial Resistance: Black Women, Media, and the Uses of Strategic Ambiguity*, New York: New York University Press.

Kaba, M. (2021), *We Do This 'Til We Free Us: Abolitionist Organizing and Transforming Justice,* Chicago: Haymarket Books.

Kalinga, C. (2016), 'Confronting the black jezebel stereotype: The contentious legacy of Brenda Fassie, South Africa's pop princess', *Dangerous Women Project*, 20 March. Available online: https://dangerouswomenproject.org/2016/03/20/confronting-black-jezebel-stereotype/.

Kalinga, C. (2018), 'A Reflection on the Past, Present and Future of Critical Health and Medical Humanities in Malawi', *Medical Humanities*. Available online: https://blogs.bmj.com/medical-humanities/2018/12/05/a-reflection-on-the-past-present- and-future-of-critical-health-and-medical-humanities-in-malawi/.

Kalinga, C (2021), 'Making Sense of Silenced Archives: Hume, Scotland, and the "debate" about the Humanity of Black People', *Retrospect Journal: Race in Retrospective*, 29: 9–10.

Kamunge, B., R. Joseph-Salisbury, and A. Johnson (2018), 'Changing Our Fate in *The Fire Now*', in A. Johnson, R. Joseph-Salisbury, and B. Kamunge (eds), *Fire Now: Anti-Racist Scholarship in Times of Explicit Racial Violence*, pp. 1–12, London: Zed Books.

Katshunga, J. (2019), 'Too Black for Canada, too white for Congo: re-searching in a (dis) placed body', *openDemocracy*, 28 June. Available online: www.opendemocracy.net/en/beyond-trafficking-and-slavery/too-black-canada-too-white-congo-re-searching-displaced-body/.

Kay, B. (2007) cited in S. Goffe-Caldeira (interviewer) 'Black Scotland', *The Black and Asian Studies Association Newsletter* 47.

Kay, J. (2019), 'Black Lesbian author Jackie Kay: Audre Lorde helped me coming out', *PinkNews*, 19 September. Available online: www.youtube.com/watch?v=uVQ5Oq2gVAk.

La Rose, J. (1976), 'We Did Not Come Alive In Britain', *Race Today*, 8(3): 62–65.

Leask, D. (2020), 'In Scotland, Loyalists lead a Black Lives Matter backlash', *openDemocracy,* 13 August. Available online: www.opendemocracy.net/en/opendemocracyuk/scotland-loyalists-lead-black-lives-matter-backlash/.

Learmonth, A. (2017), 'Father of Stephen Lawrence expresses anger at Dunoon's "Jim Crow" rock', *The National*, 30 December. Available online: www.thenational.scot/

news/15799413.father-of-stephen-lawrence-expresses-anger-at-dunoons-jim-crow-rock/.

Lewis, C. (2019a), 'Please can we stop talking about mixed-race identity (on its own)?', *Discover Society*, 23 July. Available online: https://archive.discoversociety. org/2019/07/23/please-can-we-stop-talking-about-mixed-race-identity-on-its-own/.

Lewis, C. (2019b), 'Interview – Chantelle Lewis', *E-International Relations*, 21 October. Available online: www.e-ir.info/2019/10/21/interview-chantelle-lewis/.

Lewis, C (2020), 'De-essentialising Mixed Race' *Busy Being Black* [podcast with Josh Rivers], Available online: https://player.fm/series/busy-being-black-2241434/ chantelle-lewis-de-essentialising-mixed-race.

Mac, J. and M. Smith (2018), *Revolting Prostitutes: The Fight for Sex Workers' Rights*, London: Verso.

Macwhirter, I. (2020), 'No society is free from racism but Scotland's record isn't bad', *The Herald*, 7 June. Available online: www.heraldscotland.com/news/18501176.iain-macwhirter-no-society-free-racism-scotlands-record-isnt-bad/.

Mahn, C. (2019), 'Black Scottish Writing and the Fiction of Diversity', in M. Breeze, Y. Taylor, and C. Costa (eds), *Time and Space in the Neoliberal University*, pp. 119–141. Cham: Palgrave Macmillan.

Maylor, U. (2009), 'What is the meaning of "black"? Researching "black" respondents', *Ethnic and Racial Studies*, 32(2): 369–387.

Mcilkenny, S. (2021), 'Kaukab Stewart makes history by becoming first woman of colour to serve as an MSP', *The Herald*, 8 May. www.heraldscotland.com/news/19289055. kaukab-stewart-makes-history-becoming-first-woman-colour-serve-msp/.

McKittrick, K. (2021), *Dear Science and Other Stories*, Durham. NC: Duke University Press.

McMillan Cottom, T. (2020), 'Where Platform Capitalism and Racial Capitalism Meet: The Sociology of Race and Racism in the Digital Society,' *Sociology of Race and Ethnicity*, 6(4): 441–449.

Meer, N. (2015), 'Looking up in Scotland? Multinationalism, multiculturalism and political elites,' *Ethnic and Racial Studies*, 38(9): 1477–1496.

Meer, N., S. Akhtar, and N. Davidson (eds) (2020), 'Taking Stock: Race Equality in Scotland', *Runnymede*. Available online: www.runnymedetrust.org/uploads/ publications/pdfs/TakingStockRaceEquality InScotlandJuly2020.pdf.

Mental Welfare Commission for Scotland (2021), 'Racial Inequality and Mental Health in Scotland', *Mental Welfare Commission for Scotland*, September 2021. Available online: www.mwcscot.org.uk/sites/default/files/2021-09/Racial-Inequality-Scotland_Report_Sep2021.pdf.

Miller, M., R. Laycock, J. Sadler, and R. Serdiville (2014), *As Good as Any Man: Scotland's Black Tommy*, Stroud: The History Press.

Miller, D. (2010), 'Who rules Scotland? Neoliberalism, the Scottish ruling class and its intellectuals', in N. Davidson, N., P. McCafferty, and D. Miller (eds), *Neoliberal Scotland: Class and Society in a Stateless Nation*, pp. 9 –135. Cambridge: Cambridge Scholars.

Miren, F. (2017), 'How One Woman's Death Highlighted Escorts' Devastating Distrust of the Police', *Buzzfeed*, 26 January, Available online: www.buzzfeed.com/frankiemullin/could-escort-jessica-mcgraas-murder-have-been-prevented.

Monk, E. P. (2018), 'The color of punishment: African Americans, skin tone, and the criminal justice system', *Ethnic and Racial Studies*, 49(10): 1593–1612.

Mullen, S. (2009), *It Wisnae Us: The Truth about Glasgow and Slavery*, Edinburgh: Royal Incorporation of Architects in Scotland.

Museums Galleries Scotland (2020), 'MGS Appoints Project Manager: Empire, Slavery & Scotland's Museums', *Museums Galleries Scotland*. Available online: www.museumsgalleriesscotland.org.uk/stories/mgs-appoints-project-manager-empire-slavery-scotland-s-museums/.

Mwasi Collectif (2019), 'Those Who Fight for Us Without Us are Against Us: Afrofeminist Activism in France', in A. Emejulu and F. Sobande (eds), *To Exist is to Resist: Black Feminism in Europe*, pp. 46–62. London: Pluto Press.

National Library of Scotland (date unknown), 'Scotland and the slave trade', *National Library of Scotland*. Available online: www.nls.uk/collections/topics/slavery.

National Records of Scotland (2020), 'Mid-2019 population estimates Scotland', *National Records of Scotland*, 30 April. Available online: www.nrscotland.gov.uk/statistics-and-data/statistics/statistics-by-theme/population/population-estimates/mid-year-population-estimates/mid-2019.

Not One Rogue Cop (2021), 'Huge police presence in Pollokshields supporting the work of Home Office as locals resist the eviction and detention of members ..', *Twitter*, 13 May. Available online: https://twitter.com/NotOneRogueCop/status/1392803011668365313.

Nwonka, C. J. (2020), 'The black neoliberal aesthetic', *European Journal of Cultural Studies*. December 2020. DOI:10.1177/1367549420973204.

Office of the First Minister (2016), 'Scotland's New Makar' Office of the First Minister', *Gov.scot*, 15 March 2016. Available online: https://firstminister.gov.scot/scotlands-new-Makar/.

Olaloku-Teriba, A. (2018), 'Afro-Pessimism and the (Un)Logic of Anti-Blackness', *Historical Materialism*, 26(2): 96–122. Available at: www.historicalmaterialism.org/articles/afro-pessimism-and-unlogic-anti-blackness.

Olufemi, L. (2020), *Feminism, Interrupted: Disrupting Power*, London: Pluto Press.

Ong, C. (2020), 'Big brands pay us less, say Black Scottish influencers', *The Ferret*, 30 July. Available online: https://theferret.scot/black-scottish-influencers-inequalities-media/.

Osei-Oppong, M. (2020), *For the Love of Teaching: The Anti-Racist Battlefield in Education*, London: Peaches Publications.

Osuna, S (2017), 'Class Suicide: The Black Radical Tradition, Radical Scholarship, and the Neoliberal Turn', in G. T. Johnson and A. Lubin (eds), *Futures of Black Radicalism*, pp. 21–22, New York: Verso Books.

Otele, O. (2020), *African Europeans: An Untold History*, London: Hurst & Co.

Palmer, G. (2007), *The Enlightenment Abolished: Citizens of Britishness*, Penicuik: Henry Publishing.

Patel, M. (1994), 'Caring to challenge anti-racism in childcare in Scotland and beyond', in HMSO (ed) *Challenging Racism in the Early Years: The Role of Childcare Services in Scotland and Europe*. Edinburgh: HMSO.

Patrick, A. (1990), 'Talking muses', *The List*, 18 May. Available online: https://archive.list.co.uk/the-list/1990-05-18/69/.

Pitts, J. (2019), *Afropean: Notes from Black Europe*, London: Penguin Books.

Quan, H. L. T. (2017), 'It's Hard to Stop Rebels That Time Travel', in G. Johnson and A. Lubin (eds), *Futures of Black Radicalism*, pp. 21–22, New York: Verso Books.

Quan, H. L. T. (ed) (2019), *Cedric J. Robinson: On Racial Capitalism, Black Internationalism, and Cultures of Resistance*, London: Pluto Press.

Qureshi, A. (2020), 'New creative platform We Are Here Scotland officially launches', *Bella Caledonia* 1 November. Available online: https://bellacaledonia.org.uk/2020/11/01/new-creative-platform-we-are-here-scotland-officially-launches/.

Qureshi, A. (2021a), *Flip the Script: How Women Came to Rule Hip Hop*, Edinburgh: 404 Ink.

Qureshi, A. (2021b), 'People of Colour and the Creative Industries in Scotland: A Post-2020 Reflection', *Bella Caledonia*, 28 February. Available online: https://bellacaledonia.org.uk/2021/02/28/people-of-colour-and-the-creative-industries-in-scotland-a-post-2020-reflection/.

Ransby, B. (2018), *Making All Black Lives Matter: Reimagining Freedom in the 21st Century*. Oakland: University of California Press.

Refugee Survival Trust (2005), 'What's going on?' A study into destitution and poverty faced by asylum seekers and refugees in Scotland', Available online: www.rst.org.uk/wp content/uploads/2012/11/Whats_going_on_A_study.pdf.

Refugees for Justice (2021), 'Why we're fighting for justice, accountability, and change', Available online: https://www.refugeesforjustice.com/our-story-2

Rennie, A. (2010), 'Buddies can enjoy a Taste of Africa at Paisley Town Hall event', *The Daily Record*, 19 November (Updated 25 October 2013). Available online: www.dailyrecord.co.uk/news/local-news/buddies-can-enjoy-taste-africa-2580827.

Robinson, C. J. (1983), *Black Marxism: The Making of the Black Radical Tradition*, London: Zed Press.

Rocks, K. (1990), 'Tackling Racism', in S. Henderson and A. Mackay (eds), *Grit and Diamonds: Women in Scotland Making History 1980–1990*, pp. 175–176, Edinburgh: Stramullion.

Rosa-Salas, M. and Sobande, F. (2022), 'Hierarchies of knowledge about intersectionality in marketing theory and practice', *Marketing Theory*, 22(2): 175–189.

Russell, L. (2020), *Glitch Feminism: A Manifesto*, London: Verso.

Sangha, S. and hill, l.r. (2020), '#BlackLivesMatter', *The Daily Record*, 5 June. Available online: www.pressreader.com/uk/daily-record/20200605/28206339419276.

Sarwar, A. (2021), 'Nicola Sturgeon and I are on different sides in this seat, but we are all united when it comes to . .', *Twitter*, 7 May. Available online: https://twitter.com/AnasSarwar/status/1390583234854064128

Sayyid, S. (2000), 'Beyond Westphalia: Nations and Diasporas – the Case of the Muslim Umma', in B. Hesse (ed), *Un/settled Multiculturalisms: Diasporas, Entanglements, Transruptions*, pp. 33–50, London: Zed Books.

Scotland's Census (2011), 'Ethnicity', *Scottish Government*. Available online: www.scotlandscensus.gov.uk/census-results/at-a-glance/ethnicity/.

Scotland Against Criminalising Communities (SACC), (2020), 'Justice for Badreddin', SACC, 29 June. Available online: www.sacc.org.uk/articles/2020/justice-badreddin.

Scotland Is Now (date unknown), 'Safety and Inclusivity', *Scotland Is Now*. Available online: www.scotland.org/about-scotland/safety-and-inclusivity.

Scottish Green Party (2021), 'Scottish Greens Manifesto 2021: Our Common Future', *Scottish Green Party*, Available online: https://greens.scot/ourfuture.

Scottish Court and Tribunal Services (2020), 'Opinion of Lady Dorrian, the Lord Justice Clerk in the Petition by BC and Others against Iain Livingstone QPM, Chief Constable Of The Police Service of Scotland and Others', *Scottish Court and Tribunal Services*, 16 September. Available online: www.scotcourts.gov.uk/docs/default-source/cos-general-docs/pdf-docs-for-opinions/2020csih61.pdf?sfvrsn=0.

Scottish Government (2020), 'Independent Review of Complaints Handling, Investigations and Misconduct Issues in Relation to Policing', *Scottish Government*, 11 November. Available online: www.gov.scot/publications/independent-review-complaints-handling-investigations-misconduct-issues-relation-policing/documents/.

Scottish Government (2020a), 'Protecting Scotland, Renewing Scotland: The Government's Programme for Scotland 2020–2021', *Scottish Government*, 1 September. Available online: www.gov.scot/publications/protecting-scotland-renewing-scotland-governments-programme-scotland-2020-2021/.

Scottish Government (2020b), 'Migration: helping Scotland prosper', *Scottish Government*, 27 January. Available online www.gov.scot/publications/migration-helping-scotland-prosper/pages/2/.

Scottish Government (2020c), 'Scottish prison population: statistics 2019 to 2020', *Scottish Government*, 14 July. Available online: www.gov.scot/publications/scottish-prison-population-statistics-2019-20/documents/.

Scottish Government (2020d), 'Racist occurrence statistical count relating to Government employees between specific dates: FOI release', *Scottish Government*, 10 September. Available online: www.gov.scot/publications/foi-202000066981/.

Scottish Government (2021), 'International Development 2019–2020: contribution report', *Scottish Government*, 12 February. Available online: www.gov.scot/publications/contribution-international-development-report-2019-2020/.

Scottish Labour Party (2021), 'Scottish Labour's National Recovery Plan', *Scottish Labour Party*, Available online: https://scottishlabour.org.uk/where-we-stand/national-recovery-plan/.

Scottish Liberal Democrats (2021), 'Scottish Liberal Democrats: Put Recovery First', *The Liberal Democrats*, Available online: www.scotlibdems.org.uk/read_2021_manifesto.

Scottish National Party (2021), 'SNP 2021 Manifesto: Scotland's Future, Scotland's Choice', *Scottish National Party,* 15 April. Available online: www.snp.org/manifesto/.

Scottish Parliament (2020), 'Meeting of the Parliament. Parliamentary Year 5, No. 14, Session 5', *Scottish Parliament,* 10 June. Available online: www.parliament.scot/S5_BusinessTeam/Chamber_Minutes_20200610.pdf.

Scottish Police Federation (2020), 'Coronavirus – What Coronavirus?', *Scottish Police Federation*, 18 June. Available online: https://spf.org.uk/coronavirus-what-coronavirus/.

Scoutable United FC (2021), 'About', Available online: https://www.scoutableunited.org.uk/

Senedd Cymru Welsh Parliament (2020), 'Closed petition: Make it compulsory for Black and POC UK histories to be taught in the Welsh education curriculum', *Senedd Cymru Welsh Parliament*. Available online: https://petitions.senedd.wales/petitions/200034.

Shelton, A. (2001), 'Black Women's Agency in Scotland', in E. Breitenbach and F. Mackay (eds), *Women and Contemporary Scottish Politics. An Anthology*, pp. 47–53. Edinburgh: Polygon.

Shukla, N. (2016), *The Good Immigrant*, London: Unbound.

Smith, J. (2020), 'BBC to examine 1989 racist murder of man on Cowgate in Edinburgh for Black History Month,' *Edinburgh Live,* 3 October. Available online: www.edinburghlive.co.uk/news/edinburgh-news/bbc-examine-1989-racist-murder-19044927.

Snook (2015), *Dearest Scotland: Letters Written to the Future of A Nation*, Glasgow: Ringwood Publishing.

Snorton, Riley, C. (2017), *Black on Both Sides. A Racial History of Trans Identity*, Minneapolis: University of Minnesota Press.

Sobande, F. (2019), 'Awkward Black girls and post-feminist possibilities: Representing millennial Black women on television in *Chewing Gum* and *Insecure*', *Critical Studies in Television: The International Journal of Television Studies*, 14 (4): 435–450.

Sobande, F. (2020a), *The Digital Lives of Black Women in Britain*, Cham: Palgrave Macmillan.

Sobande, F. (2020b), 'Woke-washing: "intersectional" femvertising and branding "woke" bravery', *European Journal of Marketing*, 54 (11): 2723–2745.

Sobande, F. (2021a), 'On Beyond Branding "Brand Activism" and Whitewashing Critiques of Capitalism', *Margins*, 14 November. Available online: https://marginstwenty.home.blog/2021/11/14/beyond-branding-brand-activism-and-whitewashing-critiques-of-capitalism/.

Sobande, F., Schoonejans, A., Johnson, G.D., Thomas, K.D. and Harrison, A.K. (2020), 'Enacting anti-racist visualities through photo-dialogues on race in Paris', *Equality, Diversity and Inclusion*, Vol. ahead-of-print No. ahead-of print. https://doi.org/10.1108/EDI-01-2020-0019.

Sobande, F. and Wells, J. R. (2021), 'The poetic identity work and sisterhood of Black women becoming academics', *Gender, Work & Organization*. DOI: 10.1111/gwao.12747.

Spowart, N. (2019), 'Jackie Kay: 10 things that changed my life', *The National*, 8 September. Available online: www.thenational.scot/news/17887456.jackie-kay-10-things-changed-life/.

Statistics Canada (2016), 'Immigration and Ethnocultural Diversity Highlight Tables. Ethnic Origin, both sexes, age (total), Canada, 2016 Census – 25% Sample data', *Statistics Canada*, 1 November. Available online: www12.statcan.gc.ca/census-recensement/2016/dp-pd/hlt-fst/imm/Table.cfm?Lang=E&T=31&Geo=01&SO=4D#fn19.

STUC Women's Committee (2013), *Inspiring Women*, Edinburgh: Word Power Books 2013.

Tasker, Y. and Negra, D. (eds.) (2007*), Interrogating Postfeminism: Gender and the Politics of Popular Culture*. Durham, NC: Duke University Press.

Taylor, K. Y. (2021), *From #BlackLivesMatter to Black Liberation* ((Expanded Second Edition). Chicago, IL: Haymarket Books.

The National Theatre of Scotland (2020), 'Scenes for Survival: Black Scots. An Extract from First Snow/*Première neige*,' *The National Theatre of Scotland*, 14 July. Available online: www.nationaltheatrescotland.com/latest/black-scots.

The National Theatre of Scotland (2021), 'Ghosts' [Press Release sent via email].

Thomas-Smith, A. (2020), 'Podcast Transcript: Gary Younge on the Global Black Liberation Uprisings'. New Economics Foundation. Available online: https://neweconomics.org/2020/06/weekly-economics-podcast-transcript-gary-younge-on-the-global-black-liberation-uprisings.

University of Edinburgh (2021), 'Lecturer in Black British History' [job advert]. Available online: https://elxw.fa.em3.oraclecloud.com/hcmUI/CandidateExperience/en/sites/CX_1001/job/632/?utm_medium=jobshare/en/sites/CX_1001.

University of Glasgow, 'Runaway Slaves in Britain: Bondage, freedom and race in the eighteenth century'. Available online: www.runaways.gla.ac.uk/database.

University of Glasgow, 'Minority Ethnic Emerging Leaders Programme'. Available online: www.gla.ac.uk/schools/socialpolitical/johnsmith/ourwork/meelp/.

Valluvan, S. (2019), *The Clamour of Nationalism. Race and Nation in Twenty-first-Century Britain*, Manchester: Manchester University Press.

Virdee, S. (2014), *Racism, Class and the Racialized Outsider*, Basingstoke: Palgrave Macmillan.

Walcott, R. (2019), 'The End of Diversity', *Public Culture,* 31(2): 393–408.

Wallace, M. (2016), *Invisibility Blues: From Pop to Theory*. London; Brooklyn, New York: Verso.

Walker, D, (2005), 'Working in it, through it, and among it all day' Chrome Dust at J & J White of Rutherglen, 1893–1967,' *Scottish Labour History Journal*, 40: 50–69.

Warner, K. J. (2017), 'Plastic Representation,' *Film Quarterly*, 71(2).

White, N. (2021), '"Ditch Bame' Race Commission proposal broadly welcomed, but campaigners wonder what's next,' *The Independent*, 29 March. Available online: www.

independent.co.uk/news/uk/home-news/bame-race-commission-campaign-b1823825.html.

Williams, L. (2020), 'Remaking our histories: Scotland, slavery and empire', *National Galleries of Scotland*, 9 October. Available online: www.nationalgalleries.org/art-and-artists/features/remaking-our-histories-scotland-slavery-and-empire.

Wilson, D. (2017), 'Making Creative Cities in the Global West: The New Polarization and Ghettoization in Cleveland, USA, and Glasgow, UK', in U. Gerhard, M. Hoelscher and D. Wilson (eds) *Inequalities in Creative Cities: Issues, Approaches, Comparisons*, pp. 107–127. New York: Palgrave Macmillan.

Woods, Z. R. and Harrison, A. K. (2021), 'Brown Girl in the Lens', in F. Sobande, A. Schoonejans, G. D. Johnson, K. D. Thomas, A. K. Harrison and S. A. Grier (eds) *ISRF Bulletin Issue XXIII: Race and Markets*, pp. 27–32. Independent Social Research Foundation.

Wynter, S. (1990) 'Afterword: Beyond Miranda's Meanings: Un/silencing the "Demonic Ground" of Caliban's Woman', in C.B. Davies and E.S. Fido (eds), *Out of the Kumbla: Caribbean Women and Literature*, pp. 355–370. Trenton: African World Press.

Yancy, G. (2008), *Black Bodies, White Gazes: The Continuing Significance of Race*. Lanham: Rowman & Littlefield.

Younge, G. (2018), 'Britain's imperial fantasies have given us Brexit', *The Guardian*, 3 February. Available online: www.theguardian.com/commentisfree/2018/feb/03/imperial-fantasies-brexit-theresa-may.

Index

www.ingramcontent.com/pod-product-compliance
Ingram Content Group UK Ltd.
Pitfield, Milton Keynes, MK11 3LW, UK
UKHW031022040325
455779UK00001B/2